1 MONTH OF
FREE
READING

at

www.ForgottenBooks.com

By purchasing this book you are eligible for one month membership to ForgottenBooks.com, giving you unlimited access to our entire collection of over 700,000 titles via our web site and mobile apps.

To claim your free month visit:

www.forgottenbooks.com/free583798

ISBN 978-0-331-64389-3
PIBN 10583798

PRIZE LISTS

OF THE

UNIVERSITY OF GLASGOW

FROM SESSION 1777-78
TO SESSION 1832-33.

COLLECTED BY

W. INNES ADDISON,

Author of "A Roll of the Graduates of the University of Glasgow," and
" The Snell Exhibitions.'

GLASGOW:
CARTER & PRATT, PRINTERS AND PUBLISHERS,
62 BOTHWELL CIRCUS.

1902.

PREFACE.

With three exceptions (1825-26, 1828-29, and 1832-33), the Lists contained in this volume have been collected from the advertising columns of the old Glasgow newspapers, and they are now reproduced *verbatim et literatim*, with all the original vagaries of spelling, punctuation, etc. The excepted Lists were found in the intermittent *University Calendars* of the day.

From 1833-34 to 1862-63, the Prize Lists were printed annually in pamphlet form, and a complete set of these is preserved in the Matriculation Office. From 1863-64 onwards, the Lists appear yearly in the *Calendars*. By the present issue there is thus secured an unbroken series of printed Lists for a century and a quarter. None previous to 1777 have been discovered, and it is doubtful whether any ever existed.

The peculiarities of spelling above hinted at extended to the names of students, and resulted in the same person appearing under different guises, *e.g.*, Smith and Smyth, Stewart and Stuart, etc. Owing to the complications thence arising, it has, as a rule, been found advisable to give in the Index only one version of each surname. To save space, all persons of the same Christian name and surname have been indexed together—"Smith, John," for example, including one student of 1784, and another of 1824 —and this has likewise necessitated, in many cases, the omission of middle names from the Index, as, for instance, "Young, Charles," which includes Charles William Young.

W. I. A.

Matriculation Office,
    University of Glasgow,
        November, 1902.

PRIZE LISTS.

GLASGOW COLLEGE, May 6, 1778.

Yesterday, the Annual Distribution of Prizes to the Students of the LOGIC, GREEK, and HUMANITY CLASSES of Glasgow College was made, in the Common Hall, by the Principal and Professors, in presence of a numerous meeting of the University.

———

The Prizes of the LOGIC CLASS were adjudged to

Francis Stuart,	William Daling,
John Pollock,	John Barr,
Alexander Graham,	Robert Clerk,
Gavin Wodrow,	Richard Millar, and
Daniel Taylor,	Samuel Swinton,

for the best Exercises in Reasoning ; and the best Specimens of Composition on various subjects in Taste and Criticism, prescribed to them during the course of this Session.

———

The Prizes of the GREEK CLASS were adjudged to
George Wilson,
for the best Essay on the Genetive Absolute.

To James Hall,
for the best Essay on the Middle Voice, and attempt to investigate the Principle upon which that Voice may be taken in a passive signification.

To James Hall,
for an Essay on the Principle on which several different Prepositions are used, in the Greek and other Languages, to connect the passive Form of the Verb with the Noun, denoting the Agent, etc., in an oblique Case.

To John Hastie,
for excelling in the weekly grammatical Competition : and,
To John Mill,
for Propriety of Manners, and Punctuality in all the Exercises of
the Class.

———

The Prizes of the HUMANITY CLASS were adjudged to
Richard Miller,
for the best Translation from Latin into English.

To Gabriel Gordon,　　　Walter Monteath, and
　　Andrew Cowan,　　　William Anderson,
for the best Translations from English into Latin.

To James Hall,　　　William Tennant, and
　　William Daling,　　　James Turnbull,
　　George Wilson,
Students of Philosophy, for the best critical Observations on three
Odes of Horace.

To John Connel,　　　John Macpherson, and
　　Robert Edmund,　　　Walter Monteath,
　　John Higgens,
for the best Specimens of Elocution in the delivery of Speeches
from Sallust and Cæsar ; and,
To Robert Brisbane,
Thomas Dalziel, and
Hugh Maclean,
for Propriety of Manners during an attendance of two Sessions in
the public Class.

———

GLASGOW COLLEGE, MAY 6, 1779.

On Friday last, the Annual Distribution of Prizes to the
Students of the LOGIC, GREEK, and HUMANITY CLASSES of
Glasgow College was made, in the Common Hall, by the Principal
and Professors, in presence of a numerous meeting of the
University.

The Prizes of the LOGIC CLASS were adjudged to

Borlage Willocks, Manchester,
James Broadfute, Dunsyre,
William King, Baldernock,
John Mill, Montrose,
Rolland Lindsay, Covington,
James Scot, Strathaven,
Robert Earl, Ballantrae,
Stevenson M'Gill, Port-Glasgow,
Robert Renny, Kilsyth, and
James Brown, Stirling,

for the best specimens of Composition on various subjects of Reasoning, Taste, and Criticism, prescribed during the course of this Session.

————

The Prizes of the GREEK CLASS were adjudged to

William Tennent, A.M., Ayr,

for the best Critical Analysis of the Chœphoræ of Aeschylus.

James Hall, Lochwinnoch,

for the best Essay on the generalizing and particularizing processes exhibited in the application of terms in the Greek Language.

George Wilson, Greenock,

for an Essay for reducing the Two forms of the Future Active of Greek Verbs to One original Analogy.

William King, Baldernock,

for excelling in the weekly Grammatical Competition.

Stevenson M'Gill, Port-Glasgow, and
John Higgans,

for the first and second Specimens of Elocution, in the delivery of Speeches from Homer ; and

Robert Cross, Glasgow, and
Robert Urchart, Irvine,

for Propriety of Manners, and Punctuality in the Exercises of the Class.

The Prizes of the HUMANITY CLASS were adjudged to

John Mill, Montrose,

Student of Philosophy, for the best Translation from English into Latin.

The Honourable Charles Lindsay, Fife,
Robert Hall, Cathcart, and
John Mill, Montrose,

Students of Philosophy, for the best critical Observations on one of the Odes of Horace.

The Hon. Charles Lindsay, Fife, and
William Daling, Fife,

Students of Philosophy, for the best Translation from Latin into English.

John Blackburn, Glasgow,

for the best Latin Verses.

George Kippen, Glasgow,
Andrew Pollock, ,,
James Graham, ,, and
Alexander Cooper, ,,

for the best Specimens of Elocution in the delivery of Speeches from Virgil ; and

William Anderson, Glasgow,
James Graham, ,,
John M'Pherson,
Thomas Cunningham, ,,
Thomas Muir,
Robert Edmond,
Robert Cross, and
Robert Mitchell, ,,

for good behaviour during an attendance of two Sessions in the public Class.

GLASGOW COLLEGE, May 4, 1780.

On Monday last the Annual Distribution of Prizes to the Students of the LOGICK, GREEK, and HUMANITY CLASSES of Glasgow College, was made, in the Common Hall, by the Principal and Professors, in presence of a numerous Meeting of the University.

———

The Prize, in the LOGICK CLASS, for the best Criticism on the Paper of the *Guardian*, No. 130, was adjudged to
William King, Baldernock.

The Prizes for the best Specimens of Composition on various Subjects of Reasoning, Taste, and Criticism, prescribed during the Course of the Session, were adjudged as follows :—

John Alexander Higgins, Airth.
William Crichtone, England.
Israel Clarke, Ireland.
Robert Urquhart, Irvine.
Hugh Fraser, Aberdeenshire.
James Swan, Ireland.
Robert Edmond, Glasgow.
George Muirhead, Dysart.
John M'Kinlay, Perthshire.
Patrick Mushet, Stirling.
Sir William Cockburn, Edinburgh.
Robert Mitchel, Glasgow.
James Grahame, Glasgow.

———

The Prizes of the GREEK CLASS were adjudged as follows :—
The Prize for the best Essay on the Greek Prepositions, to
William Crichtone, England.

For the best Essay on the Greek Particles, to
James Hall, Renfrewshire.

For the best Essay on The Effect of Reasoning and Inference in particularizing general Terms, as illustrated by the Greek Language, to
Niel Jamieson, Virginia.

For the best Essay on the Helps towards the Elucidation of Syntax, derived from the Analysis of Complex Words into their Parts, to

Stevenson M'Gill, Port-Glasgow.

For excelling in the Weekly Grammatical Competition, to

Robert Cross, Glasgow.

For the first and second Specimens of Elocution, in the Delivery of Speeches from Homer, to

Robert Edmond, Glasgow.
James Grahame, Glasgow.

For Propriety of Manners, and Punctuality in the Exercises of the Class, to

Robert M'Leod, Ross-shire.
John Murray, Glasgow.

The Prizes of the HUMANITY CLASS were adjudged as follows:—

The Prizes for Critical Observations on the Aulularia of Plautus, to

James Hall, Renfrewshire.
John Mill, Montrose.

For the best Translations from English into Latin, to

John Blackburn, Glasgow.
George Muirhead, Dysart.

For the best Translations from Latin into English, to

John Blackburn, Glasgow.
Sir William Cockburn, Edinburgh.

For Exercises on Prosody, to

Thomas Rutherford, Glasgow.
John Murray, Glasgow.

For Latin Verses, to

Alexander Cooper, Glasgow.
Thomas Rutherford, Glasgow.

For the best Specimens of Elocution, in the Delivery of Speeches from Virgil and Livy, to

George Kippen, Glasgow.
John Murray, ,,

Andrew Pollock, Glasgow.
Lawrence M'Dowal, Renfrewshire.

For Good Behaviour, during an Attendance of two Sessions in the Public Class, to

Andrew Pollock, Glasgow.
James Gardner,   ,,
James Tennant,   ,,
John Blackburn,   ,,
John Craig.
Walter Tassie,   ,,
William Dalzell,   ,,
William Richardson, Glasgow.
William Zuill,   ,,
Thomas Rutherford,   ,.
Henry Fergus, Denny.
Hugh Montgomery, Eaglesham.
James Whiteford, Lesmahagow.
John Reyburn, Campbelton.
Neil Jamieson, Virginia.
William Grahame, Kilbryde.

GLASGOW COLLEGE, May 10, 1781.

On Tuesday, the 1st current, the Annual Distribution of Prizes, to the Students of the ETHIC, LOGIC, GREEK, and HUMANITY Classes of Glasgow College, was made, in the Common Hall, by the Principal and Professors, in presence of a numerous Meeting of the University.

The Prizes in the ETHIC CLASS, for the best Essays on the Cardinal Virtues, were adjudged to

Hugh Frazer, Aberdeenshire.
George Muirhead, Dysart.

The Prize for the best Illustration of the Argument for the Existence of a Supreme Being, drawn from the Evidences of Design in the Universe, to

William Crichton, B.A., Northumberland.

The Prizes in the LOGIC CLASS, for the best Specimens of Composition on various Subjects of Reasoning, Taste, and Criticism, prescribed during the Course of the Session, were adjudged to

> Thomas Jefferson, Cumberland.
> Henry Glasford, Glasgow.
> William Niven, Ireland.
> William Henderson, Borrowstounness.
> Walter Tassie, Glasgow.
> John Craig,   ,,
> John Murray,   ,,
> Æneas M'Leod, Cromartie.
> William Dalziel, Glasgow.
> Thomas Wallace, Ireland.
> John Blackburn, Glasgow.
> John Reyburn, Campbeltown.
> Thomas Jamieson, Douglas.
> James Tennent, Glasgow.
> Henry Fergus, Cumbernauld.
> Andrew Pollock, Glasgow.
> William Smith, Lanark.

The Prizes of the GREEK CLASS were adjudged, for the best Abridgement of Longinus, to

> Stevenson M'Gill, A.M., Port-Glasgow.

For the best Essay on the Greek Verb and its Accidents, to

> Robert Rennie, A.M , Kilsyth.

For the best Essay on Greek Comparison, to

> William Crichton, B.A., Northumberland.

For the best Essay on the Greek Particles, to

> James Brown, Stirling.

For the best Translation of Anacreon in Verse, to

> Thomas Jefferson, Cumberland.

For the best Translation of Anacreon in Prose, to

> John Blackburn, Glasgow.

For Excelling in the Weekly Grammatical Competition, to

> John Murray, Glasgow.

For Exemplary Conduct during the Session, to
>   Henry Maxwell, Paisley.
>   John Jamieson, Port-Glasgow.

The Prizes of the HUMANITY CLASS were adjudged—

For the best Poetical Translation from Latin into English, to
>   Thomas Jefferson, Cumberland.

For the best Prose Translations from Latin into English,
>   John M'Lean, Dantzig.
>   David Lynsen, New York.

For the best Translations from English into Latin, to
>   John Blackburn, Glasgow.
>   John M'Lean, Dantzig.
>   Henry Maxwell, Paisley.

For the best Latin Verses, to
>   Thomas Jefferson, Cumberland.
>   Robert Ritchie, Glasgow.
>   Lockhart Muirhead, Dysart.
>   John Malcolm, Jamaica.

For Diligence and Exemplary Conduct, to
>   Andrew Duncan, Glasgow.
>   James Brown, Paisley.
>   James Stevenson, Glasgow.
>   John Hamilton, Cathcart.
>   John Hosier, Glasgow.
>   John Moodie, Riccartown.
>   John M'Lean, Dantzig.
>   Lockhart Muirhead, Dysart.
>   Walter Logan, Massachussetts Bay.
>   William Jamieson, Glasgow.
>   William Munro,   ,,
>   William M'Turk,   ,,
>   Robert Clark, Beith.
>   Robert Ritchie, Glasgow.
>   Thomas Ryeburn, Campbeltown.

GLASGOW COLLEGE, MAY 2, 1782.

On Wednesday, the 1st current, the Annual Distribution of Prizes, to the Students of the ETHIC, LOGIC, GREEK, and HUMANITY CLASSES of Glasgow College, was made in the Common Hall, by the Principal and Professors, in presence of a numerous meeting of the University.

The Prizes of the ETHIC CLASS were adjudged—

I. For the best Exercise, in Latin, on Self-command, to
> Thomas Jefferson, Cumberland.

II. For the best Essays in English, on subjects in Moral Philosophy, prescribed during the Session, to
> Thomas Jefferson, Cumberland.
> Thomas Cunningham, B.A., Glasgow.
> William Niven, Ireland.

The Prizes of the LOGIC CLASS were adjudged—

I. For the best Abstract, and Additional Observations on Mr. Addison's Criticisms on Milton's "Paradise Lost," to
> Henry Glasford, Glasgow.

II. For the best Criticism on the Paper of the *Spectator*, No. 418, to
> John Craig, Glasgow.

III. For the best Essay on Literary Ambition, to
> Thomas Jefferson, Cumberland.

IV. For the best Specimens of Composition on Various Subjects of Reasoning and Taste, prescribed during the Session, to
> Joseph Jefferson, Cumberland.
> Hugh Meiklejohn, Culross.
> Lockhart Muirhead, Dysart.
> Charles Stewart Hawthorn, Ireland.
> Campbell Betham, Isle of Man.
> Henry Maxwell, Paisley.
> John Martin, Barbadoes.

Robert Ritchie, Glasgow.
Robert Patrick, Beith.
Robert Clark, Beith.

The Prizes of the GREEK CLASS were adjudged—

For the best Critical Essay on the Oedipus Tyrannus of Sophocles, to

James Brown, Stirling.

For the best Essay on the Nature and Accedents of Noun, to

William Crichton, M.A., Northumberland.

For the best Essay on the Analogy of Greek Derivation, to
George Muirhead, Dysart.

For the best Essay on the Greek Prepositions, to
Henry Maxwell, Paisley.

For excelling in the weekly Grammatical Competition, to
John Robertson, Glasgow.

For Exemplary Conduct during the Session, to

William Eadie, Strathern.
Thomas Fleming, Edinburgh.

The Prizes of the HUMANITY CLASS were adjudged—

For the best Translation from Latin into English, to
Lockhart Muirhead, Dysart.

For the best Translations from English into Latin, to
William Eadie, Strathern.
Fife King, Jamaica.

For the best Latin Verses, to
John Martin, Barbadoes.
Lawrence Millar, Perthshire.
Thomas Fleming, Edinburgh.
James Smith, Glasgow.
John Sommers, Hamilton.

For the best Specimens of Elocution, in the delivery of Latin Speeches, to

> John Sommers, Hamilton.
> William Erskine, Strathern.
> Samuel M'All, Glasgow.
> James Smith, Glasgow.

For excelling in a Public Examination, to

> Henry Fergus, Cumbernauld.
> Campbell Bethem, Isle of Man.

For Exemplary Conduct, during two Sessions, to

> David Lang, Dumbartonshire.
> James Dalziell, Glasgow.
> James Smith, *minor*, ,,
> John Sommers, Hamilton.
> Nicol Brown, Glasgow.
> William Marshall, ,,
> George Pinkerton, ,,
> James Smith, *major*, ,,
> James Stirling, Dumbartonshire.
> John Robertson, Glasgow.
> Robert M'Brayne, ,,
> William Wardrope, ,,

On Saturday, 2nd March, 1782, a Gold Medal given by the Lord Chancellor of the University of Glasgow for the best English Composition awarded to

> Patrick Taylor, Student of Divinity.

GLASGOW COLLEGE, MAY 8, 1783.

On Thursday, the 1st current, the Annual Distribution of Prizes, to the Students of the ETHICK, LOGICK, GREEK, and HUMANITY Classes of Glasgow College, was made in the Common Hall, by the Principal and Professors, in presence of a numerous meeting of the University.

The Prizes of the ETHICK CLASS were adjudged—

I. For the best Latin Exercises on Progress in Social Virtue, to

Joseph Jefferson, Cumberland.
Lockhart Muirhead, Dysart.

II. For the best Essays in English, on Subjects in Moral Philosophy, prescribed during the Session, to

Joseph Jefferson, Cumberland.
Lockhart Muirhead, Dysart.
James Whitehead, St. Ninians.
Thomas Wilson, Ireland.
Andrew Crawford, New Cumnock.

The Prizes of the LOGICK CLASS were adjudged—

I. For the best Criticism on the first book of the Eneid of Virgil, to

Joseph Jefferson, Cumberland.

II. For the best Essays on Literary Ambition, to

Lockhart Muirhead, Dysart.
Joseph Jefferson, Cumberland.

III. For the best Analysis of a Literary Composition, to

Alexander Whitehead, St. Ninians.

IV. For the best Specimens of Composition on various subjects of Reasoning and Taste, prescribed during the Session, to

First Divison.

William Eadie, Strathern.
George Storie, London.
Alexander Whitehead, St. Ninians.
John Smyly, Ireland.

Second Division.

Nicol Brown, Glasgow.
Robert White, Galloway.
John Sommers, Hamilton.
Samuel Gilfillan, Stirlingshire.

Third Division.

Archibald Millar, Glasgow.
William Erskine, Strathern.
William M'Turk, Glasgow.
Richard Freebairn, Dumbarton.
Andrew Monach, Kirkcudbright.

———

The Prizes of the GREEK CLASS were adjudged—

I. For the best Critical Essay on the Choephorae of Æschylus, to

William Crichton, M A., Northumberland.

II. For the best English Translation of the same Tragedy, to
Archibald Millar, Glasgow.

III. For the best Essay on the Greek Pronouns, to
Alexander Whitehead, St. Ninians.

IV. For the best Essay on the Greek Particles, to
James Mitchell, Beith.

V. For excelling in the Grammatical Competition, to
Thomas Fleming, St. Andrews.

VI For Exemplary Conduct during the Session, to
John Glynn Wynn, N. Wales.
William Marshall, Glasgow
George Gordon,   ,,

———

The Prizes of the HUMANITY CLASS were adjudged—

I. For the best Essays on the Domestic Manners of the Romans, to
Robert Brisbane, Glasgow.
George Monro,   ,,
James Mitchell, Beith.

II. For the best Translation from Latin into English, to
Archibald Millar, Glasgow.

III. For the best Translation from English into Latin, to
Laurence Millar, Strathern.

IV. **For** the best Latin Verses, to
> John Glynn Wynn, N. Wales.
> James M'Turk, Glasgow.

V. **For** excelling in a Public Examination, to
> John Moodie, Riccartoun.
> John Mitchell, Beith.

VI. **For** the best Specimens of Elocution in the delivery of Latin Speeches, to
> John Glynn Wynn, N. Wales.
> William Erskine, Strathern.
> Samuel M'Call, Glasgow.
> Samuel Hunter, Galloway.

VII. **For** Exemplary Conduct, to
> Alexander Fulton, Renfrewshire.
> George Gordon, Glasgow.
> James Munro,   ,,
> John Glynn Wynn, N. Wales.
> John Hedley, Westmoreland.
> John How, Kilbarchan.
> John Meek, Shotts.
> Robert Aitken, Kilbarchan.
> Walter Tait, Glasgow.

GLASGOW COLLEGE, MAY 6, 1784.

On Saturday, the 1st current, the Annual Distribution of Prizes was made in the Common Hall of Glasgow College, by the Professors, in presence of a numerous meeting of the University.

Three Prizes, given for the best Latin Orations, delivered in the Common Hall, during the Session, were adjudged to
> Lockhart Muirhead, Dysart.
> William Richardson, Glasgow.
> John Moody, Ayrshire.

At the same time were distributed Prizes to the Students of the
ETHICK, LOGICK, GREEK, and HUMANITY CLASSES.

The Prizes of the ETHICK CLASS were adjudged—

I. For the best Latin Exercises on Justice, to

> Samuel Rose, Middlesex.
> William M'Turk, Glasgow.

II. For the best illustration of the argument for the Existence
of a Supreme Being, drawn from the works of nature, to

> William M'Turk, Glasgow.
> Andrew Monach, Kirkcudbright.
> John Sommers, Hamilton.

III. For the best proofs that there is a Moral Administration
established in the world, to

> Archibald M'Laughlan, Greenock.
> Robert Forrester, Cumberland.

IV. For the best account of the Epicurean doctrine concerning
the Summum Bonum, with remarks, to

> Samuel Rose, Middlesex.
> Robert Stirling, Perthshire.

V. For the best Essays on the question, Are Virtue and Interest
ever really disjoined? to

> Samuel Rose, Middlesex.
> Richard Freebairn, Dumbarton.

The Prizes of the LOGICK CLASS were adjudged—

I. For the best Criticism on a Paper of the *Guardian*, to

> John Sommers, Hamilton.

II. For the best Poetical Essay on the Siege of Gibraltar, to

> Lockhart Muirhead, Dysart.

III. For the best Analysis of a Literary Composition, to

> John Glynn Wynn, North Wales.

IV. For the best Specimens of Composition on various Subjects of Reasoning and Taste, prescribed during the Session, to

1st Division.

James Murray, Ireland.
John Smith,   ,,
Samuel Hunter, Galloway.
John Glynn Wynn, North Wales.
James Binning, Whitburn.
John Howe, Kilbarchan.
John Hedley, Westmoreland.
George Hay, Ireland.

2nd Division.

Alexander Fulton, Eaglesham.
Walter Tait, Glasgow.
Patrick Forbes, Argyleshire.

V. For the best Public Theme, to
James Binning, Whitburn.

The Prizes of the GREEK CLASS were adjudged—

I. For the best Translation of the Nubes of Aristophanes, to
Thomas Fleeming, Fifeshire.

II. For the best Essay on the Greek Prepositions, to
Robert Clark, Beith.

III. For the best Essay on the Unity of Greek Flexion, to
John Glynn Wynn, North Wales.

IV. For the best Analysis of Greek Contraction, to
Thomas Fleeming, Fifeshire.

V. For the best Poetical Translations of two Chorusses in the Medea of Euripides, to
Lockhart Muirhead, Dysart.
John Glynn Wynn, North Wales.

VI. For excelling in the Grammatical Competition, to
James Smith, Glasgow.

VII. **For** Exemplary Conduct during the Session, to

> James Smith, Glasgow.
> Thomas Thomson, Dailly.
> James Borland, Kilmarnock.
> Archibald Henderson, Glasgow.

The Prizes of the HUMANITY CLASS were adjudged—

I. For the best Critical Analysis of one of Cicero's Orations, to

> Lockhart Muirhead, Dysart.

II. For the best account of the Military Institutions of the Romans, to

> James Whitehead, Stirlingshire.

III. For the best account of the different kinds of Poetry, to

> Henry Fergus, Stirlingshire.

IV. For the best Translation trom Latin into English, to

> John Glynn Wynn, North Wales.

V. For the best Translations from English into Latin, to

> John Hunter, Paisley.
> James Maxwell, Glasgow.

VI. For the best Latin Verses, to

> Rolland Lindsay, Lanerkshire.
> Robert Kerr, Middlesex.

VII. For excelling in a public Examination, to

> Matthew Biggar, Renfrewshire.
> Samuel Rose, Middlesex.
> Walter Tait, Glasgow.

VIII. For Exemplary Conduct, to

> Alexander Cowan, Borrowstounness.
> Robert Cowan,   ,,
> John Cowan,   ,,
> Archibald Scott, Lanerkshire.
> Charles Thomson, Dumbartonshire.
> John Hunter, Paisley.

GLASGOW COLLEGE, May 5, 1785.

On Monday, the second current, the Annual Distribution of Prizes was made in the Common Hall of Glasgow College, by the Professors, in presence of a numerous Meeting of the University, and of many respectable Gentlemen of this city and neighbourhood.

The Three Silver Medals, given by the University, were adjudged as follows :—

I. For the best dissertation on the Authenticity of the Gospel of St. Matthew, especially of the first and second chapters, to

Stevenson Macgill, M.A., Port-Glasgow.

II. For the best Essay on the Ebbing and Flowing of the Sea, to

John Sommers, M.A., Hamilton.

III. For the best Specimen of Elocution, to

John Sommers, M.A., Hamilton.

Two Prizes, given for the best Latin Orations, delivered in the Common Hall, during the Session, were adjudged, to

William M'Turk, Glasgow.
Laurence Millar, Perthshire.

At the same time were distributed Prizes to the Students of the MATHEMATICK, ETHICK, LOGICK, GREEK, and HUMANITY CLASSES.

The Prizes of the MATHEMATICK CLASSES were adjudged as follows :—

I. For the best Exercises in Plain Geometry, to

Charles Foster Mustard, Essex.
George Lloyd, Worcestershire.
Samuel Waud, York.
John Murray, Newcastle.
William Penrose, Corke.
Duncan Macfarlane, Stirlingshire.
John Macarthur, Renfrewshire.

II. For the best Exercises in Solid Geometry, to
Patrick Macdowal, Glasgow.
John Smith, Ireland.

III. For the best Exercises in Geography, to
Robert Maccubbin, Lanarkshire.
James Nielson, Ireland.

The Prizes of the ETHICK CLASS were adjudged—.

I. For the best Account of the Doctrine of the Stoicks, and of the Peripateticks concerning the Summum Bonum, to
Samuel Rose, Middlesex.

II. For the best Latin Exercises on Conscience, to
John Glynn Wynn, North Wales.
James Binning, Linlithgowshire.

III. For the best Exercises on various Subjects in Natural Theology and Ethicks, prescribed during the Session, to
John Glynn Wynn, North Wales.
James Binning, Linlithgowshire.
James Smith, Glasgow.
Alexander Fulton, Renfrewshire.

The Prizes of the LOGICK CLASS were adjudged—

I. For the best Criticism on a Paper of the *Spectator*, to
James Binning, Linlithgowshire.

II. For the best Essay on Genius, to
John Glynn Wynn, North Wales.

III. For the best Analysis of a Literary Composition, to
George Gordon, Glasgow.

IV. For the best Specimens of Composition on various Subjects of Reasoning and Taste, prescribed during the Session, to

First Division.
John Alexander Hunter, York.
Thomas Thomson, Ayrshire.
Charles Foster Mustard, Essex.
George Gordon, Glasgow.
John Robertson, Lanarkshire.

Second Division.

James Green, Yorkshire.
William Oliphant, Dumbarton.
George Lloyd, Worcester.
George Campbell, Argyleshire.
Archibald Scott, Lanarkshire.
John Hunter, Paisley.
John Caw, Perthshire.

V. For the best Publick Theme, to
Thomas Thomson, Ayrshire.

———

The Prizes of the GREEK CLASS were adjudged—

I. For the best Exercise on the General Analogy of the Greek Language, to
John Glynn Wynn, North Wales.

II. For the best Essay on the Middle Verb, to
John Alexander Hunter, York.

III. For the best Essay on the Prepositions, to
John Sommers, M.A., Hamilton.

IV. For the best Translation of a Chorus from the Oedipus Tyrannus of Sophocles, to
Richard Henderson, Glasgow.

V. For excelling in the Grammatical Competition, to
George Gordon, Glasgow.

VI. For Exemplary Conduct during the Session, to
John Alexander Hunter, York.
William Patrick, Ayrshire.
James Glasford, Glasgow.

———

The Prizes of the HUMANITY CLASS were adjudged—

I. For the best Account of the Civil Institutions of the Romans, to
John Mitchell, Ayrshire.

II. For the best Translation from Latin into English, to
John Hunter, Paisley.

III. For the best Translation from English into Latin, to
James Glasford, Glasgow.

IV. For the best Latin Verses, to
John Palmer, Bengal.
James Campbell, Jura.
John Campbell, Jura.

V. For the best Essays on the Nature and Beauty of Arrange-
ment in Fine Writing, to
John Glynn Wynn, North.Wales.
James Binning, Linlithgowshire.

VI. Far the best Specimens of Elocution in the delivery of
Latin Speeches, to
John Maxwell, Glasgow.
Archibald Hamilton, Glasgow.
Moncrief Thripland, Edinburgh.

VII. For Excelling in a Publick Examination, to
William Rose, Galloway.
Duncan Macfarlane, Stirlingshire.

VIII. For Exemplary Conduct, to
William Patrick, Ayrshire.
John Watt, Dumbartonshire.
James Glasford, Glasgow.
James Henderson, ,,
George Brown, London.
Robert Brown,   ,,

GLASGOW COLLEGE, MAY 4, 1786.

On Monday, the first current, the Annual Distribution of Prizes
was made in the Common Hall of Glasgow College, by the
Principal, Dean of Faculty, and Professors, in presence of a
numerous meeting of the University, and of many respectable
Gentlemen of the City and neighbourhood.

The Three Silver Medals, given by the UNIVERSITY, were adjudged—

I. For the best Dissertation on "The Evidence from Miracles of the Divine Mission of Jesus," to

Robert Rennie, M.A., Stirlingshire.

II. For the best Essay on "The Annual Motion of the Earth round the Sun," to

John Glynn Wynn, M.A., North Wales.

III. For the best Specimen of Elocution, to

John Glynn Wynn, M.A., North Wales.

———

Two Prizes, given for the best Latin Orations, delivered in the Common Hall, during the Session, were adjudged to

John M'Cubbin, Dumfries-shire.
John Glynn Wynn, M.A., North. Wales.

For the best Essay on the Second Georgick of Virgil, to

Thomas Thomson, Ayrshire.

———

At the same time were distributed Prizes to the Students of the LAW, MATHEMATICK, ETHICK, LOGICK, GREEK, and HUMANITY CLASSES.

———

The Prize of the LAW CLASS for the best Essay on this question, "Is it expedient that the National Representatives in Parliament should be obliged to follow the instructions of their constituents?" was adjudged to

Adam Gillies, Forfarshire.

———

The Prizes of the MATHEMATICK CLASS were adjudged as follows :—

First Mathematick Class.

Richard Chenevix, Ireland.
Thomas Thomson, Ayrshire.
Patrick Maxwell, Forfarshire.
Charles Robertson, Perthshire.
Archibald. Scot, Lanarkshire.
Archibald Cameron, Glasgow.
John Caw, Stirlingshire.

Second Mathematick Class.

James Ferguson, Dumfries-shire.
Duncan M'Farlane, Stirlingshire.

Geography Class.

Charles Foster Mustard, Essex.
John Glynn Wynn, North Wales.
Patrick Forbes, Argyleshire.

———

The Prizes of the ETHICK CLASS were adjudged—

I. For the best Latin Exercises on the following subject, "Oderunt peccare boni, virtutis amore," to

John Alexander Hunter, York.
John Hunter, Renfrewshire.

II. For the best Essays on "The Goodness of the Supreme Being," to

John Hunter, Renfrewshire.
Charles Foster Mustard, Essex.
James Maxwell, Glasgow.

III. For the best Exercises in confutation of the doctrine, that all our actions proceed from Self-Love, to

John Hunter, Renfrewshire.
John Alexander Hunter, York.
William Oliphant, Dumbartonshire.

IV. For the best Essays on the influence which Fortune, Custom, and Utility have upon our judgments concerning conduct, to

George Lloyd, Worcester.
William Oliphant, Dumbartonshire.

V. For the best Illustrations of the Epicurean Doctrine concerning the Summum Bonum, with suitable remarks, to

John Alexander Hunter, York.
George Gordon, Glasgow.

———

The Prizes of the LOGICK CLASS, proposed at the end of last Session, and executed during the vacation, were adjudged—

I. For the best Essay on the Influence of Attention on Genius, to

Charles Foster Mustard, Essex.

II. For the best Essay on Simplicity of Style, to
John Alexander Hunter, York.

III. For the best Specimens of Composition, on various Subjects of Reasoning and Taste, prescribed and executed during this Session, to

1st Division.

James Ferguson, Dumfries-shire.
George Cranstoun, Roxburghshire.
James Glasford, Glasgow.
William Rose, Galloway.
Moncreif Threipland, Edinburgh.

2nd Division.

John Lloyd, Worcester.
Archibald Cameron, Glasgow.
Duncan M'Farlane, Stirlingshire.
Donald Turner, Argyleshire.
Trafford Campbell,   ,,
Patrick Maxwell, Forfarshire.
Richard Chenevix, Ireland.

For the best Analysis of a Literary Composition, to
Trafford Campbell, Argyleshire.

For the best public Theme, to
William Rose, Galloway.

————

The Prizes of the GREEK CLASS were adjudged—

I. For the best Exercise on the General Analogy of the Greek Language, to
John Alexander Hunter, York.

II. For the best Translation of Longinus, to
John Anderson, Dumbartonshire.

III. For the best Translation of an Oration of Lysias, to
John Hunter, Paisley.

IV. For the best Critical Essay on the Oedipus Tyrannus of Sophocles, to
Samuel Rose, Middlesex.

V. For the best Essay on the Poetical Character of Homer, to
Alexander Fulton, Renfrewshire.

VI. For the best Essay on the Style and Manner of
Theophrastus, to
James Ferguson, Dumfries-shire.

VII. For the best Translation of the Fifth Book of Homer's
Iliad, to
James Bryce, Lanarkshire.

VIII. For the best Essay on the Language of Homer, to
George Lloyd, Worcester.

IX. For the best Account of the Versification of the Ancient
Drama, to
John Lloyd, Worcester.

X. For excelling in the Grammatical Competition, to
Thomas Thomson, Ayrshire.

XI. For Exemplary Conduct during the Session, to
George Cranstoun, Roxburghshire.
George Hunter, York.
Robert Smith, Ayrshire.
Laurence Dinwiddie, Glasgow.

———

The Prizes in the HUMANITY CLASS were adjudged—

For the best Translation of Plautus's Mostellaria, to
James Smith, Glasgow.

For the best Essays on the nature of Poetical Composition, to
John Alexander Hunter, York.
George Lloyd, Worcester.

For the best Translations from English into Latin, to
Richard Alexander Oswald, Renfrewshire.
John Campbell, Jura.
James Glasford, Glasgow.

For the best Latin Verses on the death of the late Reverend
Principal Leechman, to
George Lloyd, Worcester.
James Smith, Glasgow.

For the best Exercise in Prosody, to
George Hunter, York.

For the best Translations of a speech from Livy, to
John Henderson, North America.
John Kilby, York.

For the best Specimens of Elocution, in the delivery of Latin·
Speeches, in an Interlude selected from Virgil, to
Bazil Herron, Glasgow.
John Meek, Lanarkshire.
Archibald Maxwell, Glasgow.

And for Exemplary Behaviour and Diligence, to
Alexander Houstoun, Glasgow.
Benjamin Mathie,   „
James Henderson, North America.
John M'Doual, Glasgow.
Robert Marshal,   „
William Ramsay, North America.
William Thomson, Stirlingshire.

On Tuesday last, Mr. M'NAB's two Prizes for the best Essays·
on the Principles of Reading and Speaking were adjudged to
James Smith, Glasgow.
James Binning, Linlithgowshire.

GLASGOW COLLEGE, MAY 1, 1787.

This day the Annual Distribution of Prizes was made in the
Common Hall of Glasgow College, by the Principal and Professors, in presence of a numerous Meeting of the University, and
of many respectable Gentlemen of this City and neighbourhood.

Two Silver Medals, given by the University, were adjudged—

I. For the best Essay on the Natural History of the Winds, to
Andrew Crawfurd, M.A., Ayrshire.

II. For the best Specimen of Elocution, to
            William Erskine, M.A., Perthshire.

———

A Gold Medal given by ROBERT GRAHAⅯE, Esq., of Gartmore, Lord Rector of the University, for the best Essay on the Excellence of the British Constitution, was adjudged to
            John Glynn Wynn, M.A., North Wales.

———

Two Prizes, given for the best Latin Orations, delivered in the Common Hall during the Session, were adjudged to
            George Wotherspoon, Glasgow.
            William Oliphant, M.A., Dumbarton.

———

At the same time, were distributed Prizes to the Students of the LAW, HEBREW, MATHEMATICK, ETHICK, LOGICK, GREEK, and HUⅯANITY CLASSES.

———

The Prize of the LAW CLASS, for the best Essay on the question, "Whether is a popular Government favourable or unfavourable to the Fine Arts?" was adjudged to
            James Fergusson, Dumfries-shire.

———

The Prize of the HEBREW CLASS, for the best Essay on the Hebrew Pronoun, was adjudged to
            William Richardson, M.A., Glasgow.

———

The Prizes of the MATHEMATICK CLASS were adjudged as follows :—

First Mathematick Class.

            Moncrief Thriepland, Edinburgh.
            Robert Linton, Northumberland.
            Robert Blackadder, Perthshire.
            Thomas Godfrey, Lancashire.
            Trafford Campbell, Argyleshire.
            Archibald Campbell,   „
            Donald Turner,   „
            James Ritchie, Glasgow.
            Angus Leitch, Argyleshire.

Robert Smith, *major*, Ayrshire.
Robert Smith, *minor*,   „
William Hood,   „
Thomas Taylor, Kinross-shire.

Second Mathematick Class.

Richard Chenevix, Ireland.
George Cranstoun, Roxburghshire.

Geographical Class.

Archibald Scot, Lanarkshire.
William Oliphant, Dumbarton.

The Prizes of the ETHICK CLASS were adjudged—

I. For the best Essay on the Doctrine of the Peripateticks concerning the Summum Bonum, to

John Alexander Hunter, York.

II. For the best Latin Exercises on the following subject :—
Summum crede, nefas, animam praeferre pudori, to

James Fergusson, Dumfries-shire.
William Rose, Galloway.

III. For the best Vindication of Divine Justice and of a Moral Administration, to

George Cranstoun, Roxburghshire.
Trafford Campbell, Argyleshire.

For a Poetical Exercise on the same subject, to

John Leech, Ireland.

IV. For the best Essay on the Qualities requisite in an Agent that is accountable for his behaviour, to

James Fergusson, Dumfries-shire.
Moncrief Thriepland, Edinburgh.

V. For the best Illustration of the Natural Rights of Mankind, to

George Cranstoun, Roxburghshire.
James Henderson, Perthshire.

VI. For the best Essay "On the Regard that is due to Considerations of Utility in our Conduct," to

John Lloyd, Worcester.

The Prizes of the LOGICK CLASS, proposed at the end of last Session, and executed during the vacation, were adjudged—

I. For the best Essay on the Nature and Effects of Habit, to
James Fergusson, Dumfries-shire.

II. For the best Essay on Sublimity of Style, to
George Cranstoun, Roxburghshire.

III. For the best Specimens of Composition on various Subjects of Reasoning and Taste prescribed during this Session, to

Richard Henderson, Glasgow.
George Hunter, York.
Samuel Martin, Nottingham.
William Strang, Glasgow.
Finlay Macfarlane, Perthshire.
William Stirling, Perthshire.
Robert Broun, London.
Daniel Mackenzie, Perthshire.
Robert Linton, Northumberland.
John Kilby, York.
John Meek, Lanarkshire.
Richard Alex. Oswald, Renfrewshire.
Robert Ure, Stirlingshire.

IV. For the best Solution of the Dilemma of Protagoras, to
James Glasford, Glasgow.

V. For the best Analysis of a Literary Composition, to
George Hunter, York.

VI. For the best Public Theme, to
George Hunter, York.

VII. For the best Profession at the General Examination, to
Finlay Macfarlane, Perthshire.

VIII. For the best Poem on the Invention of the Balloon, to
William Erskine, M.A., Perthshire.

———

The Prizes of the GREEK CLASS were adjudged—

I. For the best Critical Essay on the Nubes of Aristophanes, to
George Cranstoun, Roxburghshire.

II. For the best Translation of the same Comedy, to
James Glasford, Glasgow.

III. For the best Translation of the Sixth Book of Homer's Iliad, to
Charles Foster Mustard, Essex.

IV. For the best Translation of the Characters of Theophrastus, to
James Glasford, Glasgow.

V. For the best Poetical Translation of the First Chorus of the Choëphorae of Æschylus, to
George Cranstoun, Roxburghshire.

VI. For the best Critical Essay on the Twenty-Fourth Book of Homer's Iliad, to
Thomas Thomson, Ayrshire.

VII. For the best Essay on Ancient Tragedy, to
Thomas Thomson, Ayrshire.

VIII. For Excelling in the Grammatical Competition, to
Archibald Macfarlane, Stirling.

IX. For Exemplary Conduct, during the Session, to
George Hunter, York.
John Tassie, Glasgow.
James Oswald, Glasgow.
Charles Addie, Dumbartonshire.

————

The Prizes in the HUMANITY CLASS were adjudged—

I. For the best Essay on the Nature of Poetical Composition, to
James Fergusson, Dumfries-shire.

II. For the best Essays on the Beauty of Language, to
Alexander Fulton, Renfrewshire.
George Hunter, York.

III. For the best Translations of Cicero's Oration for Ligarius, to
Henry Duncombe, Yorkshire.
Samuel Martin, Nottingham.

IV. For the best Translation of the First Book of Lucan's Pharsalia, to
>Archibald Maxwell, Glasgow.

V. For the best Translations from English into Latin, to
>Mottrom Ball, Virginia.
>James Sergeantson, Yorkshire.
>Allan Love, Virginia.
>Alexander Houstoun, Glasgow.

VI. For the best Exercises in Prosody, to
>Colin Campbell, Jura.
>Charles Addison, Borrowstounness.

VII. For Excelling at the Black Stone Examination, to
>Æneas Macleod, Edinburgh.
>Robert Macfarlane, Perthshire.
>James Oswald, Renfrewshire.

VIII. For Exemplary Behaviour and Diligence, to
>Nathaniel Stevenson, Glasgow.
>John Tassie,   ,,
>Mottrom Ball, Virginia.
>Colin Campbell, Jura.

GLASGOW COLLEGE, MAY 1, 1788.

This day the Annual Distribution of Prizes was made, in the Common Hall, by the Principal, Dean of Faculty, and Professors, in presence of a numerous meeting of the University, and of many respectable Gentlemen of this City and neighbourhood.

Three Silver Medals, given by the UNIVERSITY, were adjudged,

I. For the best Account of the Arian Controversy, during the Fourth Century, to
>William Richardson, M.A., Glasgow.

II. For the best Essay on Vulcanoes to
>George Cranstoun, Roxburghshire.

III. For the best Specimen of Elocution, to

John Murray, Northumberland.

———

Ten Pounds, given by an eminent CLERGYMAN of the Church of Scotland, for the best Sermon on Titus ii. 6, to

John Thomson, Stirlingshire.

———

Two Prizes given for the best Latin Orations, delivered in the Common Hall, during the Session, to

James Neilson, M.A., Ireland.
Moncrief Threipland, Edinburgh.

———

At the same time were distributed Prizes to the Students of the HEBREW, ETHICK, LOGICK, GREEK, and HUMANITY CLASSES.

———

The Prize of the HEBREW CLASS, for the best Scheme of the Conjugation of the Defective Verbs, to

Thomas Rowat, Lanarkshire.

———

The Prizes of the ETHICK CLASS were adjudged—

I. For the best Ethick Exercises in Latin, to

George Hunter, York.
John Frisselle, Isle of Man.

II. For the best Essay on the Summum Bonum, to

James Henderson, Perthshire.

III. For the best Essays on various Subjects, prescribed during the Session, to

John Meek, Lanarkshire.
John Frisselle, Isle of Man.
Thomas Thomson, Ayrshire.
Robert Linton, Cumberland.
William Gossip, Leicestershire.
Mungo Taylor, Perthshire.
John Cumming, Ayrshire.

The Prizes of the LOGICK CLASS, for Exercises proposed at the End of last Session, and executed during the Vacation, were adjudged—

I. For the best Essay on Induction, to
George Hunter, York.

II. For the best Essay on Style, to
Samuel Martin, Nottingham.

III. For the best Specimens of Composition on various Subjects of Reasoning and Taste, prescribed and executed during this Session, to

First Division.

Thomas Godfrey, Lancashire.
Francis Jeffery, Edinburgh.
James Serjeantson, York.
John Banks, Ayrshire.
Matthew Galt, Glasgow.
Hugh Laird, Renfrewshire.
William Shaw, Stirlingshire.
Patrick Whyte, Perthshire.
William Thomson, Stirlingshire.
John Cupples, Berwickshire.

Second Division.

Robert Smith, Ayrshire.
Æneas Macleod, Edinburgh.
William Cook, Perthshire.

IV. For the best Publick Theme, to
Robert Hill, Glasgow.

For excelling at the Black Stone Examination, to
James Serjeantson, York.

The Prizes of the GREEK CLASS were adjudged—
I. For the best Specimens of Translation, to
Samuel Martin, Nottingham.
Thomas Godfrey, Lancashire.

II. For the best Specimen of Criticism, to
Thomas Thomson, Ayrshire.

III. For excelling in the Grammatical Competition, to

Hugh Laird, Ayrshire.

IV. For Exemplary Conduct during the Session, to

Matthew Galt, Glasgow.
James Muir, Stirlingshire.
William Wardlaw, Glasgow.

The Prizes in the HUMANITY CLASS were adjudged—

I. For the best Specimens of Criticism, to

John Frisselle, Isle of Man.
George Hunter, York.

II. For the best Specimens of Translation from Latin into English, to

John Frisselle, Isle of Man.
William Gossip, Leicestershire.
Archibald Scott, M.A., Lanarkshire.
James Stirling, Lanarkshire.
Thomas Brown, Glasgow.

III. For the best Translations from English into Latin, to

Mottrum Ball, Virginia.
John Stevenson, Glasgow.

IV. For the best Exercise in Prosody, to

William Crawford, Glasgow.

V. For excelling at the Black Stone Examination, to

Robert Marshal, Glasgow.

VI. For Exemplary Behaviour and Diligence, to

Archibald Hamilton, Lanarkshire.
Charles Addie, Dumbartonshire.
James Dalyel, Linlithgowshire.
James Hamilton, Lanarkshire.
James Dickson, Dumbartonshire.
Robert Semple, North America.
William Wilson, Ayrshire.

GLASGOW COLLEGE, May 1, 1789.

This day the Annual Distribution of Prizes was made in the Common Hall, by the Principal, Dean of Faculty, and Professors, in presence of a numerous meeting of the University, and of many respectable Gentlemen of this City and neighbourhood.

———

The Silver Medals, given by the UNIVERSITY, were adjudged—

I. For the best Essay on the Phenomenon of the Rainbow, to
Thomas Thomson, Ayrshire.

II. For the best Specimen of Elocution, to
Walter Tait, A.M., Glasgow.

———

The Gartmore Gold Medal, for the best Essay on the Revolution, to
George Cranstoun, Roxboroughshire.

———

Ten Pounds, given by an eminent Clergyman of the Church of Scotland, for the best Sermon on Isaiah xxviii. 22, to
John Sommers, A.M., Lanarkshire.

For the best Latin Oration, delivered in the Common Hall, during this Session, to
William Stirling, Perthshire.

———

At the same time were distributed Prizes to the Students of the HEBREW, MATHEMATICK, ETHICK, LOGICK, GREEK, and HUMANITY CLASSES.

———

The Prize of the HEBREW CLASS, for the best Analysis of the Irregular Verb, to
James Kyle, Kinross-shire.

———

The Prizes of First MATHEMATICK CLASS were adjudged to
William Gossip, Leicestershire.
William M'Arthur, Perthshire.
John Campbell, Mid Lothian.

Walter Moodie, Ayrshire.
William Crawfurd, Lanarkshire.
John Banks, Ayrshire.

The Prizes of the Second MATHEMATICK CLASS were adjudged to

Robert Hill, Glasgow.
Dykes Smith, Stirlingshire.

———

The Prizes of the ETHICK CLASS were adjudged—

I. For the best Abridgment of Butler's Analogy, written during last Vacation, to

John Frisselle, A.M., Isle of Man.

II. For the best Essays on various Subjects, prescribed during the Session, to

Burnet Bruce, Clackmannanshire.
Robert Auld, Ayrshire.
Thomas Godfrey, Lancashire.
James Serjeantson, York.
William Simpson, Forfarshire.
William Shaw, Stirlingshire.
Walter Moodie, Ayrshire.
John Fergus, Stirlingshire.
Patrick Whyte, Perthshire.

———

The Prizes of the LOGICK CLASS were adjudged—

I. For the best Essay on the Socratick Mode of Reasoning, to
Thomas Godfrey, Lancashire.

II. For the best Essay on the Construction, and Use, of the Syllogism, to
Glynn Wynn, North Wales.

III. For the best Specimens of Composition, on various Subjects of Reasoning and Taste, prescribed and executed during the Session, to

First Division.

Robert Marshal, Glasgow.
John Wilson Rae,   ,,
George Middlemore, Nottinghamshire.

Daniel M'Naughton, Argyleshire.
James Muir, Stirlingshire.
Jonathan Ranken, Glasgow.
Glynn Wynn, North Wales.
Robert Scott, Lanarkshire.

Second Division.

Charles Addie, Dumbartonshire.
John Bell, Paisley.
William Black, Lanarkshire.
James Burns, Linlithgowshire.

IV. For the best Publick Theme, to
James Muir, Stirlingshire.

V. For excelling at the Black Stone Examination, to
William Wilson, Renfrewshire.

––––––

The Prizes of the GREEK CLASS were adjudged—

I. For the best Specimens of Translation, to
Thomas Godfrey, Lancashire.

II. For Exemplary Conduct, and distinguished Diligence, during the Session, to
Archibald Wilson, Lanarkshire.
Duncan Clark, Argyleshire.
William Wilson, Renfrewshire.
Richard Cowan, Glasgow.
James Ewing,   „
James Sims, Somersetshire.
James Hamilton, Lanarkshire.
William M'Ilquham, Glasgow.

––––––

The Prizes in the HUMANITY CLASS were adjudged—

I. For the best Specimens of Criticism on some of the Odes of Horace, to
Alexander Easton, Stirlingshire.
Robert Marshal, Glasgow.

II. For the best Specimen of Translation from Latin into English, to
William M'Ilquham, Glasgow.

III. For the best Specimen of Translation from English into Latin, to

> Colin Dunlop, Glasgow.

IV. For the best Latin Verses, to

> W. C. Graham, Perthshire.

V. For excelling at the Black Stone Examination, to

> Andrew Mitchel, Ayrshire.

VI. For Exemplary Conduct, and distinguished Diligence, to

> Colin Dunlop, Glasgow.
> John Douglas, Dumbartonshire.
> John Muir, Glasgow.
> John Williamson, Glasgow.
> Michael Linning, Lanarkshire.
> Robert Drummond, Stirlingshire.
> Richard Cowan, Glasgow.
> William Crawfurd,   ,,
> W. C. Graham, Perthshire.
> William M'Dowal, Glasgow.
> William M'Ilquham, Glasgow.

GLASGOW COLLEGE, MAY 1, 1790.

This day the Annual Distribution of Prizes was made in the Common Hall, by the Principal and Professors, in presence of a numerous meeting of the University.

Three Silver Medals, given by the UNIVERSITY, were adjudged—

I. For the best Essay on the Argument for the Divine Mission of Jesus Christ, drawn from the Prophecies of the Old Testament, to

> Mungo Taylor, Perthshire.

II. For the best Essay on the Composition of Water, to

> James Watt, M.A., Ireland.

III. For the best Specimen of Elocution, to

> Thomas Freebairn, M.A., Dumbartonshire.

For the two best Latin Orations delivered in the Common Hall, during this Session, to

James Watt, M.A., Ireland.
William Heron, Galloway.

At the same time were distributed Prizes to the Students of the MATHEMATICK, ETHICK, LOGICK, GREEK, and HUMANITY CLASSES.

The Prizes of the MATHEMATICK CLASSES were adjudged to

Robert Haldane, Perthshire.
Michael Linning, Lanarkshire.

The Prizes of the ETHICK CLASS were adjudged—

I. For the best Account of the Doctrine of the Peripateticks concerning the Summum Bonum, written during the vacation, to

Patrick Whyte, Perthshire.

II. For the best Essays on various Subjects, prescribed during the Session, to

Archibald Wilson, Dumfries-shire.
William Wilson, Renfrewshire.
Glynn Wynn, North Wales.
Thomas Alexander, Ireland.
Jonathan Rankin, Glasgow.
John Bell, Renfrewshire.
Quintin Bowman, Lanarkshire.
William Black, Lanarkshire.

The Prizes of the LOGICK CLASS, proposed at the end of last Session, and executed during the vacation, were adjudged—

I. For the best Essay on the Essential Qualities of Poetical Composition, to

Glynn Wynn, North Wales.

II. For the best Essay on Method, to

Glynn Wynn, North Wales.

III. For the best Specimens of Composition, on various Subjects of Reasoning and Taste prescribed and executed during this Session, to

First Division.

James Simms, Somersetshire.
Samuel Knox, Ireland.
William M'Ilquham, Glasgow.
Robert Graham, Perthshire.
Duncan Clark, Argyleshire.
Thomas Burton, Yorkshire.
John Jamieson, Ayrshire.
Robert Semple, Lanarkshire.

Second Division.

James Ewing, Glasgow.
Andrew Mitchel, Ayrshire.
John Colquhoun, Renfrewshire.
Thomas Brown, Glasgow.
William Wardlaw, Glasgow.
William Craufurd, ,,

The Prizes of the GREEK CLASS were distributed—

I. For the best Translation of a Chorus from the Clouds of Aristophanes, to

James Simms, London.
Samuel Knox, Ireland.

II. For the best Translation of two Scenes from the same Comedy, to

Alexander Edgar, Hamilton.

III. For the best Translation of certain passages of Longinus, to

Archibald Scott, Carluke.

IV. For Exemplary Conduct, and Distinguished Diligence, during the Session, to

Duncan Clark, Argyleshire.
James Simms, Somersetshire.
Colin Dunlop, Glasgow.
James Douglas, Kelso.
James Scot, Glasgow.
Robert Douglas, Kilpatrick.
John Graham, West Indies.
Thomas Meek, Cambuslang.

The Prizes in the HUMANITY CLASS were adjudged—

I. For the best account of the Domestic Manners of the Romans, to
> Finlay M'Farlane, Perthshire.

II. For the best Translation from English into Latin, to
> James Simms, Somersetshire.
> William Moncrief, Perthshire.

III. For the best Translation from Latin into English, to
> William Stirling, Perthshire.
> Colin Dunlop, Glasgow.
> William M'Ilquham, Glasgow.
> Masterton Robertson, Inverness-shire.

IV. For excelling at the Blackstone Examination, to
> John Alex. Graham, Jamaica.

V. For the best Exercise in Prosody, to
> Colin Dunlop, Glasgow.

VI. For Exemplary Conduct, and distinguished Diligence, to
> Alexander Campbell, Dumbartonshire.
> Archibald Livingston, Stirlingshire.
> Colin Dunlop, Glasgow.
> James Donald,   ,,
> James Forbes, Argyleshire.
> James Hamilton, Lanarkshire.
> James Scot, Glasgow.
> John Douglas, London.
> Robert M'Kenzie, Dumbartonshire.

GLASGOW COLLEGE, MAY 2, 1791.

This day the Annual Distribution of Prizes was made in the Common Hall, by the Principal, Dean of Faculty, and Professors, in presence of a numerous meeting of the University, and of many respectable Gentlemen of this City and neighbourhood.

Two Silver Medals, given by the UNIVERSITY, were adjudged—

I. For the best Essay on the Argument in favour of Christianity, from the Prophecies of the New Testament, to

Thomas Taylor, A.M., Kinross.

II. For the best Specimen of Elocution, to

John Macalpine, A.M., Glasgow.

The Gartmore Gold Medal, for the best Essay on the Effects of the Union of Scotland and England, to

James Watt, A.M., Ireland.

A Prize from the Funds of a Donation for the encouragement of Literature by the late JAMES COULTER, Esq., of Glasgow, was given for the best Sermon on Phil. iv. and 5, to

Alexander Easton, Stirlingshire.

Three Prizes given for the best Latin Orations, delivered in the Common Hall, during the Session, to

Archibald Wilson, Lanarkshire.
John Wilson Rae, London.
William Black, Douglas.

At the same time were distributed Prizes to the Students of the MATHEMATICK, ETHICK, LOGICK, GREEK, and HUMANITY CLASSES.

The Prizes in the MATHEMATICAL CLASSES were adjudged—

I. In the Senior Methematical Class,

For the Invention of Geometrical Demonstrations, and the Solution of Algebraical Problems, to

Robert Haldane, Dumblane.

II. In the Junior Mathematical Class,

For the Invention of Geometrical Demonstrations, and the Solution of Algebraical Problems, to

William M'Ilquham, Glasgow.
Samuel Mundell, Ireland.
Andrew Wilson,   „

For the best appearances in the Daily Examinations during the Session, to

Andrew Mitchell, Ayrshire.

III. In the Geography Class, to

James Douglas, Kelso.

The Prizes of the ETHICK CLASS were adjudged—

I. For the best Abridgement of Bishop Butler's Sermons on Human Nature, to

Jonathan Rankin, Glasgow.
John Wilson Rae, London.

II. For the best Ethick Exercises in Latin, to

William Craufurd, Glasgow.   .
Samuel Knox, Ireland.

III. For the best Essays on various Subjects, prescribed during the Session, to

Samuel Knox, Ireland.
William Craufurd, Glasgow.
William M'Ilquham,   ,,
James Muir, Stirlingshire.
James Struthers, Strathaven.
William Aitchison, Glasgow.
Thomas Burton, Yorkshire.

The Prizes of the LOGICK CLASS, proposed at the end of last Session, and executed during the vacation, were adjudged—

I. For the best Illustration of Lord Bacon's Division of Prejudices, to

William M'Ilquham, Glasgow.

II. For the best Criticisms on a Paper of the *Spectator*, to

Thomas Burton, Yorkshire.
James Ewing, Glasgow.

III. For the best Specimens of Composition, on various Subjects prescribed during this Session.

First Division.

Colin Dunlop, Glasgow.
James Douglas, Kelso.

Randal Gossip, Yorkshire.
Michael Linning, Lanarkshire.
William M'Dowal, Glasgow.
John Gemmil, Paisley.

Second Division.

William Moncrieff, Edinburgh.
James Moncrieff   ,,
Archibald Livingston, Stirlingshire.
John Williamson, Glasgow.
James Forbes, Argyleshire.

The Prizes of the GREEK CLASS were adjudged—

I. For the best Translation, in Verse, of the Third Chorus of the Choephorae of Æschylus, to

Samuel Knox, Ireland.

II. For the best Translation, in Verse, of the First Chorus of the Choephorae of Æschylus, to

John Wilson Rae, London.

III. For the best Prose Translation of the same Chorus, to

Duncan Clark, Argyleshire.

IV. For the best delineation of a Character, according to the manner of Theophrastus, to

William M'Ilquham, Glasgow.

V. For Eminence, and Exemplary Conduct, during the Session, to

John Waddell, Lanarkshire.
John Gemmil, Paisley.
Randal Gossip, Yorkshire.
Ralston Caldwell, Renfrewshire.
Edward Marjoribanks, Berwickshire.
James Thomson, Strathaven.
James Scot, Glasgow.
John Jardine,   ,,
George Dunlop, ,,
Robert Morehead, Stirlingshire.
Robert M'Lachlan, Glasgow.
William Irvine,   ,,
John Muir,

The Prizes in the HUMANITY CLASS were adjudged—

I. For the best Essays on the Military Institutions of the Romans, to

> Daniel Macnaughtan, Argyleshire.
> William Moncrief, Perthshire.

II. For the best Translations of Tacitus's Life of Agricola, to

> William M'Ilquham, Glasgow.
> W. C. Graham, Perthshire.

III. For the best Translations, in Verse, of Select Passages from Lucan, to

> Thomas Gilpin, Middlesex.
> Samuel Knox, Ireland.
> John Wilson Rae, London.

IV. For the best Exercise in Prosody, to

> William Irvine, Glasgow.

V. For Exemplary Behaviour and Diligence, to

> Christopher Greig, Fifeshire.
> Duncan Campbell, Island of Tyrie.
> George Dunlop, Glasgow.
> George Williamson, ,,
> Hamilton Paul, Ayrshire.
> James Brownlie, Lanarkshire.
> John Jardine, Glasgow.
> John Wedderburn, Mid-Lothian.
> Ralston Caldwell, Renfrewshire.

GLASGOW COLLEGE, MAY 1, 1792.

This day the Annual Distribution of Prizes was made in the Common Hall, by the Principal and Professors, in presence of a numerous meeting of the University, and of many respectable Gentlemen of this City and neighbourhood.

Three Silver Medals, given by the University, were adjudged—

I. For the best Discourse on the Argument in support of Christianity, from its extensive propagation amidst all the opposition which it had to encounter, till the Conversion of Constantine, to

James Somerville, Lanarkshire.

II. For the best Explanation of Sir Isaac Newton's Rules of Philosophising, to

William M'Ilquham, A.M., Glasgow.

III. For the best Specimen of Elocution, to

John Wilson Ray, Glasgow.

————

Prizes given from a Donation of the late JAMES COULTER, Esq., were adjudged—

I. For the best Lecture on St. Paul's Discourse at Athens, Acts xvii., to

Donald M'Kenzie, Perthshire.

II. For the best Essay on the Importance and Usefulness of the Hebrew Language, to

William Black, Lanarkshire.

III. For the best Illustration of the Mechanic Powers, to

John Jamieson, Ayrshire.

IV. For the best Essay on the Nature and Effects of Habit, to

Andrew Mitchell, Ayrshire.

V. For the best Account of the Facts respecting the Fallacy of the Senses, to

James Scott, Glasgow.

VI. For the best Latin Orations delivered in the Common Hall, during this Session, to

James Muir, Ayrshire.
Duncan Clarke, Argyllshire.

————

At the same time, were distributed Prizes to the Students of the MATHEMATICK, ETHICK, LOGICK, GREEK, and HUMANITY CLASSES.

The Prizes of the MATHEMATICAL CLASSES were adjudged—

I. Of the Senior Class, for the Solution of Theorems and Problems in Geometry and Algebra, to

Colin Dunlop, Glasgow.
James Scott,   ,,
Edward Marjoribanks, Roxburghshire.
Charles Addison, Linlithgowshire.

II. Of the Junior Class, for the Solution of Theorems and Problems in Geometry and Algebra, to

Thomas Walker, Ireland.
John Menish,   ,,

For the best Appearances in the Daily Examinations during the Session, to

James Forbes, Argyllshire.

III. Of the Geography Class, to

James Moncrieff, Edinburgh.

The Prizes of the ETHICK CLASS were adjudged—

I. For the best Account of the Peripatetick Philosophy concerning the Summum Bonum to

James Muir, Ayrshire.

II. For the best Latin Themes, to

Colin Dunlop, Glasgow.
William Moncrieff, Edinburgh.

III. For the best Essays on various Subjects of Morals, prescribed during the Session, to

Andrew Mitchell, Ayrshire.
William Moncrieff, Edinburgh.
James Moncrieff,   ,,
John Oughterson, Ayrshire.
Andrew Harley, Paisley.

The Prizes of the LOGICK CLASS, proposed at the end of last Session, and executed during the Vacation, were adjudged—

I. For the best Illustration of the Rules for composing a Theme, to

Colin Dunlop, Glasgow.

II. For the best Essay on the Qualities of the Epic Action, to William Moncrieff, Edinburgh.

III. For the best Specimens of Composition, on various Subjects prescribed during this Session.

First Division.

Robert Kay, Stirlingshire.
Hamilton Paul, Ayrshire.
Ralston Caldwall, Renfrewshire.
Thomas Linning, Lanarkshire.
James Olive, London.
James Scott, Glasgow.
Thomas Potter, Ireland.

Second Division.

Humphrey Crombie, Glasgow.
William Jamieson, Paisley.
Lord Spencer S. Chichester, England.
Charles Babington, Dumfries.
Robert Scott, Glasgow.

The Prizes of the GREEK CLASS were adjudged—

I. For the best Account of the Versification of the Greek Lyrick Poetry, to

James Olive, London.

II. For the best Translation of a Chorus from the Medea of Euripides, to

Thomas Potter, Ireland.

III. For Exemplary Diligence, and Propriety of Conduct during the Session, to

John Young, Stirlingshire.
John Cook,   ,,
James Olive, London.
John Gardner, Glasgow.
Robert Morehead, Stirlingshire.
George Dunlop, Glasgow.
Archibald Nisbet, Lanarkshire.
Ralph Wardlaw, Glasgow.
William Wallace,   ,,

Andrew Wedderburn, Mid-Lothian.
John M. Robertson, Glasgow.
Robert Hamilton,   ,,

The Prizes in the HUMANITY CLASS were adjudged—

I. For the best Account of the Domestick Institutions of the Romans, to

James Moncrieff, Edinburgh.

II. For the best Translations of Latin into English, to

John Young, Stirlingshire.
Hamilton Paul, Ayrshire.

III. For the best Translations of English into Latin, to

Ralph Wardlaw, Glasgow.
Patrick M'Dougald, Dumbartonshire.

IV. For excelling at the Black Stone Examination, to

John Murdoch Robertson, Glasgow.

V. For the best Exercise in Prosody, to

William Chrystel, Stirlingshire.

VI. For exemplary Conduct, and distinguished Diligence, to

Francis Snodgrass, Renfrewshire.
Henry Ritchie, Glasgow.
James Chapman, Stirlingshire.
James Hood, Glasgow.
John Crawford, Ayrshire.
John Graham, Glasgow.
John Muir,   ,,
William Chrystel, Stirlingshire.

GLASGOW COLLEGE, MAY 1, 1793.

This day, the Annual Distribution of Prizes was made in the Common Hall, by the Principal and Professors, in presence of a numerous meeting of the University, and of many respectable Gentlemen of this City and neighbourhood.

The Gartmore Gold Medal was adjudged—

For the best Essay on the true interests of Great Britain, with regard to Foreign Alliances, to

John Wilson Rae, Glasgow.

———

Three Silver Medals, given by the UNIVERSITY, were adjudged—
I. For the best Essay on the Credibility of the Gospel History, to

Donald M'Kenzie, Perthshire.

II. For the best Essay on the Steam Engine, to
James Ewing, Glasgow.

III. For the best Specimen of Elocution, to

Patrick Macvicar, A.M., Argyllshire.

———

Prizes given from a Donation of the late JAMES COULTER, Esq., were adjudged—

I. For the best Sermon on John i. 17, to
Jonathan Rankin, Lanarkshire.

II. For the best Solution of the Hydrostatical Paradoxes, to
William M'Ilquham, A.M., Glasgow.

III. For the best Abridgment of the First Part of Butler's Analogy, to
James Muir, Ayrshire.

IV. For the best Essay on the Syllogism, to
John Jardine, Glasgow.

V. For the best Essay on Literary Composition, to
James Muir, Ayrshire.

VI. For the best Abstract of Cicero's First Book de Legibus, to
John Wilson Rae, Glasgow.

For the best Latin Orations in the Common Hall, to
Michael Linning, Lanarkshire.
Colin Dunlop, Glasgow.

At the same time, were distributed, Prizes to the Students of the MATHEMATICK, ETHICK, LOGICK, GREEK, and HUMANITY CLASSES.

———

The Prizes of the MATHEMATICK CLASS were adjudged—

I. For the Solution of Theorems and Problems in Geometry and Algebra, prescribed as Exercises during the Session, to

> John Jardine, Glasgow.
> Thomas Jackson, Dumfries.
> Thomas Hogg, Ireland.

II. For the best appearances in the Daily Examinations, during the Session, to,

> John Cook, Stirlingshire.

———

The Prizes of the ETHICK CLASS were adjudged—

I. For the best Account of the Peripatetick Philosophy, to

> James Moncrieff, Edinburgh.

II. For the best Latin Themes, to

> Thomas Jackson, Dumfries-shire.
> James Olive, Middlesex.

III. For the best Essays on various subjects of Morals, prescribed during the Session, to

> Robert Douglas, Dumbartonshire.
> Hamilton Paul, Ayrshire.
> James Scott, Glasgow.
> Christopher Greig, Perthshire.
> John Cook, Stirlingshire.
> William Jamieson, Paisley.
> William Irvine, Glasgow.

———

The Prizes of the LOGICK CLASS, proposed at the end of last Session, and executed during the Vacation, were adjudged—

I. For the best Essay on the advantages arising from the Study of History, to

> Thomas Meek, Lanarkshire.
> Arch. Livingston, Stirlingshire.

For the best Illustration of Horace's Advice to Authors, " Sumite Materiem," etc., executed this Session, to

George Dunlop, Glasgow.
Arch. Livingston, Stirlingshire.
Henry Cha. Boisragon, Ireland.

II. For the best Specimens of Composition, on various Subjects, prescribed during this Session.

First Division.

Henry Ch. Boisragon, Ireland.
Rich. Boyle Adderley, England.
Robert Hill, Ayrshire.
George Dunlop, Glasgow.
William Dunlop,   ,,
George Strong, England.
Thomas Campbell, Glasgow.

Second Division.

John Gilmore, Ireland.
J. Murdoch Robertson, Glasgow.
Robert Jafferay, Ayrshire.
William Wallace, Glasgow.
Robert Shaw, Ireland.

———

The Prizes of the GREEK CLASS were adjudged—

I. For the best Translations, in verse, of the Second Chorus of the Oedipus Tyrannus of Sophocles, to
Robert Kay, Stirlingshire.
Rich. Boyle Adderley, Ireland.

II. For the best Translations, in prose, of the same Chorus, to
Stephen C. Rice, Ireland.
John Cook, Stirlingshire.

III. For the best Translation, in verse, of the Fourth Chorus of the Oedipus Tyrannus, to
Robert Kay, Stirlingshire.

IV. For Exemplary Diligence, and Propriety of Conduct, during the Session, to
John Muir, Glasgow.
William Wallace, Glasgow.
Thomas Campbell,   ,,

Ralph Wardlaw, Glasgow.
Robert Robison, Stirlingshire.
Archibald Nisbet, Lanarkshire.
William Robinson, Stirlingshire.
James Corkendale,   „
George Blackwell, Glasgow.
John Dunlop,   „
Gregory Watt, England.
James Robison, Stirlingshire.

————

The Prizes of the HUMANITY CLASS were adjudged—

I. For the best Essays on the Historical Compositions of the Ancients, to

Arch. Livingston, Stirlingshire.
Robert Douglas, Dumbartonshire.
Samuel Mundel, A.M., Ireland.

II. For the best Translation, in Verse, of Claudian's Epithalamium on the Marriage of Honorius and Maria, to

Hamilton Paul, Ayrshire.

III. For the best Translation of Cicero's Dream of Scipio, and Paradoxes, to

John Jardine, Glasgow.

IV. For the best Translations from English into Latin, to

Joseph Finlayson, Glasgow.
David Aird, West Indies.

V. For the best Exercise in Prosody, to

George Blackwell, Glasgow.

VI. For Excelling at the Black Stone Examination, to

George Blackwell, Glasgow.
John Dunlop,   „
William Smellie, Lanarkshire.
Hugh Ker, Ayrshire.

VII. For Exemplary Conduct, and Distinguished Diligence, to
    Andrew Hamilton, Glasgow.
    Archibald Nisbet, Lanarkshire.
    George Blackwell, Glasgow.
    John Brown,   ,, ,
    John Dunlop,   ,,
    Lewis M'Kenzie, Ayrshire.
    Robert Robison, Stirlingshire.
    William Robinson,   ,,

GLASGOW COLLEGE, May 1, 1794.

This day, the Annual Distribution of Prizes was made in the Common Hall, by the Principal and Professors, in presence of a numerous meeting of the University, and of many respectable Gentlemen of this city and neighbourhood.

Three Silver Medals, given by the University, were adjudged—

I. For the best Essay on the Credibility of the Gospel History, to
    John Henderson, Perthshire.

II. For the best Historical and Philosophical Account of the Thermometer, to
    Thomas Meek, Lanarkshire.

III. For the best Specimen of Elocution, to
    Matthew Galt, M.A., Glasgow.

Prizes given from a Donation of the late James Coulter, Esq., were adjudged—

I. For the best sermon on Matthew v. 16, to
    Jonathan Rankin, Lanarkshire.

II. For the best Essay on the Oratorial Compositions of the Ancients, to
    Archibald Livingston, M.A., Stirlingshire.

III. For the best Translation of Cebe's Table, to
                Nathaniel Alexander, Ireland.

Prizes were also given for the best Latin Orations delivered in
the Common Hall, to
                Thomas Jackson, M.A., Dumfries-shire.
                Hamilton Paul, Ayrshire.

———

At the same time, were distributed, Prizes to Students of the
MATHEMATICK, ETHICK, LOGICK, GREEK, and HUMANITY
CLASSES.

———

The Prizes of the MATHEMATICAL CLASS were adjudged—

For the best Solutions of various Theorems and Problems in
Geometry and Algebra, proposed during the Session, to
                Gregory Watt, Birmingham.
                James Lewis, Jamaica.
                Matthew Heron, Ireland.
                David Grier, Ireland.

For the best Appearances in the Daily Examinations during the
Session, to
                John Gilmore, Ireland.

———

The Prizes of the ETHICK CLASS were adjudged—
I. For the best Latin Themes, to
                Stephen Rice, Ireland.
                Robert Jeffray, Ayrshire.

II. For the best Essays on the Origin of Evil, to
                John Jardine, Glasgow.
                Henry Boisragon, Ireland.
                John Graham, Renfrewshire.

III. For a Poetical Essay on the same Subject, to
                Thomas Campbell, Glasgow.

IV. For the best Illustrations of the Effect of Voluntary
Determination in rendering an Action morally good or evil, to
                Alexander Fleming, Ayrshire.
                Stephen Rice, Ireland.
                John Graham, Renfrewshire.

V. For the best Essays on Entails, to

> John Jardine, Glasgow.
> William Dunlop, „
> Robert Jeffray, Ayrshire.

VI. For the best Essay on Conduct, as it may be influenced by Views of Utility, to

> William Wallace, Glasgow.

———

The Prizes of the LOGICK CLASS were adjudged—

I. For the best Essay on Imitation, as it respects the Fine Arts, proposed at the end of last Session, and executed during the Vacation, to

> William Dunlop, Glasgow.

II. For the best Specimens of Composition on various Subjects, prescribed and executed this Session, to

First Division.

> James Corkindale, Stirlingshire.
> Robert Robison,   „
> Hugh Kennedy, Ireland.
> Archibald Nisbet, Lanarkshire.
> George Palmer, Yorkshire.
> Robert M'Kenzie, Dumbartonshire.

Second Division.

> Andrew Taylor, Glasgow.
> Ralph Wardlaw,   „
> John Brown,   „
> James Hume Purves, Berwickshire.
> John M'Kenzie, Ayrshire.
> John M'Gill,   „
> Henry Kennedy, Ireland.

III. For the best Illustration of Quintilian's Marks of Early Genius, Mihi ille Puerdetur, etc., executed this Session by the Students, both of the Private and Publick Class, to

Private Class.

> William Dunlop, Glasgow.
> J. W. Birch, Berkshire.

Publick Class.

Archibald Nisbet, Lanarkshire.
James Hume Purves, Berwickshire.

IV. For the best Profession at the Black Stone Examination, to

Robert Robison, Stirlingshire.

V. For the best Public Theme, to

Andrew Wedderburn, Mid-Lothian.

The Prizes of the GREEK CLASS were adjudged—

I. For the best Critical Essay on the 24th Book of Homer's Iliad, to

Thomas Jackson, Dumfries-shire.
John Jardine, Glasgow.

II. For the best Translation of Passages selected from the Clouds of Aristophanes, to

Thomas Campbell, Glasgow.
Gregory Watt, Birmingham.

III. For Propriety of Conduct, and Exemplary Diligence, during the Session, to

James Corkindale, Stirlingshire.
Robert Mackenzie, Dumbartonshire.
Robert Tait, Jamaica.
Hugh Kerr, Ayrshire.
James Robison, Stirlingshire.
James Thomson, Lancashire.
William Wilson, Paisley.
Andrew Simpson, Kinross-shire.
William Macqueen, Ayrshire.
William Stirling, Glasgow.
John Campbell, Ayrshire.
John Wright, Glasgow.

The Prizes of the HUMANITY CLASS were adjudged—

I. For the best Critical Account of Oratorial Composition among the Romans, to

Archibald Livingston, A.M., Stirlingshire.

II. For the best Account of the Domestic Manners of the Romans, to
John Brown, Glasgow.

III. For the best Essay on the Structure of Latin Verse, to
John Graham, Renfrewshire.

IV. For the best Translations from Latin into English, to
John Young, Stirlingshire.
John Dunlop, Glasgow.
Hugh Kerr, Ayrshire.
George Meek, Stirlingshire.
Joseph Amory, West-Indies.
Lorn Campbell, Argyllshire.

V. For the best Translation from English into Latin, to
William Stirling, Glasgow.

VI. For Excelling at the Black Stone Examination, to
James Robison, Stirlingshire.

VII. For Exemplary Diligence and Behaviour, to
George Meek, Stirlingshire.
Hugh Kerr, Ayrshire.
James Lister, Glasgow.
J. M. Campbell, ,,
John Scot,
John Wallace, ,,
John Wright, ,,
Matthew Shaw, ,,
Thomas Easton, Stirlingshire.

GLASGOW COLLEGE, MAY 1, 1795.

This day, the Annual Distribution of Prizes was made in the Common Hall, by the Principal and Professors, in presence of a numerous meeting of the University, and of many respectable Gentlemen of this City and neighbourhood.

Three Silver Medals, given by the UNIVERSITY, were adjudged—

I. For the best Essay on the Intrinsick Excellence and Tendency of Christianity, to

Robert Auld, Ayrshire.

II. For the best Historical and Philosophical Account of the Barometer, to

Henry Boisragon, Ireland.

III. For the best Specimen of Elocution, to

Matthew Gardner, A.M., Glasgow.

THE GARTMORE GOLD MEDAL,

For the best Account of the Origin and Nature of the Feudal System, was adjudged to

Andrew Mitchel, A.M., Ayrshire.

Prizes given from a Donation of the late JAMES COULTER, Esq., were adjudged—

I. For the best Lecture on the Parable of the Good Samaritan, Luke x. to

Andrew Mitchel, A.M., Ayrshire.

II. For the best Account of the Epicurean Philosophy, with Observations on its Defects, to

Archibald Nisbet, Lanarkshire.

III. For the best Literal Translation of the First Book of Cicero's Offices, to

William Dunlop, A.M., Glasgow.

Prizes were also given for the best Latin Orations, composed for the Common Hall, to

John Jardine, Glasgow.
Joseph Finlayson, Glasgow.

At the same time were distributed Prizes to Students of the MATHEMATICK, ETHICK, LOGICK, GREEK, and HUMANITY CLASSES.

The Prizes of the MATHEMATICAL CLASS were adjudged—

For the best Appearances in the Daily Examinations, and the best Exercises prescribed during the Session, to

> Samuel Lang, Ireland.
> James Corkendale, Stirlingshire.
> Alexander Carson, Ireland.
> George Palmes, Yorkshire.
> James Auld, Renfrewshire.
> John Campbell, Ayrshire.

The Prizes of the ETHICK CLASS were adjudged—

I. For the best Essay on the Peripatetick Philosophy, to

> John Jardine, Glasgow.

II. For the best Latin Themes, to

> James Corkendale, Stirlingshire.
> John Brown, Glasgow.

III. For the best Essays on the Evidences from Reason for the Goodness of God, to

> James Corkendale, Stirlingshire.
> George Palmes, Yorkshire.
> Hugh Kennedy, Ireland.

IV. For the best Essays on the Nature and Comparative Value of those things upon which Human Happiness depends, to

> Ralph Wardlaw, Glasgow.
> John Brown,   „

V. For the best Essays on Natural Rights, as distinguished from those that are Adventitious, to

> James Corkendale, Stirlingshire.
> George Palmes, Yorkshire.
> Andrew Taylor, Stirlingshire.

VI. For the best Accounts of the Doctrine of the Stoicks concerning the Summum Bonum, to

> John Brown, Glasgow.
> John M'Gill, Ayrshire.

The Prizes of the LOGICK CLASS were adjudged—

I. For the best Essay on the difference between Prose and Poetry, executed during the Vacation, to

Archibald Nisbet, Lanarkshire.

II. For the best Specimens of Composition on various Subjects, prescribed and executed this Session.

First Division.

Hugh Kerr, Ayrshire. ·
Gregory Watt, Birmingham.
James Templeton, Ayrshire.
William Patrick, Stirlingshire.
Henry Kennedy, Ireland.
James Robison, Stirlingshire.
Joshua Field, Yorkshire.

Second Division.

Francis Clason, London.
John Dunlop, Glasgow.
James Lister,   ,,
John Stewart, Ireland.
George Meek, Stirlingshire.
Matthew Shaw, Glasgow.
Sir James Colquhoun, Edinburgh.
Samuel Allen, Ireland.

III. For the best Essay on Abstraction and Generalisation, to

Ralph Wardlaw, Glasgow.
James Corkendale, Stirlingshire.
Gregory Watt, Birmingham.

IV. For the best Profession at the Black Stone Examination, to

James Robison, Stirlingshire.

V. For the best Publick Theme, to

Gregory Watt, Birmingham.

The Prizes of the GREEK CLASS were adjudged—

I. For the best Translation, in Verse, of the Clouds of Aristophanes, to

Thomas Campbell, Glasgow.

II. For the best Critical Essay on the First Book of Homer's Iliad, to

James **Corkendale**, Stirlingshire.

III. For the best Translations, in Verse and Prose, of certain select passages of Aeschylus, to

Gregory Watt, Birmingham.

IV. For the best Translation, in Verse, of the first Chorus of the Choephorae of Aeschylus, to

Thomas Campbell, Glasgow.

V. For Propriety of Conduct, and Exemplary Diligence, during the Session, to

William Ballingall, Kinross-shire.
Matthew Shaw, Glasgow.
Francis Clason, London.
George Blackwell, Glasgow.
William Wilson, Paisley.
Robert Boyle, Glasgow.
John Nimmo,   ,,
James Hutcheson, Hamilton.
Robert Nimmo, Glasgow.
William Freeland, ,,
James Oswald,   ,,
John Cunningham, Port-Glasgow.
John Oswald, Glasgow.
Alexander Douglass, Dumfries-shire.

———

The Prizes of the HUMANITY CLASS were adjudged—

I. For the best Account of the Religious Institutions of the Romans, to

Joseph Finlayson, Glasgow.

II. For the best Translations from Latin into English, to

James Robison, Stirlingshire.
John Oswald, Glasgow.
John Scot,   ,,
John Brown,   ,,
Alexander Campbell, Jamaica.
John Young, Glasgow.

E

III. For the best Translations from English into Latin, to
Ludovic Houstoun, Renfrewshire.
John Nimmo, Glasgow.
James Dennistoun, Glasgow.
Joseph Amory, West-Indies.

IV. For the best Latin Verses, entitled " Afri Lamentatio in Servitutem Abrepti," to
John Nimmo, Glasgow.
Alexander M'Arthur, Argyleshire.

V. For the best Translation in Verse of Claudian's Epithalamium on the Marriage of Honorius, to
Thomas Campbell, Glasgow.

VI. For Excelling at the Black Stone Examination, to
James Oswald, Glasgow.
John Nimmo, ,,
Thomas Rose, Aberdeenshire.

VII. For Exemplary Diligence and Regularity, to
James M'Rindell, Glasgow.
John Dick, ,,
John M'Dougald, ,,
John Nimmo,
Robert Nimmo, ,,

GLASGOW COLLEGE, May 2, 1796.

This day, the Annual Distribution of Prizes was made in the Common Hall, by the Lord Rector, Principal and Professors, in presence of a numerous meeting of the University, and of many respectable gentlemen of this City and neighbourhood.

Three Silver Medals, given by the UNIVERSITY, were adjudged:

I. For the best Essay on the Pelagian Controversy, to
Andrew Mitchell, A.M., Airshire.

II. For the best Essay on Electricity, to
      James Corkendale, Stirlingshire.

III. For the best Specimen of Elocution, to
      Archibald Livingston, A.M., Stirlingshire.

———

Prizes given from a Donation of the late JAMES COULTER, Esq., were adjudged—

I. For the best Sermon, to
      Andrew Mitchell, A.M., Airshire.

II. For the best Translation from the Greek, to
      Gregory Watt, Birmingham.

———

Prizes were also given for the best Latin Orations, delivered in the Common Hall, to
      George Palmes, Yorkshire.
      James Corkendale, Stirlingshire.
      Alexander Carson, A.M., Ireland.

———

At the same time were distributed Prizes to Students of the MATHEMATICK, ETHICK, LOGICK, GREEK, and HUMANITY CLASSES.

The Prizes of the MATHEMATICAL CLASS were adjudged to

I. *Seniores.*
      James Templeton, Airshire.
      Francis Clason, London.
      Henry Simson, Ireland.
      George Penrose,   „

II. *Juniores.*

      William Houstoun, Renfrewshire.
      John Nimmo, Glasgow.
      Ludovic Houstoun, Renfrewshire.

———

The Prizes of the ETHICK CLASS were adjudged—

I. For the Lest Latin Themes, to
      James Templeton, Airshire.
      William Moore, Ireland.

II. For the best Illustration of the Arguments for the Goodness of the Supreme Being, to

Gregory Watt, Birmingham.
James Lister, Glasgow.

III. For a Poetical Essay on the Goodness of God, to

William Drummond, Ireland.

IV. For the best Essays on the Origin of Polytheism, to

John Dunmore Napier, Stirlingshire.
Henry Kennedy, Ireland.

V. For the best Essays on the Natural Laws of Succession among Descendants, to

Samuel Allen, Ireland.
Francis Clason, London.

VI. For the best Essays on Justice, in the sense in which it was understood by the Ancient Philosophers, to

James Templeton, Airshire.
William Moore, Ireland.

———

The Prizes of the LOGICK CLASS were adjudged—

I. For the best Illustration of the Peripatetick Division of the Intellectual Habits, executed during the Vacation by the Students of the former Session, to

James Templeton, Airshire.

II. For the best Essay on the Socratick Dialogue, with a Specimen in the manner of Socrates, executed also during the vacation, to

John Brown, Glasgow.
Gregory Watt, Birmingham.

III. For the best Specimens of Composition on Various Subjects, prescribed and executed during the Course of this Session, to

First Division.

Hugh Thomson, Kilmarnock.
William Stirling, Glasgow.
Robert Boyle,   ,,
William Freeland,   ,,
John Roxburgh, Hamilton.
Samuel Walker, Yorkshire.
William Lamb, Lanarkshire.

Second Division.

William Wilson, Paisley.
Thomas Easton, Stirlingshire.
George Blackwell, Glasgow.
David Blackadder, Dumbartonshire.
Alexander Campbell, Argyllshire.

The Prizes of the GREEK CLASS were adjudged—

I. For the best Translations of the First Book of Homer's Iliad, in Verse, to

Hugh Kennedy, Ireland.
James Lister, Glasgow.

II. For the best Translation of the same Book, in Prose, to

John Brown, Glasgow.

III. For the best Poetical Translations of the Choephorae of Aeschylus, to

Thomas Campbell, Glasgow.
Gregory Watt, Birmingham.

IV. For the best Critical Examination of the Choephorae, to

Gregory Watt, Birmingham.

V. For the best Account of the Principle upon which Long Vowels and Diphthongs are, in certain cases, estimated as Short, in Greek Metres, to

James Corkendale, Stirlingshire.

VI. For the best Translations, in Verse, of a Chorus in the Medea of Euripides, to

Gregory Watt, Birmingham.
Thomas Campbell, Glasgow.

VII. For Exemplary Conduct, and Eminence in the Prosecution of Study during the Session, to

George Blackwell, Glasgow.
William Freeland,   „
William Lamb, Lanarkshire.
John Nimmo, Glasgow.
James Oswald,   „
John Oswald,   „
John Hodgson, Lanarkshire.

Colin Campbell, Glasgow.
William Bogle, Lanarkshire.
Devonshire Penrose, Ireland.
Michael Stirling, Perthshire.
James Baird, Renfrewshire.

The Prizes of the HUMANITY CLASS were adjudged—

I. For the best Essays on the Beauties of Language, to
    Archibald Livingston, A.M., Stirlingshire.
    Joseph Finlayson, Glasgow.
    John Graham, A.M., Glasgow.

II. For the best Account of the Rank and Duties of Roman Magistrates, to
    John Muir, Glasgow.

III. For the best Translations from Latin into English, to
    William Agur, Glasgow.
    Colin Douglas,   ,,

IV. For the best Translation from English into Latin, to
    John Young, Glasgow.

V. For Excelling at the Black Stone Examination, to
    Colin Campbell, Glasgow.
    Patrick Cumin,   ,,
    Robert Bell,   ,,
    William M'Aulay,   ,,

VI. For Exemplary Diligence and Regularity, to
    James Walker, Stirlingshire.
    Colin Campbell, Glasgow.
    William Bruce, Stirlingshire.

GLASGOW COLLEGE, MAY 1, 1797.

This day, the Annual Distribution of Prizes was made in the Common Hall, by the Principal, Dean of Faculty, and Professors, in presence of a numerous meeting of the University, and of many respectable Gentlemen of this City and neighbourhood.

Three Silver Medals, given by the UNIVERSITY, were adjudged:

I. For the best Essay on the Rise and Progress of the Reformation, during the Sixteenth Century, to

Christopher Greig, Fifeshire.

II. For the best Historical and Philosophical Account of the Application of the Barometer to the Mensuration of Heights, to

David Warden, A.M., Ireland.

III. For the best Specimen of Elocution, to

James Chapman, Stirlingshire.

The Gartmore Gold Medal, for the best Account of the Pro gress and Nature of the Roman Constitution, from the foundation of the City to the death of the Gracchi, was adjudged to

Thomas Jackson, Dumfries-shire.

Prizes given from a Donation of the late James Coulter, Esq., were adjudged—

I. For the best Lecture on Matt. vii. 24-29, to

Robert Douglas, Stirlingshire.

II. For the best Account of the Philosophical Doctrines in Cicero's Fifth Book of Tusculan Questions, to

Hugh Ker, Airshire.

III. For the best Translation of Cicero's Dialogue on Old Age, to

William Ballingall, Fifeshire.

Prizes were also given for the best Latin Orations composed for the Common Hall, to

George Meek, M.A., Falkirk.
Francis Clason, London.

A Prize in the ANATOMY CLASS, for a Dissertation on Hernia, was adjudged to

Andrew Ure, Glasgow.

At the same time were distributed Prizes to Students of the MATHEMATICK, NATURAL PHILOSOPHY, ETHICK, LOGICK, GREEK, and HUMANITY CLASSES.

The Prizes of the MATHEMATICK CLASS were adjudged, to

I. *Seniores*,

         Hugh Kerr, Airshire.
         William Freeland, Glasgow.
         John Oswald,   ,,
         George Waddell, Stirlingshire.
         Thomas Greer, Ireland.
         James Oswald, Glasgow.

II. *Juniores*,

         Samuel Stephenson, Ireland.

———

The Prizes of the NATURAL PHILOSOPHY CLASS were adjudged:

I. For General Eminence during the Session, to

         Samuel Wylie, Ireland.
         Francis Clason, London.
         David Warden, A.M., Ireland.
         William Wilson, Ireland.

II. For the best Essays on the Mechanical Powers, to

         Samuel Wylie, Ireland.
         William Stewart, Paisley.

III. For the best Public Theme, to

         Francis Clason, London.

———

The Prizes of the ETHICK CLASS were adjudged —

I. For the best Latin Themes, to

         Hugh Ker, Airshire.
         William Wilson, Paisley.

II. For the best Illustration of the Argument for the Existence of a Supreme Being, from the Evidences of Design in the Works of Nature, to

         Hugh Ker, Airshire.
         John Roxburgh, Hamilton.
         William Freeland, Glasgow.

III. For the best Essays on the Nature and Operations of the Moral Faculty, to

         Thomas Easton, Stirlingshire.
         Richard Gouldsmith, London.

IV. For the best Essays on the Right to Property acquired by Occupancy, to

> William Freeland, Glasgow.
> Andrew Hamilton,   ,,

V. For the best Illustration of the Cardinal Virtues, to

> John Wallace, Glasgow.
> Hugh Tomson, Kilmarnock.

The Prizes of the LOGICK CLASS, proposed at the end of last Session, and executed during the Vacation, were adjudged—

I. For the best Essay on Personal Merit, to

> Hugh Tomson, Kilmarnock.

For the best Abridgement of Mr. Addison's Papers in the *Spectator* on the Pleasures of the Imagination, to

> Hugh Tomson, Kilmarnock.

II. For the best Specimens of Composition on Various Subjects prescribed during the Session, and for distinguished Eminence in the general business of the Class, to

> The Hon. Charles Kinnaird, London.
> James Hutcheson, Hamilton.
> John Oswald, Glasgow.
> James Walker, Stirlingshire.
> Francis Popham, Somersetshire.
> James Oswald, Glasgow.
> John Nimmo,   ,,
> Francis Steel, Airshire.
> Thomas Rose, Glasgow.
> John Allen, Northumberland.
> John Young, Glasgow.
> James Young,   ,,
> Michael Stirling, Perthshire.
> John Stenhouse, Glasgow.
> John Eyre, York.
> Lewis Houstoun, Renfrewshire.
> John Hodson, Lanarkshire.
> John Donaldson, Airshire.
> Colin Douglas, Glasgow.

III. For the best Essay on the Fallacies of the Senses, to

> John M'Donald, Glasgow.

The Prizes of the GREEK CLASS were adjudged—

I. For the best Translation of the Medea of Euripides, executed during the Vacation, as prescribed to the Students of last Session, to
William Stewart, Paisley.

II. For the best Translation of the Characters of Theophrastus, executed during the Vacation, to
James Hutcheson, Hamilton.

III. For the best Translation of the 14th Olympick of Pindar, in Latin Verse, to
The Hon. Charles Kinnaird, London.

IV. For the best Translation of the same Olympick in English Verse, to
Ralph Wardlaw, Glasgow.

V. For the best Translation of the same Ode in Prose, to
James Hutcheson, Hamilton.

VI. For the best Translation of a Chorus in the Oedipus Tyrannus of Sophocles, in English Verse, to
Hugh Tomson, Kilmarnock.

VII. For the best Translation of the same Chorus in Prose, to
John Graham, Killearn.

VIII. For Exemplary Conduct in the Publick Class, and Eminence in the Prosecution of Study, during the Session, to
>   John Hodson, Lanarkshire.
>   William Bogle,   ,,
>   Michael Stirling, Perthshire.
>   Robert M‘Kechnie, Paisley.
>   Charles Logan, Airshire.
>   Hugh Bone,   ,,
>   Patrick Tennent, Glasgow.
>   William Banks,   ,,
>   John Pollock,   ,,
>   William G. Mack, Lanarkshire.
>   George Stirling, Glasgow.
>   James Turnbull, Lanarkshire.

The Prizes of the HUMANITY CLASS were adjudged—

I. For the best Inquiry into the Nature of Figurative Language, to

Thomas Easton, Stirlingshire.

II. For the best Account of the Domestic Manners of the Romans, to

Peter Aitkin, Glasgow.

III. For the best Translation from English into Latin, to

John Lockhart, Glasgow.

IV. For the best Translation from Latin into English, to

John Donaldson, Airshire.
John Pollock, Glasgow.

V. For Excelling at the Black Stone Examination, to

Patrick Tennent, Glasgow.

VI. For Exemplary Diligence and Regularity, to

Hugh Bone, Airshire.
John Pollock, Glasgow.
Wm. Mack, Lanarkshire.

GLASGOW COLLEGE, 1st MAY, 1798.

This day, the Annual Distribution of Prizes was made in the Common Hall, by the Principal, Dean of Faculty, and Professors, in presence of a numerous meeting of the University, and of many reverend and respectable Gentlemen of this City and neighbourhood.

Three Silver Medals, given by the UNIVERSITY, were adjudged—

I. For the best Historical View of Theological Opinions entertained by Reformers during the sixteenth and seventeenth Centuries, to

Christopher Greig, Fifeshire.

II. For the best Essay on the Construction of the Pump, to

Hugh Ker, Airshire.

III. For the best Specimen of Elocution, to
        John Muir, A.M., Glasgow.

Prizes given from a Donation of the late JAMES COULTER, Esq.,
were adjudged—
  I. For the best Sermon on 2nd Timothy iii. 4, to
        Robert Douglas, Kilpatrick.

  II. For the best Essay on Lord Bacon's Idols or Prejudices, to
        William Freeland, Glasgow.

  III. For the best Translation of Xenophon's Defence of
Socrates, to
        Alexander Macarthur, Argyllshire.

Prizes were also given for the best LATIN ORATIONS delivered
in the Common Hall, to
        James Templeton, Airshire.
        Hugh Ker,   ,,

A Prize in the ANATOMY CLASS,
For the best Essay on the Theory and Cure of the Cataract, to
        James Tennant, Lanarkshire.

A Prize in the CIVIL HISTORY CLASS,
For the best Essay on the Government of Sparta, to
        John Oswald, Glasgow.

At the same time were distributed Prizes to the Students of the
MATHEMATICK, NATURAL PHILOSOPHY, ETHICK, LOGICK, GREEK,
and HUMANITY CLASSES.

The MATHEMATICAL PRIZES were adjudged—
  I. In the *Senior Class*, to
        Hugh Ker, Airshire.
        William Freeland, Glasgow
  II. In the *Junior Class*, to
        James Walker, Falkirk.
        John Craig, Airshire.
        William Drummond, Ireland.

Samuel Caldwell, Ireland.
Duncan Blair, Balfron.
John Sym, Stirlingshire.

The Prizes of the NATURAL PHILOSOPHY CLASS were adjudged—

For general eminence during the Session, to

Hugh Ker, Airshire.
James Templeton, Airshire.
William Freeland, Glasgow.
William Lamb, Lanarkshire.
Thomas Grier, Ireland.
James M'Crindell, Glasgow.
Patrick M'Master, Stranraer.

The Prizes in the ETHICK CLASS were adjudged—

I. For exemplary Conduct in the Class, and for Eminence in the prosecution of Study during the Session, to

James Hutchison, Hamilton.
John Hodgson, Lanarkshire.
John Brown, Argyllshire.
Michael Stirling, Perthshire.
Alexander M'Arthur, Argyllshire.
James Walker, Falkirk.
Francis Steel, Airshire.
John Eyre, York.

II. For the best Exercises read in the Class on different Subjects presented during the Session, to

James Hutchison, Hamilton.
John Brown, Argyllshire.
Alexander M'Arthur, Argyllshire.
Francis Steill, Airshire.

The Prizes of the LOGICK CLASS, proposed at the end of the last Session, and executed during the Vacation—

I. For the best Essay on the Principles of Classification, and their connection with Reasoning, to

Colin Douglas, Glasgow.

II. For the best Essay on the Limits and Laws of Fiction in Epick Poetry, to

> James Hutchison, Hamilton.

III. For the best Specimens of Composition on various Subjects of Reasoning, Taste, and Criticism, prescribed during this Session, and for distinguished Eminence in the general business of the Class, to

> John White, Paisley.
> Hugh Bone, Kirkmichael.
> Charles White, England.
> David Snodgrass, Dreghorn.
> William Gordon Mack, Airdrie.
> Robert Richardson, Stirling.
> John Willock, Riccartown.
> Thomas Ballingal, Fifeshire.
> Robert Buchanan, Stirling.
> George Moncrief, Edinburgh.

The Prizes of the GREEK CLASS were adjudged—

For the best Translation, in verse, of two Choruses from the Clouds of Aristophanes, to

> William H. Drummond, Ireland.

II. For the best Translation of the same Choruses, in prose, to

> Alexander Telfer, Lanarkshire.

III. For the best Essay on the Optative Processes, recognised in the Structure, and Phraseologies of the Greek Language, to

> Alexander Carson, Ireland.

IV. For Exemplary Conduct in the Publick Class, and Eminence in the prosecution of Study during the Session, to

> Robert Richardson, Stirling.
> William Parker, Glasgow.
> William G. Mack, Lanarkshire.
> John Donaldson, Airshire.
> Patrick Tennent, Glasgow.
> John Pollok,   ,,
> William Pollok,   ,,
> George Stirling,   ,,
> Thomas M'Kenzie, Galloway.

John Riddell, Glasgow.
John Finlay,   ,,
Daniel Fisher, Stirling.
Robert Dunlop, Airshire.
Dugald M'Gibbon, Argyllshire
Andrew Campbell, Airshire.
Robert Finlay, Glasgow.
David Ran. Dickson, Peebles-shire.

The Prizes in the HUMANITY CLASS were adjudged—

I. For the best Translations of Latin into English, to

Alexander Carson, A.M., Ireland.
Hugh Bone, Galloway.
Thomas Ballingal, Fifeshire.
William G. Mack, Lanarkshire.

II. For the best Translation of English into Latin, to

John Pollok, Glasgow.
John White, Paisley.
Patrick Tennent, Glasgow.

III. For the best Essay on Poetical Composition, to

J. Donaldson, Airshire.

IV. For the best Essays on Epick Poetry, to

W. H. Drummond, Ireland.
J. Donaldson, Airshire.

V. For Excelling at the Black Stone Examination, to

Colin Smith, Campbeltown.
Donald Cuthbertson, Glasgow.
Jo. Finlay,   ,,

VI. For exemplary Diligence and Regularity, to

Andrew Russell, Renfrewshire.
Dugald Macgibbon, Inveraray.
George Dick, Glasgow.
James Ramsay, Airshire.
John Finlay, Glasgow.
John Wilson, Paisley.

VII. For the best English Verses, to
>   James Clason, Lanarkshire.
>   W. H. Drummond, Ireland.

VIII. For the best Translations of Buchanan's Psalms, to
>   David Fleming, Glasgow.
>   John White, Paisley.

GLASGOW COLLEGE, 1st May, 1799.

This day, the Annual Distribution of Prizes was made in the Common Hall, by the Principal, Dean of Faculty, and Professors, in presence of a numerous meeting of the University, and of many Reverend and respectable Gentlemen of this City and neighbourhood.

Two Silver Medals, given by the UNIVERSITY, were adjudged—
I. For the best Essay on the Invention and Improvement of Telescopes, to
>   William Freeland, Glasgow.

II. For the best Specimen of Elocution, to
>   Joseph Finlayson, Glasgow.

THE GARTMORE GOLD MEDAL,
For the best Account of the State of the Roman Government from the death of the Gracchi to the death of Augustus, to
>   Robert Douglas, Stirlingshire.

Prizes given from a Donation of the late JAMES COULTER, were adjudged—

I. For the best Lecture on the History of the Temptation, Matthew iv. chapter, to
>   Mathew Grahame, Glasgow.

II. For the best Account of the Epicurean Philosophy, to
>   Alexander M'Arthur, Argyllshire.

III. For the best Translation of the Fifth Book of Cicero de Finibus, to

Thomas Ballingall, Glasgow.

IV. A Prize in the ANATOMY CLASS,

For the best Essay on Fractures, to

Andrew Cooper, Lanarkshire.

———

Prizes were also given for the best LATIN ORATIONS, composed for the Common Hall, to

Alexander M'Arthur, Argyllshire.
Francis Steel, Airshire.

——— .

At the same time were distributed Prizes to Students of the MATHEMATICK, NATURAL PHILOSOPHY, ETHICK, LOGICK, GREEK, and HUMANITY CLASSES. .

———

The Prizes for the SECOND MATHEMATICAL CLASS were adjudged to

James Walker, Stirlingshire.
John Craig, Airshire.

Those of the FIRST MATHEMATICAL CLASS, to

1. *Seniores.*

John Jefferys, Worcestershire.
Gilbert Wright, Glasgow.
John Whiteside, Ireland.
David Murray Snodgrass, Airshire.
James Phillips, Ireland.

2. *Juniores.*

William Pollock, Glasgow.
Thomas Edington,   ,,

———

The Prizes of the NATURAL PHILOSOPHY CLASS were adjudged—

For general eminence during the Session, to

James Walker, Stirlingshire.
John Craig, Airshire.
James Ritchie, Air.
John Sym, Stirlingshire.
John Duncan, Ireland.

The Prizes of the ETHICK CLASS were adjudged—

I. For the two best Essays on the Immortality of the Soul, to
> Thomas Millar, Ireland.
> John Donaldson, Airshire.

II. Prizes were also given for General Eminence during the Session, to
> Robert Richardson, Stirling.
> John Donaldson, Airshire.
> Thomas Millar, Ireland.

———

The Prizes of the LOGICK CLASS, proposed at the end of last Session, and executed during the Vacation, were adjudged—

I. For the best Essay on the Influence of Attention on the other Powers of the Mind, to
> John Donaldson, Ballantrae.

II. For the best Essay on Figurative Language, to
> John Donaldson, Ballantrae.

III. The Prizes for the best Specimens of Composition, on various Subjects prescribed to the Students of this Session, and for distinguished Eminence in the General Business of the Class, to
> David Davis, Carmarthenshire.
> Alexander Blair, London.
> John Ross, Yorkshire.
> Charles Logan, Kirkmichael.
> Lant Carpenter, Worcestershire.
> John Whitelaw, Bothwel.
> George Stirling, Glasgow.
> Patrick Tennent,   ,,
> William Poole, Cumbertrees.
> David Coulter, Stranraer.
> Archibald M'Ewen, Argyllshire.

———

The Prizes of the GREEK CLASS were adjudged—

I. For the best Translation, in Verse, of a Chorus in the Choephorae of Æschylus, to
> James Smith, Glasgow.

. II. For the best Essay on the Interrogative and Indefinite application of the Relative Pronoun and Article, to
Robert Richardson, Stirling.

III For the best Essay on the Versification of Homer, to
Alexander Blair, London.

IV. For Exemplary Conduct in the Publick Class, and Eminence in the Prosecution of Study, during the Session, to
Patrick Tennent, Glasgow.
Alexander Blair, London.
William Glen, Airshire.
William Poole, Annandale.
John Riddell, Glasgow.
Robert Findlay, ,,
John Findlay, ,,
Robert Dunlop, Airshire.
John Wilson, Paisley.
William Cumin, Glasgow.
Andrew Whyte, Paisley.
William Robertson, Glasgow.
Robert Black, Galloway.
William Stewart, Airshire.
James Kirkwood, Dumbartonshire.
Mark Marshall, Stirlingshire.

———

The Prizes of the HUMANITY CLASS were adjudged—

I. For the best Essay on Historical Composition, to
John Donaldson, Airshire.

II. For the best Translation from Latin into English, to
David Coulter, Galloway.
John Wilson, Paisley.
Robert Findlay, Glasgow.
Allan Fleming, ,,
Patrick Mitchel, Airshire.

III. For the best Translations from English into Latin, to
John Wilson, Paisley.
James Hoggan, Dumfries-shire.
Archibald Hamilton, Glasgow.

IV. For Excelling at the Black Stone Examination, to
> John Wilson, Paisley.
> Robert Findlay, Glasgow.

V. For Excelling at the Examinations on Roman Antiquities, to
> John Wilson, Paisley.
> Robert Findlay, Glasgow.

VI. For Exemplary Diligence and Regularity, to
> John Wilson, Paisley.
> Robert Findlay, Glasgow.
> Robert Dunlop, Airshire.
> Thomas Haggart, Glasgow.
> Thomas M'Kenzie, Galloway.

VII. For the best Latin Verses, to
> William Cumin, Glasgow.
> James Gray, Airshire.

VIII. For the best English Verses, to
> Alexander M'Arthur, Argyllshire.

GLASGOW COLLEGE, 1st MAY, 1800.

This day, the Annual Distribution of Prizes was made in the Common Hall, by the Principal, Dean of Faculty, and Professors, in presence of a numerous meeting of the University, and of many respectable Gentlemen of this City and neighbourhood.

Two Silver Medals, given by the UNIVERSITY, were adjudged :

I. For the best Essay on the Figure of the Earth, to
> William Freeland, Glasgow.

II. For the best Specimen of Elocution, to
> David Wilson, Glasgow.

Prizes given from a Donation by the late JAMES COULTER, Esq., were adjudged—

I. For the best Sermon on Matthew xxii. 37, 38, to
> Andrew Hamilton, Glasgow.

II. For the best Account of the Stoical System of Philosophy, respecting the Summum Bonum, to

Thomas Ballingall, Glasgow.

III. For the best Translation of the Enchiridion of Epictetus, to

Alexander M'Arthur, Argyllshire.

Prizes were also given for the best Latin Orations, composed for the Common Hall, to

Thomas Millar, Ireland.
Joseph Maxwell, Georgia.

The Prizes of the MATHEMATICAL CLASSES were adjudged—

For General Eminence during the Session, to

Second Class.

Robert Boyle, Lanarkshire.
Lant Carpenter, Birmingham.

First Class—Seniores.

Hutcheson M'Fadyen, Ireland.
John Paul, Ireland.
William Poole, Dumfries-shire.
Andrew Malcom, Ireland.

First Class—Juniores.

Archibald Johnston, Port-Glasgow.
William Orr, Ireland.

The Prizes of the NATURAL PHILOSOPHY CLASS were adjudged:

For Exemplary Behaviour, and Assiduity in the Business of the Class, to

William John Stavely, Ireland.
John Whiteside,   ,,
Thomas Millar,   ..
Hugh Bone, Airshire.
Gilbert Wright, Glasgow.

The Prizes in the ETHIC CLASS were adjudged—

I. For the best Exercises, read in the Class during the Session,. to

>Lant Carpenter, Birmingham.
>Alexander Blair, London.

III. For Eminence in Translation, in the Public Class, during the Session, to

>Alexander Blair, London.
>Lant Carpenter, Birmingham.

II. For General Merit and Eminence, in Answering in Examinations, and in the other Business and Duties of the Class, to

>John Ross, Rotheram, Yorkshire.
>Robert Boyle, Lanarkshire.

———

The Prizes of the LOGICK CLASS, for Exercises proposed at the end of last Session, and executed during the Vacation, were adjudged—

I. For the best Essays on Memory, and on the Means of its Culture, to

>John Ross, Yorkshire.
>Lant Carpenter, Birmingham.

II. For the best Specimens of Composition on various Subjects of Reasoning and of Taste, prescribed and executed during this Session, to

>John Finlay, Glasgow.
>Thomas Mackenzie, Port-Patrick.
>James Smith, Glasgow.
>Richard Blair, London.
>John Riddell, Glasgow.
>Robert Findlay,   ,,
>Alexander Higginson, London.
>Isaac Lodge Toms, Suffolk.
>James Russel, Glasgow.
>Edward S. Lees, Dublin.
>William E. Lees,   ,,
>David Ramsay, Kirkmichael.

III. For the best Public Theme, to

>Thomas Haggart, Glasgow.

IV. For the best Appearance at the Public Examination, to
John Riddell, Glasgow.

· The Prizes of the GREEK CLASS were adjudged—

I. For the best Translation, in Verse, of the Second Chorus of
the Medea of Euripides, to
Alexander Blair, London.

II. For the best Translation, in Prose, of the same Chorus, to
Alexander Telfer, Lamington.

III. For the best Translation, in Verse, of the Third Chorus of
the Medea, to
Alexander Blair, London.

IV. For the best Translation, in Prose, of the same Chorus, to
Archibald M'Ewen, Kilmartin.

V. For Propriety of Conduct, and General Eminence in the
Business of the Course, during the Session, to
John Riddell, maj., Glasgow.
John Finlay,　　　　　　 ,,
Andrew Campbell, Kilmarnock.
David Ramsay, Kirkmichael.
Andrew Malcolm, Ireland.
Edward S Lees, Dublin.
John Wilson, Paisley.
William Cumin, Glasgow.
William Easton, Strathaven.
Andrew Whyte, Paisley.
James Buchanan, Glasgow.
James Reid,　　　　　　 ,,
Oliver G. Fehrszen, Cape of Good Hope.
John Riddell, *min.*, Glasgow.
Robert Buchanan,　　　 ,,
William Boyd, Fenwick.
Mungo N. Campbell, Port-Glasgow.
Claud Marshall, Glasgow.

The Prizes of the HUMANITY CLASS were adjudged—

I. For the Camilliad, a Poem on the Recovery of Rome from
Gauls, to
John Finlay, Glasgow.

II. For the best Translation from Latin into English, to
    Robert Findlay, Glasgow.
    William Cumin,   ,,
    John Wilson, Paisley.
    Thomas Haggart, Glasgow.
    Thomas Mackenzie, Galloway.
    David Ballingall, Glasgow.
    William Liston, Linlithgowshire.
    John Craigie, Glasgow.
    O. G. Fehrszen, Cape of Good Hope.
    William Smith, Glasgow.

III. For the best Translation from English into Latin, to
    David Ballingall, Glasgow.

IV. For Latin Verses, and Exercises in Prosody, to
    William Brownlee, Stirlingshire.
    Morris Pollock, Glasgow.
    John Richmond, Irvine.

V. For Excelling at the Examination on Roman Antiquities, to
    James Angus, Glasgow.
    John Riddell,   ,,

VI. For excelling at the Black Stone Examination, to
    James M'Nair, Glasgow.

VII. For Exemplary Diligence and Regularity, to
    James Buchanan, Glasgow.
    Robert Buchanan,   ,,
    O. G. Fehrszen, Cape of Good Hope.
    James M'Nair, Glasgow.
    John Riddell,   ,,

GLASGOW COLLEGE, 1st MAY, 1801.

This day, the Annual Distribution of Prizes was made in the Common Hall, by the Principal, Dean of Faculty, and Professors, in presence of a numerous meeting of the University, and of many Reverend and respectable Gentlemen of this City and neighbourhood.

One Silver Medal, given by the UNIVERSITY, was adjudged :
For the best account of the beneficial effects of Christianity to
the World, to

Alexander M'Arthur, Argyllshire.

THE GARTMORE GOLD MEDAL,

For the best Essay on the political effects resulting to Europe
from the discovery of America, to

James Moor, Kilmarnock.

Prizes given from a Donation of the late JAMES COULTER, Esq. :
I. For the best Lecture on the Apostle' Paul's discourse to
the Athenians, Acts xvii. 22, to

William Freeland, Glasgow.

II. For the best Essay on " The Association of Ideas," to

Lant Carpenter, Birmingham.

III. For the best Translations of Cicero's first Oration against
Catiline, to

William Liston, Linlithgowshire.
David Coulter, Stranraer.
John Wilson, Paisley.

Prizes for the best LATIN ORATIONS, delivered in the Common
Hall, were adjudged to

Alexander Blair, London.
David Davies, South Wales.
Archibald M'Ewing, A.M., Argyllshire.

The Prizes of the NATURAL PHILOSOPHY CLASS were adjudged
to

Lant Carpenter, Birmingham.
Robert Boyle, Lanarkshire.
Charles Logan, Airshire.
James Ramsay,   ,,

The Prizes of the SECOND MATHEMATICAL CLASS were
adjudged to

Andrew Malcom, Ireland.
Robert Findlay, Glasgow.

Those of the First Class, to

I. *Seniores.*

John Ritchie, Airshire.
Andrew Campbell, Airshire.
John Davis, Ireland.
David Ramsay, Airshire.

II. *Juniores.*

Robert Tennent, Glasgow.
Alexander Garden, Glasgow.

The Prizes of the ETHICK CLASS were adjudged—

I. For Superior Eminence, during the Session, in all the departments of the business of the Class, to

Robert Findlay, Glasgow.

II. For the best Exercises, read in the Class, during the Session, to

John Riddell, Glasgow.
Andrew Malcom, Ireland.

III. For the best Translations of Cicero in the Class, during the Session to

John Finlay, Glasgow.
John Davis, Ireland.

The Prizes of the LOGIC CLASS, for the best specimens of Composition, on various subjects of Reasoning and of Taste, prescribed during the course of the Session, and for Distinguished Eminence in the general business of the Class, were adjudged to

John Wilson, Paisley.
Edward Reid, Ireland.
James Strange Butson, Ireland.
William Cumin, Glasgow.
William Horton Lloyd, Suffolk.
James Auld, Renfrewshire.
Olof Fehrszen, Cape of Good Hope.
James Currie, Stewarton.
Robert Anderson, Perthshire.
William Brounlee, Lanarkshire.
Andrew Symington, Paisley.

For the best Essays on the Socratic Dialogue, to
>William Horton Lloyd, Suffolk.
>John Wilson, Paisley.

The Prizes of the GREEK CLASS were adjudged—

I. For the best Critical Exercises on the 24th Book of Homer's Iliad, to
>*Alexander Blair*, London.
>John Muir, Glasgow.

II. For the best Translation, in Verse, of a Chorus from the "Oedipus Tyrannus," to
>Alexander Blair, London.

III. For the best Translation in Prose of the same Chorus, to
>John Russel, Stirling.

IV. For the best Translation, in Verse, of another Chorus from the Oedipus Tyrannus, to
>John Finlay, Glasgow.

V. For the best Translation in Prose, of the same Chorus, to
>Charles Herbert, Ireland.

VI. For Propriety of Conduct, Diligence, and Eminent Abilities, displayed during the whole of the Session, to
>*James Currie*, Stewartown.
>Mark Marshall, Baldernock.
>William Easton, Evandale.
>William Russel, Glasgow.
>*William Boyd*, Fenwick.
>James Buchanan, Glasgow.
>Mungo Campbell, Port-Glasgow.
>Robert Buchanan, Callander.
>*William Reid*, St. Quivox.
>Norman MacLeod, Essex.
>John Craigie, Glasgow.
>William Henderson, Kilmarnock.
>James Sample, Barbadoes.
>John Stirling, London.
>*James Whyte*, Paisley.
>James Waddell, Govan.

The Prizes of the HUMANITY CLASS were adjudged—

I. For the best Account of the Roman Comitia, to
        James Phillips, Ireland.
        Archibald M'Ewing, A.M., Argyllshire.
        David Ballingall, Glasgow.

II. For the best Translations from Latin into English, to

        George James, Barbadoes.
        James Buchanan, Glasgow.
        John M'Call,   ,,

III. For the best Translations from English into Latin, to

        David Ballingall, Glasgow.
        Robert Anderson, Perthshire.
        Archibald Rogerson.
        O. G. Fehrszen, Cape of Good Hope.
        Archibald Morton, Lanarkshire.

IV. For excelling at the Examination on Roman Antiquities, to

        Robert Buchanan, Perthshire.

V. For the best Latin Verses, to

        John Smith, Airshire.
        Andrew Tennant, Glasgow.
        Robert Thomson, Stirling.

VI. For Excelling at the Black Stone Examination, to

        John Craigie, Glasgow.
        William Reid, Airshire.

VII. For Exemplary Diligence and Regularity, to

        William Boyd, Airshire.
        John M'Call, Glasgow.
        Mungo Campbell, Greenock.
        William Barclay, Dumbartonshire.
        William Taylor, Glasgow.
        George James, Barbadoes.
        James Cooper, Dumbartonshire.
        William Wilson, Renfrewshire.

GLASGOW COLLEGE, May 1, 1802.

This day, the Annual Distribution of Prizes was made in the Common Hall, by the Principal, Dean of Faculty, and Professors, in presence of a numerous meeting of the University, and of many Reverend and respectable Gentlemen of this City and neighbourhood.

Two Silver Medals, given by the UNIVERSITY, were adjudged:

I. For the best Essay on the Tides, to
William Freeland, Glasgow.

II. For the best Specimen of Elocution, to
Æneas M'Kellar, Greenock.

Prizes given from a Donation of the late JAMES COULTER, Esq.

I. For the best Sermon on 1 Pet. i. 15, to
William Freeland, Glasgow.

II. For the best Essay on the Active Powers of Man, to
Andrew George Malcolm, A.M., Ireland.

III. For the best Translation of the Timon of Lucian, to
Archibald M'Ewing, A.M., Argyllshire.

ANATOMY.

A Prize was given for the best Essay on the Diseases of the Spine, to
John Nimmo, Glasgow.

Prizes for the best LATIN ORATIONS delivered in the Common Hall, were adjudged to
James Strange Butson, A.M., Ireland.
Andrew George Malcolm, A.M., „ .

The Prizes of the SENIOR MATHEMATICAL CLASS were adjudged to
Alexander Pollok, Airshire.
Robert Tennent, Glasgow.

Those of the JUNIOR MATHEMATICAL CLASS, to

1. *Seniores.*

>James Ferguson, Ireland.
>David Muir, ,.
>James Barclay, Dysart.
>James Currie, Stewartown.

2. *Juniores.*

>Maurice Pollok, Glasgow.
>Thomas Reid, Ireland.

The Prizes of the NATURAL PHILOSOPHY CLASS were adjudged to

>Andrew George Malcolm, A.M., Ireland.
>{ Robert Findlay, A.M., Glasgow.
>{ John Davies, A.M., Ireland.
>William Parker, Airshire.
>Charles Robb, Stirlingshire.

The Prizes of the ETHIC CLASS were adjudged to

>William Horton Lloyd, Suffolk.
>John Wilson, Paisley.
>William Cumin, Glasgow.
>Andrew Symington, Paisley.
>George Hay, Ireland.
>Robert Anderson, Perthshire.

The Prizes of the LOGIC CLASS were adjudged—

I. For the best Analysis of the Faculty of Imagination, prescribed at the end of last Session, to

>John Wilson, Paisley.
>Edward Reid, Ireland.
>Andrew George Malcolm, Ireland.

II. The Prizes for the best Specimens of Composition on various Subjects of Reasoning and of Taste, prescribed during the course of the present Session, and for distinguished eminence and proficiency, in the general business of the Class, were adjudged, in the following order of merit, to

>James Ledlie, Ireland.
>John Campbell, Cardross.
>Robert Buchanan, Callander.

William Boyd, Finnick.
Samuel Stirling, Campsie.
John Richmond, Irvine.
Mungo Campbell, Port-Glasgow.
Robert Bennet, Ireland.
James Buchanan, Glasgow.
James Aird, Lowdon.
Alexander Russel, Stirling.
David Ballingall, Glasgow.

For the best Solution of the celebrated Dilemma of Protagoras and Euathlus, to

James Ledlie, Ireland.

The Prizes of the GREEK CLASS were adjudged :—

I. For a Translation in Verse, of the Oedipus Tyrannus of Sophocles, to

Alexander Blair, London.

II. For the best Translation of the Alcibiades secundus of Plato, to

Archibald M'Ewing, Argyllshire.

III. For the best Critical Essays on the First Book of Homer's Iliad, to

Henry Anderson, Stirlingshire.
John Wilson, Paisley.

IV. For the best Translation in Verse of a Chorus from the Clouds of Aristophanes, to

William Brownlee, Lanarkshire.

V. For the best Translation in Prose of the same Chorus, to

William Easton, Lanarkshire.

VI. For Propriety of Conduct, Diligence, and Eminent Abilities, displayed during the whole of the Session, to

William Boyd, Airshire.
Archibald Morton, Lanarkshire.
James Ledlie, Ireland.
Robert Bennet,   ,,
James Couper, Stirlingshire.
William Reid, Airshire.
John Smith,   ,,

Samuel Ferguson, Ireland.
William Ewing, Glasgow.
Campbell Robertson, Stirlingshire.
John M'Call, Glasgow.
William Wilson, Paisley.
Andrew Tennent, Glasgow.
Michael Russell, Stirlingshire.
Thomas Glas Sandeman, Glasgow.
Robert Neilson, Glasgow.
{ John Glassford Hopkirk, Glasgow.
{ John Dunlop, Greenock.

———

The Prizes of the HUMANITY CLASS were adjudged—

I. For the best Translation from Latin into English, to

Thomas Miller, A.M., Ireland.
James Phillips,   ,,
O. G. Fehrzen, Cape of Good Hope.
John Steel, Lanarkshire.

II. For the best Translation from English into Latin, to

John Couper, Stirlingshire.

III. For the best Essays, giving an account of the Patria Potestas, among the Romans, to

James Phillips, Ireland.
Thomas Miller, A.M., Ireland.
David Ballingall, Glasgow.
Charles Herbert, Ireland.
Robert Bennet,   ,,
Daniel Macbeth, Lanarkshire.

IV. For excelling at the examination on Roman Antiquities, to

William Ewing, Glasgow.
John Hamilton, Lanarkshire.
Michael Russel, Stirlingshire.

V. For excelling at an Examination in the Private Humanity Class, to

Campbell Robertson, Stirlingshire.

VI. For excelling at the Blackstone Examination, to

John Macall, Glasgow.
John Heenan, Ireland.

VII. For Exemplary Diligence and Regularity, to
        William Wilson, Renfrewshire.
        William Ewing, Glasgow.
        Michael Russel, Stirlingshire.
        John Harvey, Renfrewshire.
        Jacob Runnels, Island of St. Thomas.
        Alexander Macfarlane, Hebrides.
        John Hamilton, Lanarkshire.

VIII. For the best Latin Verses, to
        Thomas G. Sandeman, Glasgow.

GLASGOW COLLEGE, 2nd MAY, 1803.

This day, the Annual Distribution of Prizes was made, in the Common Hall, by the Principal, Dean of Faculty, and Professors, in presence of a numerous meeting of the University, and of many Reverend and respectable Gentlemen of this City and neighbourhood.

Three Silver Medals, given by the UNIVERSITY, were adjudged—

I. For the best Essay on the Socinian Controversy, to
        Daniel Wilkie, Rutherglen.

II. For the best Essay on the Theory and Construction of the Common Pump, to
        Andrew George Malcolm, A.M., Ireland.

III. For the best Specimen of Elocution, to
        Archibald Telfer, Lanarkshire.

The GARTMORE GOLD MEDAL was adjudged—

For the best Essay on the Advantages to be derived to Great Britain and Ireland, from the Union of these Kingdoms, to
        Hugh Moffat Norris, London.

G

Prizes given from a Donation of the late JAMES COULTER, Esq.—

I. For the best Lecture on 1 Cor. xiii. 1-8, to

William Freeland, Glasgow.

II. For the best Essay on the Causes and Phenomena of the Wind, to

William Freeland, Glasgow.

————

Prizes for the best LATIN ORATIONS, delivered in the Common Hall, to

John Wilson, Paisley.
William H. Lloyd, Suffolk.

————

The Prizes of the *Senior* MATHEMATICAL CLASS were adjudged to

John Ritchie, Air.
Morrice Pollok, Glasgow.
James Currie, Airshire.

Those of the *Junior* MATHEMATICAL CLASS, to

1. *Seniores.*

Charles Herbert, Ireland.
Archibald Morton, Lanarkshire.
James Ledlie, Ireland.
Thomas Jardin, Ireland.
Niel Somerville, Glasgow.

2. *Juniores.*

Charles Gray, Ireland.
John M'Caul, Glasgow.
George Alex. Stevenson, Ireland.

————

Prizes of the NATURAL PHILOSOPHY CLASS were adjudged to

Andrew Symington, Paisley.
Alexander Pollock, Airshire.
Robert Adams, Ireland.
William H. Lloyd, Suffolk.
William Easton, Evandale.

The Prizes of the ETHICK CLASS were adjudged to
>Robert Buchanan, Callender.
>James C. Ledlie, Ireland.
>James Aird, Stewarton.
>Archibald Rogerson, Cumnock.
>William Boyd, Fenwick.
>John Campbell, Cardross.
>John Richmond, Irvine.

The Prizes of the LOGIC CLASS were adjudged—

I. For the best Essay on Imitation, as a principle in the Fine Arts, prescribed at the end of last Session, to
>William Leechman Taylor, Glasgow.

II. The Prizes for the best Specimens of Composition, on various Subjects of Reasoning and Taste, prescribed and executed during the course of the present Session, and for distinguished eminence and proficiency in the whole business of the Class, were adjudged to
>James Couper, Baldernock.
>Robert Burns, Mauchline.
>Robert Henry, Ireland.
>Robert Rayner Young, Glasgow.
>William Dun Barclay, Kirkintilloch.
>Joseph Lowry, Ireland.
>William Muir, Glasgow.
>John Harvey, Kilpatrick.
>George Spence, London.
>David Logan, W. Kilpatrick.
>John Johnston, Ireland.
>James White, Paisley.
>William Ewing, Glasgow.
>Thomas Charretie, London.
>Michael Russel, Stirlingshire.

The Prizes of the GREEK CLASS were adjudged—

I. For the best Translation, in Verse, of a Chorus from the Choephorae of Æschylus, to
>John Richmond, Irvine.

II. For the best Translation, in Prose, of the same Chorus, to
>John Monteith, Houston.

III. For the best Translation in Verse, of another Chorus from the Choephorae, to

James Airds, Stewarton.

IV. For the best Translations, in Prose, of the same Chorus, to

Andrew Symington, Paisley.
John Monteith, Houston.

V. For Propriety of Conduct, Diligence, and Eminent Abilities displayed during the whole of the Session, to

William Wilson, Paisley.
William Reïd, St. Quivox.
Robert Burns, Mauchline.
William Barclay, Cadder.
Thomas Sandeman, Glasgow.
John M'Caul, Glasgow.
Campbell Robertson, Gargunnock.
John G. Hopkirk, Glasgow.
James Carlisle, Paisley.
Robert Smith, Kilmaurs.
William Robertson, Rothesay.
John Hamilton, Glasgow.
Thomas Robertson, Glasgow.
Robert Ralston, Paisley.
Gavin Fullerton, Dalry.
Andrew Glen, Lochwinnoch.

The Prizes of the HUMANITY CLASS were adjudged—

For the best Translations from Latin into English, to

Robert Bennet, Ireland.
And. G. Malcom, A.M., Ireland.
Thomas Charretie, London.
James Ledlie, Ireland.
William Lockhart, Glasgow.
T. G. Sandeman,   „
John Hamilton, Lanarkshire.
Samuel Wilson, Glasgow.
Robert Muir, Kilmarnock.

II. For the best Translations from English into Latin, to

George Monteith, Houston.

III. For excelling at the Examination on Roman Antiquities, to

John Hamilton, Lanarkshire.

IV. For excelling at the Blackstone Examination, to

John Hamilton, Lanarkshire.
T. G Sandeman, Glasgow.
Robert Neilson,   ,,
John Hopkirk,   ,,

V. For exemplary Diligence and Regularity, to

John Hamilton, Lanarkshire.
T. G. Sandeman, Glasgow.
Robert Neilson,   ,,
Jacob Runnels, Island of St. Thomas.
Campbell Robertson, Stirlingshire.
Richard Fulk S. Greville, Hampshire.
Alexander Buchanan, Glasgow.

GLASGOW COLLEGE, 1st May, 1804.

This day, the Annual Distribution of Prizes was made in the Common Hall, by the Principal and Professors, in presence of a numerous meeting of the University, and of many Reverend and respectable Gentlemen of this city and neighbourhood.

Three Silver Medals, given by the University, were adjudged—

I. For the best Essay on the controversy with regard to future punishments, to

Andrew George Malcolm, A.M., Ireland.

II. For the best Essay on the most approved methods of finding the Latitude at Sea, to

Robert Adams, A.M., Ireland.

III. For the best Specimen of Elocution, to

John Willock, Airshire.

Prizes given from the Donation of the late JAᴍES COULTER, Esq.

I. For the best Sermon on Mat. xxii. 39, "The second is like unto it, Thou shalt love thy neighbour as thyself," to

Thomas Easton, Strathblane.
Andrew George Malcolm, A.M., Ireland.

II. For the best account of the Analytic and Synthetic methods of Investigation, to

Robert Buchanan, Perthshire.

III. For the best Translation of Cicero's Somnium Scipionis et Paradoxa, to

James White, Paisley.

Prizes for the best LATIN ORATIONS, delivered in the Common Hall, to

James Couper, Glasgow.
William Boyd, Airshire.

The Prizes of the *Senior* MATHEᴍᴀTICAL CLASS were adjudged to

A. Symington, Renfrewshire.
James Couper, Glasgow.

Those of the *Junior* MATHEᴍᴀTICAL CLASS, to

1. *Seniores.*

William Turner, Newcastle.
M. Adam, Greenock.
George Haig, South Carolina.
George Spence, London.
Geo. C. Monteath, Houston.
John Kyle, South Carolina.
John Johnston, Ireland.

2. *Juniores.*

A. Alexander, Glasgow.
William Kidston, Nova Scotia.
William Wilson, Hawkhead.

The Prizes of the NATURAL PHILOSOPHY CLASS were adjudged to

Archibald Morton, Cambusnethan.
David Moore, A.M., Ireland.
Archibald Rogerson, A.M., Airshire.

Robert Bennett, A.M., Ireland.
Thomas Jardine, A.M.,   ,,
John Craig, A.M ,   ..

The Prizes in the ETHIC CLASS were adjudged to
Michael Russell, Stirlingshire.
John Harvie, Dumbartonshire.
Joseph Lowry, Ireland.
George Forsyth,   ,,
John Steele, Lanarkshire.
John Kell, America.
William Dunn Barclay, Cadder.

The Prizes of the LOGIC CLASS were adjudged—

I. For the best Essay on the Reflex Sense of Beauty, prescribed at the end of the last Session, to
Michael Russel, Stirlingshire.
William Dunn Barclay, Cadder.

II. For the best Specimens of Composition on Various Subjects of Reasoning and Taste, prescribed and executed during the course of the present Session, and for distinguished eminence and proficiency in the whole business of the Class, to
William Hogg, Air.
William Hamilton, Glasgow.
James Carlisle, Paisley.
William Turner, Newcastle.
John M'Caul, Glasgow.
John Gibb, Bothwell.
John Moorhead, Ireland.
James Runnels, Island of St. Thomas.
Campbell Robertson, Gargunnock.
Francis Somerveil, Glasgow.
John Glasford Hopkirk, Glasgow.
John Dunlop, Greenock.
David Dunlop, Airshire.

The Prizes of the GREEK CLASS were adjudged—

I. For the best translation, in verse, of the Military Fragments of Tyrtæus, to
John Richmond, Irvine.

II. For the best Translation, in Verse, of a Chorus from the Medea of Euripides, to

        Andrew George Malcolm, A.M., Ireland.

III. For the best Translation, in Prose, of a scene from the Medea, to

        William Hogg, Ayr.

IV. For Propriety of Conduct, Diligence, and Eminent Abilities, displayed during the whole of the Session, to

        Samuel Herron, Ireland.
        Campbell Robertson, Gargunnock.
        James Carlisle, Paisley.
        John Hamilton, Lanarkshire.
        Gavin Fullarton, Dalry.
        William Douglas, Ireland.
        John MacBeath, Greenock.
        John Russel, Hamilton.
        Daniel M'Beth, Lanarkshire.
        John Fleming, Glasgow.
        Andrew Baillie, Dalziell.
        James Alexander, Girvan.

———

The Prizes in the HUMANITY CLASS were adjudged—

I. For the best Account of the Distinctions of Ranks among the Romans, to

        James C. Ledlie, Ireland.

II. For the best Translation from English into Latin, to

        James Monteath, Renfrewshire.

III. For the best Translations from Latin into English, to

        Andrew Alexander, Glasgow.
        John Monteith, A.M., Renfrewshire.
        Tho. G. Sandeman, Glasgow.
        Hugh Wallace,   ,,
        James Monteath, Renfrewshire.

IV. For the best Latin Verses, to

        Thomas Hamilton, Glasgow.
        James Graham,   ,,
        James Ure,

V. For exemplary Diligence and Behaviour, to
> Alex. Buchanan, Glasgow.
> Gavin Fullarton, Dalry.
> James Russel, Glasgow.
> And. Galloway,   ,,
> Wm. Austin,   ,,
> And. Wilson,   ,,
> John Russel, Hamilton.
> Wm. Gray, Glasgow.
> Somersal M'Kechnie, West Indies.

VI. For excelling at the Blackstone Examination, to
> Daniel Macbeth, Lanarkshire.
> James Russel, Glasgow.
> John Russel, Hamilton.

VII. For excelling at the Examination on Roman Antiquities, to
> James Russel, Glasgow.
> Alexander Buchanan, Glasgow.
> Gavin Fullarton, Dalry.
> James Edington, Glasgow.

GLASGOW COLLEGE, 1st MAY, 1805.

This day, the Annual Distribution of Prizes was made, in the Common Hall, by the Principal, Dean of Faculty, and Professors, in presence of a numerous Meeting of the University, and of many Reverend and respectable Gentlemen of this City and neighbourhood.

Two Silver Medals, given by the UNIVERSITY, were adjudged—

I. For the best Essay on the Evidence from Miracles for the Truth of Christianity, to
> James Crawford Ledlie, A.M., Ireland.

II. For the best Specimen of Elocution, to
> George Haig, South Carolina.

THE GARTMORE GOLD MEDAL,

For the best System of Defence for Great Britain, in the present state of Europe, to

William Dunn Barclay, Lanarkshire.

Prizes given from a Donation of the late JAMES COULTER, Esq.

I. For the best Lecture on the first five verses of the 12th Chapter of the Epistle to the Romans, to

Thomas Easton, A.M., Stirlingshire.

II. For the best Account of the Systems which derive the Principle of Moral Approbation, from Reason, to

John Harvey, Renfrewshire.

III. For the best Translation of the Funeral Oration of Pericles, from Thucydides, to

George Cunningham Monteath, A.M., Renfrewshire.

Prizes given by the Rev. CLAUDE BUCHANAN, D.D., Vice-Provost of the College of Fort William in Bengal, etc., etc., etc.

I. One hundred pounds, for the best English Dissertation on the means of civilizing the Subjects of the British Empire in India, and for diffusing the Light of the Christian Religion throughout the Eastern World, to

The Rev. John Mitchell, A.M., Anderston.

II. Twenty-Five Pounds, for the best Latin Ode or Poem: subject, Collegium Bengalense, to

Alexander M'Arthur, Argyllshire.

Prizes for the best LATIN ORATIONS were adjudged to

George Spence, A.M., London.

William Dunn Barclay, Lanarkshire.

The Prizes of the Senior MATHEMATICAL CLASS were adjudged to

George Haig, South Carolina.

John M'Caul, Glasgow.

Those of the Junior MATHEMATICAL CLASS, to
1. *Seniores.*

> John Grenside, London.
> George Payne, Northampton.
> Henry Forster Burder, London.
> Henry Holland, Lancashire.
> John Dunlop, Greenock.
> William Hogg, Ayr.
> Robert Stewart, Ireland.

2. *Juniores.*

> William Hunter, Glasgow.
> James Monteath, Renfrewshire.

The Prizes of the NATURAL PHILOSOPHY CLASS, for Propriety of Conduct, Diligence, and Ability during the whole Session, were adjudged to

> John Steel, A.M., Shotts.
> William Stewart Anderson, A.M., Greenock.
> Matthew Adam, Ayrshire.
> William Wilson, Paisley.
> George Haig, South Carolina.
> George Spence, A.M., London.

The Prizes of the MORAL PHILOSOPHY CLASS were adjudged to

> William Hogg, Ayr.
> William Turner, Newcastle.
> Samuel Butler, Ireland.
> Hugh Woods,   „
> James Watson, Glasgow.
> Robert Stewart, Ireland.

The Prizes of the LOGIC CLASS were adjudged—

I. For the best Essay on the Causes of Diversity of Style in Composition, prescribed at the end of last Session; to

> William Turner, Newcastle.

II. For the best Imitation of the Socratic Dialogue, to

> Henry Forster Burder, London.
> Richard Ross, Monaghan.

III. For the best Specimens of Composition on various subjects of Reasoning and Taste, prescribed and executed during the course of the present Session, and for Distinguished Eminence and Proficiency in the whole business of the Class, to

Henry Forster Burder, London.
Joseph Fletcher, Chester.
John Barr, Ayrshire.
George Payne, Northampton.
James Fergusson, Belfast.
John M'Beth, Greenock.
Gavin Fullarton, Ayrshire.
Thomas Glas Sandeman, Glasgow.
John Grenside, London.
Thomas Chrystie, Glasgow.
John Hamilton,   ,,
John Hercy, London.
John Russel, Hamilton
Alexander Buchanan, Glasgow.

The Prizes of the GREEK CLASS were adjudged—

I. For the best Translation, in Verse, of a Chorus from the Oedipus Tyrannus of Sophocles, to

Henry Holland, Lancashire.

II. For the best Translation, in Verse, of another Chorus from the Oedipus Tyrannus, to

William Muir, Glasgow.

III. For Propriety of Conduct, Diligence, and Eminent Abilities, displayed during the whole of the Session, to

John M'Beath, Greenock.
John Russell, Hamilton.
James Wright, Ireland.
John Smith, Glenurchy.
James Russell, Glasgow.
John Fleming,   ,,
Andrew Baillie, Lanarkshire.
Andrew Glen, Renfrewshire.
John Millar, W. Lothian.
John Muir, Kilmarnock.
John Ross, Island of St. Thomas.

Gabriel J. M. de Lys, St. Malo.
Archibald Bruce, W. Lothian.
William Craig, Paisley.
Adam Boyd, Ayrshire.
Alexander Simpson, Glasgow.

The Prizes of the HUMANITY CLASS were adjudged—

I. For the best Account of the Patria Potestas, among the Romans, to

Andrew Alexander, Glasgow.

II. For the best Translation from English into Latin, to

William Sym, Dumbartonshire.

III. For the best Translation from Latin into English, to

William Sym, Dumbartonshire.
John Davidson,   ,,
James Monteath, Renfrewshire.
Peter Chalmers, Glasgow.

IV. For the best Latin Verses, to

Peter Chalmers, Glasgow.
William Sym, Dumbartonshire.
James Ure, Glasgow.
John Lyon, Lanarkshire.
James Campbell Hozier, Glasgow.

V. For excelling at the Examinations on Roman Antiquities, to
John M'Kerrow, Ayrshire.

VI. For excelling at the Blackstone Examination, to

James Graham, Glasgow.
Andrew Glen, Renfrewshire.
Gavin Semple, Lanarkshire.
Jo. Simson, Lanarkshire.
Peter Chalmers, Glasgow.
William Stewart,   ,,
John Ross, Island of St. Thomas.

VII. For Exemplary Diligence and Regularity, to

Robert Muir, Glasgow.
William Sym, Dumbartonshire.
Peter Chalmers, Glasgow.

James Barr, Ayrshire.
Andrew Glen, Renfrewshire.
Andrew Baillie, Lanarkshire.
George Buchanan, Glasgow.
James Alexander, Ayrshire.
John M'Kerrow,   ,,
George Donaldson, Glasgow.
Adam Boyd, Ayrshire.

GLASGOW COLLEGE, 1st MAY, 1806.

This day, the Annual Distribution of Prizes was made in the
Common Hall, by the Principal, Dean of Faculty, and Professors,
in presence of a numerous meeting of the University, and of
many Reverend and respectable Gentlemen of this City and
neighbourhood.

Two Silver Medals, given by the University, were adjudged—
I. For the best Critical Dissertation and Commentary on the
Original Text of the Song of Moses, Exodus, chap. xv., to
Robert Buchanan, Callander, Monteith.

II. For the best Specimen of Elocution, to
Richard Ross, A.M., Ireland.

The Prizes on Mr. COULTER's Donation.

I. For the best Sermon on 1st Cor. xiii. 13. Now abideth
Faith, Hope, Charity, etc., to
Thomas Easton, Stirlingshire.

II. For the best Translation of Cicero's Oration for Archias, to
John Barr, Beith, Airshire.

The Prizes for the best LATIN ORATIONS in the Common Hall,
during the Session, were adjudged to
David Dunlop, A.M., Airshire.
William Robertson, A.M., Rothesay.

Two Prizes proposed, for Excelling in the Daily Examination, to those Students in the SCOTS LAW CLASS who chose to be examined, were adjudged to

John Dunlop, Greenock.
William Graham, Lanarkshire.

———

In the ASTRONOMY CLASS, a Prize for the best Essay on Dr. Herschell's Theory of the Construction of the Heavens, was adjudged to

William Turner, A.M., Newcastle.

———

The Prizes of the *Senior* MATHEMATICAL CLASS were adjudged to

John Dunlop, Greenock.
William Hunter, Glasgow.
James Yates, Liverpool.

———

Those of the *Junior* MATHEMATICAL CLASS to

David Fleming, Paisley.
George Forsyth, Ireland.
James Stevenson, Neilston.
Thomas Sandeman, Glasgow.
William Sym, Dumbartonshire.
James Grahame, Glasgow.
Peter Whyte, Ireland.
Mathew Reid, Airshire.
Robert Gass, Ireland.
John Barr, Beith.
Gavin Fullarton, Glasgow.
Henry Preston, Yorkshire.

———

The Prizes of the NATURAL PHILOSOPHY CLASS were adjudged,

I. For the best Essay on the Barometer written during the Vacation, to

William Glendy, A.M., Ireland.

II. For General Eminence during the Session, to

William Turner, A.M., Newcastle.
James Watson, Glasgow.
Robert Stewart, A.M., Ireland.

William Hogg, A.M., Ayr.
Robert Smith, Ayrshire.
James Carlisle, Paisley.
James Smith, Stirling.

The Prizes in the ETHIC CLASS were adjudged—

I. For the best Account of the Doctrine contained in Smith's Theory of Moral Sentiments, prescribed at the end of last Session, to

William Turner, A.M., Newcastle.

II. For the best Specimens of Composition on various Subjects connected with Moral Philosophy, and for distinguished eminence and proficiency, to

Joseph Fletcher, Chester.
John M'Beth, Greenock.
Henry Foster Burder, London.
George Payne, London.
John Barr, Beith, Ayrshire.
John Russel, Hamilton.
Gavin Fullarton, Ayrshire.

The Prizes of the LOGIC CLASS were adjudged—

I. For the best Essay on the Reflect Sense of Ridicule, prescribed at the end of last Session, to

John M'Beth, Greenock.

II. For the best Specimens of Composition, on various Subjects of Reasoning and of Taste, connected with the Course of Lectures, prescribed and executed during the present Session, and for distinguished eminence and proficiency in the whole business of the Class, to

First Division.

Thomas Francis Kennedy, Daily.
James Yates, Liverpool.
James Russell, Glasgow.
George Rennie, Sutherlandshire.
John M'Kerrow, Mauchline.
James Alexander, Girvan.
Gabriel de Lys, France.

Daniel M'Beth, Lanark.
Andrew Glen, Lochwinnoch.
Robert Ker, Dalry.
James Davis, Ireland.
Thomas Hamilton, Glasgow.
John Muir, Kilmarnock.
James Harvie, Ireland.

Second Division.

Patrick Chalmers, Glasgow.
John Fleming,   ,,
Robert M'Nair, Slamannan.
William Sym, New Kilpatrick.

The Prizes of the GREEK CLASS were adjudged—

I. For the best Essay on the Analogy of Greek Verbal Nouns, to

James Yates, Lancashire.

II. For the best Translation, in Prose, of a scene from the Clouds of Aristophanes, to

Andrew Symington, A.M., Paisley.

III. For the best Translation, in Verse, of certain Choral Passages from the same Comedy, to

William Muir, Glasgow.

IV. For the best Translation, in Latin Verse (*Alcaic*) of the Fourteenth Olympic of Pindar, to

Thomas F. Kennedy, Daily.

V. For the best Translation, in English Verse, of the same Olympic, to

John Richmond, A.M., Irvine.

VI. For propriety of conduct, diligence, and eminent abilities displayed during the whole Session, to

Patrick Chalmers, Glasgow.
William Stewart,   ,,
William Craig,   ,,
James Davies, Ireland.
Adam Boyd, Fenwick.
Robert Gregor, Methven.

H

John Ross, St. Thomas'.
James Grahame, Glasgow.
Archibald Browning, Strathaven.
George Donaldson, Glasgow.
William Thomson, Ayrshire.
David Wilkie, Nielston.
John Armour, Strathaven.
Hugh Hamilton, Lanarkshire.
James Armour, Fenwick.
John Verter, St. Thomas'
Richard Thomson, Glasgow.

The Prizes of the HUMANITY CLASS were adjudged—

I. For the best Historical Accounts of the Rise, Progress, and Termination of the Decemviral Power at Rome, to

William Muir, Glasgow.
David Logan, East Kilpatrick.
John Simson, Strathaven.

II. For the best Translations from English into Latin, to

Thomas Brisbane, Dunlop.
William Couper, Glasgow.

III. For the best Translations from Latin into English, to

William Sym, East Kilpatrick.
John Simson (for two different exercises), Strathaven
John Muir, Kilmarnock.
John Lyon, Lanarkshire.

IV. For the best Latin Verses, to

Adam Boyd, Fenwick.
George Macintosh, Glasgow.

V. For excelling at the Examinations on Roman Antiquities, to

George Oswald Sym, East Kilpatrick.

VI For Excelling at the Black Stone Examination, to

Alexander Simson, Northumberland.
Archibald Browning, Strathaven.
David Wilkie, Neilston.
Donald Manson, Lanark.

George Donaldson, Glasgow.
John Armour, Strathaven.
Thomas Grahame, Glasgow.

VII. For exemplary Diligence and Regularity, to
Adam Boyd, Fenwick.
Alexander Simson, Northumberland.
George Donaldson, Glasgow.
John Lyon, Lanark.
Hugh Hamilton, Strathaven.
John Baird, Fintry.
Daniel Maclean, Glasgow.
Richard Senior,   ,,
Robert Gregor, Methven.
Archibald Browning, Strathaven.
Henry Rainey, Sutherland.
John Towers, Glasgow.

The number of Prizes, given on this occasion, was greater than usual, on account of the great increase of Students attending the University this Session. The numbers, upon an accurate enumeration, are—Gown Students, 452 ; Students not wearing gowns, 417 ; Total, 869, none of them, though attending different classes, being counted more than once.

GLASGOW COLLEGE, 1st MAY, 1807.

This day, the Annual Distribution of Prizes was made in the Common Hall, by the Principal, Dean of Faculty, and Professors, in presence of a numerous meeting of the University, and of many Reverend and respectable Gentlemen of this City and neighbourhood.

Three Silver Medals, given by the University, were adjudged—
I. For the best dissertation on the Inspiration of the Writings of the New Testament, to
Charles Logan, Airshire.

II. For the best Historical and Philosophical Account of the Telescope, to

James Watson, Glasgow.

III. For the best Specimen of Elocution, to

James Carlisle, Paisley.

The GARTMORE GOLD MEDAL,

For the best Account of the Rise, Progress, and Present State of the National Debt, adjudged to

Andrew Aléxander, Glasgow.

The Prizes on Mr. COULTER'S Donation.

I. For the best Lecture on the Parable of the Marriage Supper, Matt. xxii. 1, to

Andrew Symington, A.M., Paisley.

II. For the best Illustration of the first fifty Aphorisms of Lord Bacon's Novum Organum, to

John M'Beth, Greenock.

III. For the best Translation of the Moral Characters of Theophrastus, to

John Barr, Beith.

The Prizes for the best Latin Orations, in the Common Hall, during the Session, were adjudged to

Robert Walkinshaw, Glasgow.
John Russell, A.M., Hamilton.

In the ASTRONOMY CLASS a Prize for the best Account of the principal Systems invented to explain the Planetary Motions, was adjudged to

Matthew Adam, Glasgow.

The Prizes of the *Senior* MATHEMATICAL CLASS were adjudged to

David Fleming, Paisley.
James Stevenson, Neilston.

Those of the *Junior* MATHEMATICAL CLASS to

George Phillips, Pembrokeshire.
Edward Gibb, Lanarkshire.
Peter Chalmers, Glasgow.
Alexander Smith, Renfrewshire.
James Kirk, Stirlingshire.
James Reid, Airshire.
William Craig, Glasgow.
John Simpson, Strathaven.
John Muir, Kilmarnock.
Alexander Carlisle, Paisley.

The Prizes of the NATURAL PHILOSOPHY CLASS, for General Eminence during the Session, were adjudged to

Robert Walkinshaw, Glasgow.
Samuel Butler, A.M., Ireland.
James Huey, Ireland.
David Fleming, Paisley.
William Cowan, Old Monkland.
William Hogg, A.M., Ireland.

The Prizes of the MORAL PHILOSOPHY CLASS were—

I. For the best Essay on the Origin and Progress of Civil Society, a subject proposed at the end of last Session, and executed during the Vacation, adjudged to

John M'Beth, Greenock.

II. For the best Specimens of Composition on various Subjects, prescribed to the Students of this Session, and for Distinguished Eminence in the business of the Class, adjudged to

James Yates, Liverpool.
James Russell, Glasgow.
Robert M'Nair, Glasgow.
John M'Kerrow, Mauchline.
Edward Prenter, Ireland.
James Davies,   ,,
William Stuart, Glasgow.

III. For the best Essay on the Policy of a Bounty on the Exportation of Grain, a Subject prescribed to the Students of Political Economy, adjudged to

William Dunn, A.M., Glasgow.

The Prizes of the LOGIC CLASS were adjudged—

I. For the best Essay on Lord Bacon's Division of Idols, prescribed at the end of last Session, to

James Russell, Glasgow.

II. For the best Specimens of Composition on various Subjects of Reasoning and of Taste, prescribed and executed during the course of this Session, and for distinguished Eminence and Proficiency in the whole business of the Class, to

First Division.

George Phillips, Pembrokeshire.
John Clunie, London.
John Hooper, Dorsetshire.
Hon. Wm. Lennox Bathurst, Gloucestershire.
Robert Gregor, Perthshire.
John Wood, Manchester.
Adam Boyd, Fenwick.
Alexander Simpson, Northumberland.
Edward Bromhead, Lincolnshire.
Right Hon. H. Lord Apsley, Gloucestershire.
James Grahame, Glasgow.
Henderson Wightman, Ireland.

Second Division.

John Andrews, Ireland.
David Wilkie, Neilston.
Mungo Currie, Strathallan.
William M'Kenzie, Glasgow.
George Donaldson,   ,,

III. For the best Latin Poem on the Christmas Holidays, to
Hon. Wm. Lennox Bathurst, Gloucestershire.

For the best English Poem on the same Subject, to
George Phillips, Pembrokeshire.

For the best Prose Essay on the same Subject, to
John Wood, Manchester.

For the best Profession at the Public Examination, to
James Grahame, Glasgow.

For the best Theme, to
Edward Bromhead, Lincolnshire

The Prizes of the GREEK CLASS were adjudged—

I. For the best Translation in Latin Verse (*Alcaics*), of a Chorus from the Choephoræ of Aeschylus, to
Right Hon. Lord Apsley, Gloucestershire.

II. For the best Translation, in English Verse, of the same Chorus, to
William Muir, Glasgow.

III. For the best Translation, in English Verse, of another Chorus from the same Tragedy, to
David Fleming, Paisley.

IV. For the best Translation of part of the Oration of Aeschines against Ctesipho, to
William Hogg, A.M., Ayr.

V. For the best Criticism on the Interview between Hector and Andromache (Iliad VI.) to
William Muir, Glasgow.

VI. For the best Essay on the Principle on which the Long Vowel and the Diphthong are, occasionally, estimated as Short, in Greek Prosody, to
James Yates, Liverpool.

VII. For propriety of Conduct, Diligence, and Eminent Abilities displayed during the whole Session, to
Robert Gregor, Methven.
Adam Boyd, Fenwick.
George Donaldson, Glasgow.
David Wilkie, Neilston.
James Armour, Fenwick.
Archibald Browning, Strathaven.
George Sym, Kilpatrick.
John Armour, Strathaven.
George Smith, Galston.
Henry Rainy, Sutherland.
George Glass Sandeman, Glasgow.

John Frazer, Rothesay.
James Campbell, Carsphairn.
James Young, Cambusnethan.
William M'Farlane, Paisley.
James M'Nair, Slamannan.
William Galbraith, Kippen.

———

The Prizes of the HUMANITY CLASS were adjudged—

I. For the best Account of the Rules and Structure of Latin Verse, to

David Dunlop, Ayrshire.

II. For the best Translations from Latin into English, to

John M'Kerrow, Ayrshire.
Patrick Chalmers, Glasgow.
John Simpson, Strathaven.
George Oswald Sym, Kilpatrick.
Henry Rainy, Sutherland
James Miller, Anderston.
George Donaldson, Glasgow.

III. For the best Translation from English into Latin, to

Adam Boyd, Fenwick.

IV. For excelling at the Examinations on Roman Antiquities, to

John Towers, Glasgow.
John Lockhart,   ,,

V. For the best Account of the Doric Order of Architecture; with a particular Illustration of the Building, erected within the College, for receiving the Hunterian Museum, to

John M'Kerrow, Ayrshire.
James Kirk, Stirlingshire.

VI. For the best Latin Verses, entitled Apri Lamentatio in servitutem abrepti, to

Hon. Wm. Lennox Bathurst, Gloucestershire.
Edward Bromhead, Lincolnshire.
David Dunlop, Ayrshire.
Andrew Dewar,   ,,
John Stirling Lapslie, Campsie.

VII. For Excelling at the Blackstone Examination, to
    James Armour, Ayrshire.
    Thomas Brown, ,,
    John Fleming, Strathaven.

VIII For Exemplary Diligence and Regularity, to
    John Towers, Glasgow.
    James Armour, Ayrshire.
    George Oswald Sym, Kilpatrick.
    Henry Rainy, Sutherland.
    John Lockhart, Glasgow.
    George Smith, Ayrshire.
    William M'Farlane, Paisley.

GLASGOW COLLEGE, 2nd MAY, 1808.

This day, the Annual Distribution of Prizes was made, in the Common Hall, by the Principal, Dean of Faculty, and Professors, in presence of a numerous meeting of the University, and of many Reverend and respectable Gentlemen of this City and neighbourhood.

Three Silver Medals, given by the UNIVERSITY, were adjudged:

I. For the best Essay on the credibility of the Mosaic History, to
    Andrew Alexander, Glasgow.

II. For the best Essay on Sir Isaac Newton's Rules of Philosophising, to
    John M'Beth, Greenock.

III. For the best Specimen of Elocution, to
    William Muir, Glasgow.

The Prizes on Mr. COULTER's Donation.

I. For an Essay on the credibility of the Mosaic History, to
    William Muir, Glasgow.

II. For the best Analysis of Dr. Smith's Theory of Moral Sentiments, to

James Russell, Glasgow.

III. For the best Translation of an Extract from Quintilian, to

James Couper, Glasgow.

A Prize of Twelve Guineas, by a learned and respectab'e Gentleman, an Alumnus of this University,

For the best Dissertation on Party Spirit, to

Robert Buchanan, Callander.

The Prizes for the best Latin Orations in the Common Hall were adjudged to

James Russell, Glasgow.
John Muir, Ayrshire.
James Harvey, A.M., Ireland.

Two Prizes proposed, for Excelling in the Daily Examinations, to those Students in the SCOTCH LAW CLASS who chose to be examined, were adjudged to

Patrick Murray, Crieff, Perthshire.
Duncan Turner, Luss, Dumbartonshire.

In the CLASS of POLITICAL ECONOMY, a Prize, for the best Essay on the policy of the Laws respecting the monopolizing and forestalling of Grain, was adjudged to

James Yates, Liverpool.

In the ASTRONOMY CLASS, a Prize for the best Essay on the Figure of the Earth, to

Matthew Adam, A.M , Ayrshire.

The Prizes of the *Senior* MATHEMATICAL CLASS were adjudged to

Alexander Smith, Paisley.

Those of the *Junior* MATHEMATICAL CLASS, to

Robert Gregor, Perthshire.
John Clunie, London.

George Oswald Sym, Dumbartonshire.
John Stewart, Greenock.
George Donaldson, Glasgow.
Archibald Bruce, Linlithgowshire.

The Prizes of the NATURAL PHILOSOPHY CLASS, for Propriety of Conduct, Exemplary Diligence, and Eminent Abilities, during the Session, were adjudged to

James Russel, Glasgow.
Francis Little, Ireland.
Peter Chalmers, Glasgow.
James Davis, A.M., Ireland.
John Wills, Ayrshire.
Robert Gass, A.M., Ireland.
Alexander Smith, Paisley.
Robert M'Nair, A.M., Stirlingshire.

The Prizes in the ETHIC CLASS were adjudged—

I. For the best Translation and Illustration of the 88th, 89th, 90th, 91st, and 92nd Aphorisms of Lord Bacon's Novum Organum, prescribed at the end of last Session, to

James Yates, Liverpool.
James Russel, Glasgow.

II. For the best Specimens of Composition on various Subjects of Moral Philosophy, prescribed by the Professor, or selected by the Students, during the Session, and for Distinguished Eminence and Proficiency in the whole business of the Class, to

George Phillips, Pembrokeshire.
John Clunie, London.
Robert Gregor, Perthshire.
John M'Clelland, Ireland.
John Wood, Manchester.
Adam Boyd, Fenwick.

The Prizes of the LOGIC CLASS were adjudged—

I. For the best Essay "On the Influence of Habits of Attention on the Powers of Knowledge," to

John Burder, London.

For the best Essay " On the Principles of the Socratic Dialogue,
with a Specimen of that form of Dialogue," to

John Kenrick, Exeter.

II. For the best Specimens of Composition on various Subjects
of Reasoning and of Taste, connected with the Course of Lectures,
prescribed and executed during the present Session, and for Distinguished Eminence and Proficiency in the whole Business of the
Class.

Seniores.

John Kenrick, Exeter.
John Burder, London.
Henry Rainy, Sutherland.
Pemberton Yates, Liverpool.
John Towers, Glasgow.
John Fraser, Rothesay.
James Reid, Hamilton.
James Armour, Fenwick.
George Sandeman, Glasgow.
Thomas Grahame,   ,,
James Towers,   ,,
William Burn. Stirling.
James Cameron, Newmills.
George M'Intosh, Glasgow.

Juniores.

Alexander M'Lean, Kilfenechen.
Richard Thomson, Glasgow.
Andrew Dewar, Fenwick.
James Grahame, Glasgow.
John Jeffray, New Monkland.
Alexander Dunlop, Glasgow.
Malcolm M'Niell, Ireland.

———

The Prizes of the GREEK CLASS were adjudged—

I. For the best Critical Essay on the 24th Book of the Iliad, to

John Kenrick, Exeter.

II. For the best Translation, in Latin Verse (Hexameters) of
Bion's Lament for Adonis, to

Edward Bromhead, Lincolnshire.

III. For the best Translation, in English Verse, of a Chorus from the Medea of Euripides, to

David Fleming, A.M , Paisley.

IV. For Propriety of Conduct, Diligence, and Eminent Abilities displayed during the whole of the Session, to

Henry Rainy, Sutherland.
James Reid, Hamilton.
George G. Sandeman, Glasgow.
John Frazer, Rothesay.
George Sym, East Kilpatrick.
George Smith, Galston,
John Lockhart, Glasgow.
William Couper,　　,,
Robert Douglass, Haddington.
Alexander Guthrie, Glasgow.
Ebenezer Bradshaw Wallace, Nenthorn.
John S. Lapslie, Campsie.
David Thom, Glasgow.
Hamilton Murray, Daily.
William Houston, Glasgow.
Alexander Lochore,　　,,
James Grieve,　　　　,,

The Prizes of the HUMANITY CLASS were adjudged—

I. For the best Account of the Sacerdotal Office among the Romans, to

John Simpson, Strathaven.

II. For the best Essays on the Beauty of Language, to

Peter Chalmers, Glasgow.
John M'Kerrow, Ayrshire.

III. For excelling at the Examinations on Roman Antiquities. and Roman Literature, to

William Macfarlane, Paisley.
Alexander Guthrie, Glasgow.　,

IV. For Excelling at the Black Stone Examination, to

G. M. Sawers, Ayrshire.
J. S. Lapslie, Campsie.
Robert Lyon, Lanark.

V. For the best Latin Verses on British Liberty, to
Robert Berrie, East Indies.

VI. For the best Translation, into English Verse, of a Psalm from Buchanan, to
R. K. Douglas, East Lothian.

VII. For the best Prose Translation from English into Latin, to
G. O. Sym, Kilpatrick.

VIII. For the best Prose Translations from Latin into English, to
John Simpson, Strathaven.
John Moor, Ayrshire.
Hon. W. L. Bathurst, Gloucestershire.
J. M. Duncan, Glasgow.
David Chrystal, Stirling.
Alexander Guthrie, Glasgow.

IX. For Exemplary Diligence and Regularity, to
William Macfarlane, Paisley.
Alexander Guthrie, Glasgow.
George Smith, Ayrshire.
J. S. Lapslie, Campsie.
William Galbraith, Stirlingshire.
R. K. Douglas, East Lothian
Robert Cooke, Ireland.
James Rogers, Santa Cruz.
James Boyd, Fenwick.
Adam Forman, Carmunnock.

GLASGOW COLLEGE, 1ST MAY, 1809.

This day, the Annual Distribution of Prizes was made in the Common Hall, by the Principal, Dean of Faculty, and Professors, in presence of a numerous meeting of the University, and of many Reverend and respectable Gentlemen of this City and neighbourhood.

Two Silver Medals, given by the UNIVERSITY, were adjudged—
I. For the best Essay on the Credibility of the Old Testament History, from the death of Moses to the Babylonish Captivity, to
William Muir, A.M., Glasgow.

II. For the best Specimen of Elocution, to
Alexander James Buchanan, Glasgow.

THE GARTMORE GOLD MEDAL was adjudged—
For the best Essay on the History of the English Constitution, from the Accession of the House of Tudor to that of the House of Stuart, to
John Kenrick, Exeter.

The Prizes on Mr. COULTER's Donation.
I. For the best Lecture on Acts xxvi. and 24, etc., to
David Dunlop, A.M., Ayrshire.

II. For the best Essay on the Steam Engine, to
Peter Chalmers, A.M., Glasgow.

III. For the best Translation of the Panegyric of Isocrates, to
John Kenrick, Exeter.

In ASTRONOMY.
For the best Account of the Methods for finding the Longitude at sea, to
John Wood, Manchester.

A Prize of Five Guineas, by a learned and respectable Gentleman, an Alumnus of this University,
For the best Exercise on Select Passages in Scripture, to
James Russell, Glasgow.

The Prizes for the best Latin Orations, in the Common Hal. were adjudged to
Robert Kerr, Glasgow.
Adam Boyd, A.M., Ayrshire.

Two Prizes for excelling in the Daily Examinations, to those Students of SCOTS LAW, who chose to be examined, were adjudged to

John Fergusson, Glasgow.
Robert Wilson,   ,,

———

The Prize of the *Senior* MATHEMATICAL CLASS was adjudged to

John Stewart, Greenock.

Those of the *Junior* MATHEMATICAL CLASS to
John Burder, London.
John Hunter, Glasgow.
George Watson, Paisley.
Thomas Freeland, Glasgow.
Henry Biggar, Edinburgh.
John Lyon, New Lanark.
Alexander Henry, Ireland.
Malcolm M'Neil,   ,,
William Skelly,

———

The Prizes of the NATURAL PHILOSOPHY CLASS, for propriety of conduct, exemplary diligence, and eminent abilities, during the Session, were adjudged to

Robert Allan, A.M., Ireland.
Robert Gregor, A.M., Perthshire.
George Phillips, A.M., Pembrokeshire.
{ George Stirling, Ayrshire.
{ Robert Milligan, Wanlockhead.
Edward Gibb, Bothwell.

———

The Prizes in the ETHIC CLASS were adjudged—

For the best Specimens of Composition on various Subjects in Moral Philosophy prescribed by the Professor, or selected by the Students during the Session ; and for distinguished eminence and proficiency in the whole business of the Class, to

John Kenrick, Exeter.
John Burder, London.
John Lyon, Lanark.
William Skelly, Ireland.

John Fraser, Rothesay.
Hugh Dewar, Fenwick.
Donald Manson, Newlands

———

The Prizes of the LOGIC CLASS,

For the best Specimens of Analysis and Composition on Subjects of Reasoning and Taste, prescribed and executed during the
Session, and for distinguished eminence and proficiency in the
whole business of the Class, were adjudged to—

Seniores.

Thomas S. Crisp, England.
Robert Douglas, Haddington.
George Redford, Berkshire.
George Sym, E. Kilpatrick.
Henry Biggar, Edinburgh.
Alex. Campbell, Ireland.
John Lockhart, Glasgow.
Henry Turner, Newcastle.
Archibald Baird, Glasgow.
Henry Crompton, Lancashire.
George Kenrick, Exeter.
George Smith, Galston.
Wallis Grieve, London.
Geo. Catlin, Nottingham.

Juniores.

John Stewart, Greenock.
William M'Farlane, Paisley.
Malcolm M'Allum, Glasgow.
John Hunter, Glasgow.
James M'Farlane, Glasgow.
Patrick Broadley, Dumbartonshire.
William Couper, Glasgow.
George Watson, Paisley.
Adam Hunter, Greenock.
James Campbell, Glasgow.
John Ferrie,   ,,
Alexander Gilfillan, ,,
John Crum,   ,

The Prizes of the GREEK CLASS were adjudged—

I. For the best Critical Essay on the 1st Book of the Iliad, to
George Redford, Berkshire.

II. For the best Essay on the Metrical Constitution of the
Greek Serious Drama, to
John Kenrick, Exeter.

III. For the best Translation, in English Verse, of a Chorus
from the Oedipus Tyrannus of Sophocles, to
Robert Gregor, A.M., Perthshire.

IV. For propriety of conduct, diligence, and eminent abilities,
displayed during the Session, to

Robert K. Douglas, Haddington.
James Miller, Anderston.
Alexander Gilfillan, Glasgow.
John Lapslie, Campsie.
James Robertson, Edinburgh.
Ebenezer Bradshaw Wallace, Nenthorn.
Alexander Lohore, Glasgow.
William Houston,   ,,
Robert Kirkwood, Dalry.
Robert Ferrier, Edinburgh.
Patrick Craigie, Glasgow.
William Blackburn, ,,
Richard Lawson, Edinburgh.
James Sym, East Kilpatrick.
John Russell, Glasgow.
John Couper,   ,,

The Prizes in the HUMANITY CLASS were adjudged—

I. For the best Essays on Historical Composition, to
David Dunlop, A.M., Ayrshire.
William Stewart, Glasgow.

II. For the best Prose Translation of the 7th Book of Lucan,
to
John Burder, London.

III. For the best Translation of the same in Verse, to
J. G. Lockhart, Glasgow.

IV. For other-Translations in .Prose, from **Plautus,** Ovid, and **Cæsar**, to

William MacFarlane, Paisley.
John Brown, Ayrshire.
James Brash, Glasgow.
J. M. Duncan, ,,
Duncan Stewart, ,,
David Knox, ,,

V. For the best Translations from English into Latin, to
William Lang, Glasgow.
Patrick White, Paisley.

VI. For the best Latin Verses, to

J. G. Lockhart, Glasgow.
Robert Ferrier, Edinburgh.

VII. For the best Account of the Roman Prætor, to
Patrick Chalmers, A.M., Glasgow.

VIII. For the best Account of the Pay of the Roman Army, to
Robert Macnair, Glasgow.

IX. For the best Analysis of an Oration by Cicero, to
Andrew Dewar, Ayrshire.

X. For exemplary Diligence and Regularity, to

John Brown, Ayrshire.
Alexander Lochore, Glasgow.
Patrick Craigie, ,,
E. B. Wallace, Nenthorn.
William Houston, Glasgow.
Robert Ferrier, Edinburgh.
John Russel, Glasgow.

XI. For excelling at the Black Stone Examination, to

Mathew Leechman, Paisley.
Robert Ferrier, Edinburgh.
David Knox, Glasgow.

XII. For excelling at the Examinations on Roman Antiquities, to

James Donald, Ayrshire.

GLASGOW COLLEGE, 1ST MAY, 1810.

This day, the Annual Distribution of Prizes was made in the Common Hall, by the Principal, Dean of Faculty, and Professors, in presence of a numerous meeting of the University, and of many Reverend and respectable Gentlemen of this City and neighbourhood.

Two Silver Medals, given by the UNIVERSITY, were adjudged—
I. For the best Essay on the Aberration of Light, to
John Kenrick, A.M., Exeter.

II. For the best Specimen of Elocution, to
John Simson, A.M., Strathaven.

The Prizes on Mr. COULTER's Donation were adjudged—
I. For the best Sermon on 2nd Peter ii. 19, to
John Barr, Glasgow.

II. For the best Essay on the Classification of the Powers of the Mind, to
George Redford, Berkshire.

III. For the best Translation of Cicero's Treatise on Old Age, to
George Oswald Sym, East Kilpatrick.

A Prize of Five Guineas, by a learned and respectable Gentleman, an Alumnus of this University, for
The best Essay on the Right of Private Judgment, was adjudged to
John Macheath, Greenock.

A Prize of Ten Pounds, on a Donation by Dr. WATT of Birmingham, for
The best Essay on·Accelerated Motion, was adjudged to
James Russel, A.M., Glasgow.

The Prizes for the best Latin Orations in the Common Hall were adjudged to
John Simson, Ayrshire.
William Couper, Glasgow.

Two Prizes for excelling in the Daily Examinations proposed to those Students of SCOTS LAW who chose to be examined were adjudged to

Simon Campbell, Glasgow.
William Pearson, „

The Prizes of the *Senior* MATHEMATICAL CLASS were adjudged to

George Oswald Sym, East Kilpatrick.
Hugh Hamilton, Lanarkshire.

Those of the *Junior* MATHEMATICAL CLASS to

William Macfarlane, Paisley.
George Macintosh, Glasgow.
James Miller, Lanarkshire.
William Young, Renfrewshire.
John Crawford, Glasgow.
William Aitken, Ireland.
John MacCulloch, Comrie.
Alexander Macintosh, Glasgow.

The Prizes of the NATURAL PHILOSOPHY CLASS, for propriety of conduct, exemplary diligence, and eminent abilities during the Session, were adjudged to

John Kenrick, A.M., Exeter.
Hugh Hamilton, Lanarkshire.
Hugh Dewar, A.M., Ayrshire.
James Boyd, Perthshire.
Hugh Stirling, Strathaven.
James Young, Cambusnethan.
John Burder, A.M., London.
William Couper, Glasgow.
John Simson, Ayrshire.
James Stark, Cumbernauld.

The Prizes of the MORAL PHILOSOPHY CLASS,

I. For the best Specimens of Composition on various Subjects in Moral Philosophy, prescribed to the Students, or selected by themselves; and for distinguished eminence in the business of the Class, were adjudged to

Thomas S. Crisp, Suffolk.
George Redford, Berkshire.

George Oswald Sym, East Kilpatrick.
Henry Turner, Newcastle.
Henry B. Biggar, Edinburgh.
George Kenrick, Exeter.
George Smith, Galston.
Patrick Bradley, Ireland.

II. For the best Translation of the v., vi., vii., viii., and ixth Chapters of Cicero's III. book, de Finibus, accompanied with Notes and Illustrations for the purpose of explaining the account of the principles of the Stoical Philosophy contained in that passage, adjudged to

George Kenrick, Exeter.

The Prizes of the LOGIC CLASS,

For the best Specimens of Analysis and Composition on Subjects of Reasoning and of Taste, prescribed and executed during the Session, and for distinguished eminence and proficiency in the whole business of the Class, were adjudged to

Seniores.

John Young, Glasgow.
Joseph Turnbull, London.
Benjamin Heywood, Manchester.
Robert Kirkwood, Glasgow.
James Robertson, Edinburgh.
Ebenezer Bradshaw Wallace, Nenthorn.
James Donald, Galston.
Thos. B. Broadbent, Warrington.
Edward M'Gowan, Durham.
James Drummond, Paisley.
James Edgar, Erskine.
Robert Trail, Antrim.

Juniores.

James Trail, Caithness.
John Brown, Ayrshire.
Robert W. Melville, Edinburgh.
Patrick Craigie, Glasgow.
James Brash,   ,,
Alexander Lochore, ,,
Patrick White, Paisley.

Mathew Leishman, Paisley.
Alexander Angus, Glasgow.
Duncan Stewart,   .,
Alexander Struthers,   ,,

For the best Essay De Feriis Academicis, to
William M'Farlane, Glasgow.
Joseph Turnbull, London.
Edward M'Gowan, Durham.

For the best Specimen of Recollection, to
Ebenezer Bradshaw Wallace, Nenthorn.

The Prizes of the GREEK CLASS were adjudged—

I. For the best Essay on the Diction of Homer, to
John Burder, A.M., London.

II. For the best Critical Essay on the Oedipus Tyrannus of Sophocles, to
Thomas S. Crisp, Suffolk.

III. For the best Critical Essay on the Nubes of Aristophanes, to
Henry Turner, Newcastle.

IV. For the best Translations in English Verse, of select Choruses from the Nubes, to
Matthew Leishman, Paisley.

V. For propriety of conduct, diligence, and eminent abilities, displayed during the Session, to

{ *Thomas Broadbent*, Warrington.
Eben. Bradshaw Wallace, Nenthorn.
Hugh Young, Loudon.
David Knox, Glasgow.

{ *William Dennistoun*, Glasgow.
John Russell,   ,,
James Sym, East Kilpatrick.
John MacArthur, New South Wales.

{ *Edward Andrews*, London.
John Crosbie, Glasgow.
John Wallace,   ,,
Andrew Kessen,   ,,
James Stirling,   ,,
William Wodrow, Mauchline.

{ *David G. Sandeman*, Glasgow.
{ Andrew Sym, East Kilpatrick.
{ David Ingles, Campsie.
{ James Duncan, Glasgow.

The Prizes in the HUMANITY CLASS were adjudged—

I. For the best Account of the Dii Perigrini of the Romans, including an Illustration of the Intolerance that appeared in the Religion of Ancient Rome, to

David Dunlop, A.M., Ayrshire.

II. For the best Translation from English into Latin, to

Alexander Lochore, Glasgow.

III. For the best Translations from Cicero, Terence, and Ovid, into English, to

John Brown, Ayrshire.
John Lyon, Lanark.
Alexander Angus, Glasgow.
James Sym, East Kilpatrick.

IV. For the best Latin Verses, to

John Russell, Glasgow.
Thomas Wallace,   ,,
Robert Thomson,   ,,

V. For excelling at the Examinations in Roman Antiquities, to

James Sym, East Kilpatrick.
John Black, Glasgow.

VI. For excelling at the Black Stone Examination, to

William Harvie, Glasgow.
James Sym, East Kilpatrick.
David Brown, Ayrshire.
John Crosby, Glasgow.

VII. For Exemplary Diligence and Regularity, to

John Russel, Glasgow.
James Grieve,   ,,
John Couper,   ,,
James Sym, East Kilpatrick.
James Harvey, Glasgow.

William Stewart, Glasgow.
Alexander Stevenson, Blantyre.
Ch. M. Provand, Glasgow.
David G. Sandeman,   ,,

GLASGOW COLLEGE, 1st MAY, 1811.

This day, the Annual Distribution of Prizes was made in the Library, by the Principal, Dean of Faculty, and Professors, in presence of a numerous meeting of the University, and of many Reverend and respectable Gentlemen of this City and neighbourhood.

One Silver Medal, given by the UNIVERSITY, was adjudged—
For the best Essay on the Credibility of the Old Testament History, from the Commencement of the Babylonish Captivity to the end of the Canon, to
James Russel, A.M., Glasgow.

The GARTMORE GOLD MEDAL was adjudged—
For the best Essay on the History and Advantages of the Union between Great Britain and Ireland, to
John M'Beath, Greenock.

The Prizes, on Mr. COULTER'S Donation, were adjudged—
I. For the best Lecture on the Parable of the Rich Man and Lazarus, to
John Russell, A.M., Hamilton.

II. For the best Essay on the Immortality of the Soul, and a Future State, to
George Redford, A.M., Windsor.

III. For the best Translation of Xenophon's Lacedemonian Republic, to
George Oswald Sym, A.M., East Kilpatrick.

A Prize of FIVE POUNDS, by a learned and respectable Gentleman, an Alumnus of this University, for the best Illustration of certain Texts of Scripture, to

John Russel, A.M., Hamilton.

A Prize of TEN POUNDS, on a Donation by Dr. WATT of Birmingham, for

The best Essay on the Composition and Resolution of Forces, to

David MacGill, Port-Glasgow.

The Prizes for the best Latin Orations, in the Common Hall, were adjudged to

George Oswald Sym, A.M., East Kilpatrick.
Thomas Montgomery, A.M , Kilwinning.

Two Prizes for excelling in the Daily Examinations, proposed to those Students of SCOTS LAW, who chose to be examined, were adjudged to

John Gabriel Buchanan, Glasgow.
John Park Fleming,   ,,

The Prizes of the MATHEMATICAL CLASSES were adjudged—

Senior Class, to

William Macfarlane, Paisley.

Junior Class, to

James Sym, East Kilpatrick.
James Thomson, Ireland.
Robert Melville, Fife.
James Collins, Ireland.
William Fleming, Hamilton.
John Couper, Glasgow.
Thomas Martineau, Norwich.
Robert Park, Ireland.

The Prizes of the NATURAL PHILOSOPHY CLASS, for Propriety

of Conduct, Exemplary Diligence, and Eminent Abilities during the Session, were adjudged to

George Oswald Sym, A.M., East Kilpatrick.
David M'Gill, Port-Glasgow.
John Osburn, Ayrshire.
Hamilton Murray, ,,
George Redford, A.M., Windsor.
Gavin Struthers, Strathaven.
William Henry, A.M., Ireland.
John Gardner, Old Monkland.

The Prizes of the MORAL PHILOSOPHY CLASS—

For the best Specimens of Composition on Various Subjects, either prescribed weekly to the Students, or chosen by themselves : For Correctness and Elegance in Translating the Latin Philosophical Treatises read in the Class, and for General Eminence during the Session, were adjudged to

First Division.

John Young, Glasgow.
William Macfarlane, Paisley.
Joseph Turnbull, London.
Edward M'Gowan, Durham.
Benjamin Heywood, Manchester.
Ebenezer Bradshaw Wallace, Nenthorn.
James Robertson, Edinburgh.
Thomas Broadbent, Warrington.

Second Division.

John Brown, Ayrshire.
Duncan Stuart, Glasgow.
Matthew Leishman, Paisley.
David Knox, Glasgow.

The Prizes of the LOGIC CLASS—

I. For the best Specimens of Analysis and Composition, and for Distinguished Eminence and Proficiency in the whole business of the Class, to

Seniores.

Arthur Connell, Edinburgh.
David Jardine, Bristol.

John M'Arthur, New South Wales.
William Brown, Strathblane.
Robert M'Lintock, East Kilpatrick.
Adam Forman, Carmunnock.
William Dennistoun, Glasgow.
John Wakefield, Kendal.
Alex. Graham, Glasgow.
James M'Tear, Ireland.
William Jevons, Liverpool.
Alex. Stevenson, Blantyre.

Juniores.

John Russell, Glasgow.
James Harvey, Barony Parish.
Thomas Martineau, Norwich.
Robert Rodger, Glasgow.
Alexander Young, Glenluce.
John Morison Duncan, Glasgow.
Laurence Lockhart,   ,,
John Black,   ,,

II. For the best Description of a Diligent and Ambitious Student, to

John M'Arthur, New South Wales.
Adam Forman, Carmunnock.

II. For the best Specimen of Recollection, to

John Russel, Glasgow.

———

The Prizes of the GREEK CLASS were adjudged—
I. For the best Essay on the Versification of Homer, to

William Ewing, Dumbarton.

II. For the best Essay on the Greek Prepositions, to

Ebenezer Bradshaw Wallace, Nenthorn.

III. For the best Translation, in English Verse, of a Chorus of the Choephorae of Æschylus, to

John Young, Glasgow.

IV. For propriety of Conduct, Diligence, and Eminent Abilities, displayed during the Session, to

> *David Jardine*, Bristol.
> John Russell, Glasgow.
> John Gilchrist, Ireland.
> John Wakefield, Kendall.

> *James Sym*, East Kilpatrick.
> Richard S. Schofield, Kingston-on-Thames.
> James Stirling, Glasgow.
> William Wodrow, Mauchline.

> *Alexander Patten*, Greenock.
> Robert Young, Evandale.
> David Pirrie, Glasgow.
> Robert Thomson, Glasgow.
> Abraham G. Simpson, London.
> William Moncrieff, Glasgow.

> *James Boyd*, Paisley.
> John Denny, Glasgow.
> John Cogan, Port-Glasgow.

The Prizes in the HUMANITY CLASS were adjudged—

I. For the best Illustrations of the Structure and Connection of Parts in Horace's Art of Poetry, to

> William Macfarlane, Paisley.
> Eben. Bradshaw Wallace, Nenthorn.

II. For the best Translation from English into Latin, to

> Robert Thomson, Glasgow.

III. For the best Translations from Tacitus, Plautus, Livy, Ovid, and Cæsar, into English, to

> James Harvey, Barony.
> Jo. Couper, Glasgow.
> Ja. Glen, Ayrshire.
> Robert Thomson, Glasgow.
> Jo. Brown, Ayrshire.
> And. Sym, East Kilpatrick.
> Ja. Thompson, Ireland.

IV. For the best Latin Verses, to

> David Inglis, Glasgow.

V. For excelling at the Black Stone Examination, to

> Jo. Clarke, Glasgow.
> Ch. Grace,   „
> George Nisbet, Monkland

VI. For Excelling at the Examinations in Roman Antiquities, to

> William Wodrow, Ayrshire.

VII. For Exemplary Diligence, Regularity, and Good Behaviour, to

> Jo. Clarke, Glasgow.
> Wm. Harvey, „
> Wm. Woodrow, Ayrshire.
> Ch. Grace, Glasgow.
> And. Sym, East Kilpatrick.
> George Miller, Glasgow.
> Thomas Wallace, „
> James Craufurd, Greenock.
> George Nishet, Monkland.
> James Davidson, Dumbartonshire.

GLASGOW COLLEGE, 1st MAY, 1812.

This day, the Annual Distribution of Prizes was made, in the Common Hall, by the Principal, Dean of Faculty, and Professors, in presence of a numerous meeting of the University, and of many Reverend and respectable Gentlemen of this City and neighbourhood.

Three Silver Medals, given by the UNIVERSITY, were adjudged—

I. For the best Essay on the Inspiration of the Writings of the New Testament, to

> David Dunlop, A.M., Ayrshire.

II. For the best Essay on the Use of the Barometer in measuring Heights, to

> George Oswald Sym, A.M., East Kilpatrick.

III. For the best Specimen of Elocution, to
      Robert Balfour Graham, Glasgow.

The Prizes on Mr. COULTER's Donation were adjudged—
I. For the best Sermon on Mark ii. 27, to
      John Muir, A.M., Ayrshire.
II. For the best Essay on the Pendulum, to
      David M'Gill, A.M., Port-Glasgow.
III. For the best Translation of the Paradoxes of Cicero and the Dream of Scipio, to
      John Brown, Ayrshire.

A Prize on a Donation by Dr. WATT of Birmingham.
For the best Essay on the best mode of Heating Public Buildings, to
      David M'Gill, A.M., Port-Glasgow.

Two Prizes, by a learned and respectable Gentleman, an Alumnus of this University, were adjudged—

I. For the best Exercise, consisting of Short Discourses on Twelve Texts of Scripture, to
      John Russell, sen., A.M., Hamilton.

II. For the best Essay on the Composition of a Sermon, to
      George Oswald Sym, A.M., East Kilpatrick.

Two Prizes, for the best LATIN ORATIONS in the Common Hall, were adjudged to
      William M'Farlane, Paisley.
      David Knox, A.M., Glasgow.

Two Prizes, for excelling in the Daily Examinations proposed to those Students of SCOTS LAW who chose to be examined, were adjudged to
      John Scouller, Glasgow.
      James MacNie, Stirling.

A Prize, in the NATURAL HISTORY CLASS,
For the best Essay on Meteoric Stones, to
William Couper, A.M., Glasgow.

The Prizes of the *Senior* MATHEMATICAL CLASS were adjudged
to
James Thomson, A.M., Ireland.
Robert Park, A.M ,   ,,

Those of the *Junior* MATHEMATICAL CLASS to
John Leitch Moodie, Largs.
David Jardine, Bath.
William Dennistoun, Glasgow.
Stair Macquhae, Ayrshire.
Alexander Stevenson, Blantyre.
Andrew Sym, East Kilpatrick.
Samuel Eccles, Ireland.

The Prizes of the NATURAL PHILOSOPHY CLASS, for propriety
of conduct, exemplary diligence, and display of eminent abilities,
during the Session, were adjudged to
William M'Farlane, Paisley.
James Thomson, A.M., Ireland.
John Wakefield, Kendal.
Ebenezer Bradshaw Wallace, A.M., Nenthorn.
John Murdoch, Ayrshire.
Duncan Stewart, Lanarkshire.
Mathew Leishman, Paisley.
Robert Park, A.M., Ireland.
Thomas Mitchell, A.M., Ireland.

The Prizes in the ETHIC CLASS,
For the best Specimens of Composition on various Subjects in
Moral Philosophy, prescribed to the Students, or selected by
themselves ; and for distinguished eminence in the business of the
Class, were adjudged to
David Jardine, Bath.
William Brown, Strathblane.
John Russell, Glasgow.

Peter M'Dermont, Ayr.
William Dennistoun, Glasgow.
Stair Macquhae, Ayrshire.
John Leitch Moodie, Largs.
James Donald, Ayrshire.
Samuel Eccles, Ireland.

The Prizes of the LOGIC CLASS,
For Essays executed during the Vacation.

1. For the best Illustration of the first twelve Aphorisms of Lord Bacon's Novum Organum, to

John Rússel, Glasgow.

2. The Prizes of this Session,

For the best Specimens of Analysis and Composition on Subjects of Philosophy and Belles Lettres, prescribed and executed during this Session, and for distinguished eminence and proficiency in the whole business of the Class, to

Seniores.

Robert Bright, Bristol.
James Sym, East Kilpatrick.
Henry Lee, Birmingham.
James Stirling, Glasgow.
James Rennie, Sorn.
Archibald Connel, Islay.
William Wodrow, Ayrshire.
James Riddel, Edinburgh.
James Glen, Renfrewshire.
John Wallace, Glasgow.
Gabriel Alexander, Ayrshire.
John Couper, Glasgow.

Juniores.

John Fergus, Kirkcaldy.
James Marshal, Paisley.
David G. Sandeman, Glasgow.
Robert Thomson,   ,,
Alexander Patten, Greenock.
James Hood, Glasgow.

> John Crosbie, Dumfries.
> George Nisbett, Lanarkshire.
> Joseph Parkes, Warwick.
> James Finlay, Glasgow.
> John Buchanan, Perthshire.
> Robert Cowan, Glasgow.

3. For the best Essay on the Chr'stmas Holidays, to
> James Stirling, Glasgow.
> John Fergus, Kirkcaldy.

For the best Poetical Essay on the same Subject, to
> Robert Bright, Bristol.

———

The Prizes of the GREEK CLASS were adjudged—

I. For the best Criticisms on the III. Book of the Iliad, to
> { Duncan Stewart, Glasgow.
> { John Russel,   „

II. For the best Essay on the Interior Syntax of the Fractional
Portions of Compound Words, to
> John Wakefield, Kendal.

III. For the best Poetical Version of a Chorus from the Medea
of Euripides, to
> John Russel, Glasgow.

IV. For propriety of conduct, diligence, and eminent abilities,
displayed during the Session, to
> { *John Wallace*, Glasgow.
> { William Wodrow, Mauchline.
> { Alexander Patten, Greenock.
> { William Adair, Ireland.
> { Henry Lee, Warwickshire.
> { *Robert Young*, Evandale.
> { Andrew Sym, East Kilpatrick.
> { John Clark, Glasgow.
> { Robert Dow, Cathcart.
> { Thomas Wallace, Glasgow.
> { *John Laxon Sweet*, Worcestershire.
> { James Ballantine, Glasgow.
> { James Davidson, Kilsyth.
> { Andrew Crawford, Lochwinnoch.
> { George Davidson, Kilsyth.
> { Gilbert Wardlaw, Glasgow.

{ *Andrew Kerr*, Glasgow.
John Stevenson, Campsie.
Joseph Stewart, Luss.

The Prizes in the HUMANITY CLASS were adjudged—

I. For an Illustration of the Principles and Arrangements of Figurative Language, to

Duncan Stewart, Glasgow.

II. For the best English Poem on the Recovery of Rome from the Gauls, by Camillus, to

John Russel, Glasgow.
James Gilfillan, Perthshire.
Robert Young, Evandale.

III. For the best Historical Account, in Prose, of the same Event, to

John Russel, Glasgow.

IV. For the best Description of the March and Encampment of a Roman Army, to

James Sym, East Kilpatrick.
Duncan Stewart, Glasgow.
David Brown, Ayrshire.
John Brown, „

V. For the best Latin Verses, to

James Glen, Renfrewshire.
James Thomson, A.M., Ireland.
John Sweet, Worcestershire.
Charles Young, Glasgow.
Robert Wylde, „
Robert Allan, „

VI. For the best Translation from English into Latin, to

Andrew Sym, East Kilpatrick.
Alexander Renny, Kilsyth.

VII. For the best Translations from Cicero, Livy, Cæsar, Plautus, and Ovid, to

Robert Thomson, Glasgow.
James Thomson, A.M., Ireland.

James Hamilton, Lanarkshire.[1]
James Glen, Renfrewshire.
John Macleroy, Stirlingshire.

VIII. For excelling at the Examinations in Roman Antiquities, to

Charles Grace, Glasgow.
Arthur Ochterson, Barbadoes.

IX. For excelling at Examinations in Roman Literature, to

James Gilfillan, Perthshire.

X For excelling at the Black-stone Examination, to

James Boyd, Glasgow.
James Davidson, Kilsyth.
Charles Young, Glasgow.
John Douglas,   ,,
George Fullerton, Ayrshire.
John Graham, Glasgow.

XI. For Exemplary Diligence, Regularity, and Good Behaviour, to

Arthur Ochterson, Barbadoes.
William Macleroy, Glasgow.
James Davidson, Kilsyth.
James Boyd, Glasgow.
John Warrand,   ,,
David Reston, Lanarkshire.
James Paterson, Glasgow.
Robert Buchanan,   ,,
John French,
Henry Inglis,

GLASGOW COLLEGE, 1st MAY, 1813.

This day, the Annual Distribution of Prizes was made in the Common Hall, by the Principal, Dean of Faculty, and Professors, in presence of a numerous meeting of the University, and of many Reverend and respectable Gentlemen of this city and neighbourhood.

[1] This young Gentleman having died after the Prize was adjudged, it was delivered to his Brother.

Three Silver Medals, given by the UNIVERSITY, were adjudged—

I. For the best Exercise on the application by Christ and his Apostles, of the passages in the Old Testament respecting the Messiah, to

John Muir, A.M., Ayrshire.

II. For the best Account of Kepler's Discoveries, to

David M'Gill, A.M., Port-Glasgow.

N.B.—A second Prize for an Essay on the same subject was also given to

John Lyon, A.M., Lanark.

III. For the best Specimen of Elocution, to

John Ferrie, Glasgow.

———

The GARTMORE GOLD MEDAL was adjudged—

For the best Essay on the Constitution of the United States of America, to

John Russel, jun., Glasgow.

———

The Prizes on Mr. COULTER's DONATION were adjudged—

I. For the best Lecture on the Parable of the Prodigal Son, to

John Russel, sen., A.M., Hamilton.

N.B.—A second Prize for an Exercise on the same subject was adjudged to

Peter Chalmers, A.M , Glasgow.

II. For the best Discourse on the nature, kinds, and degrees of Evidence, to

James Riddel, Glasgow.

III. For the best Translation of the fourth book of Xenophon's Memorabilia, to

Robert Bright, Bristol.

———

A Prize on a DONATION by Dr. WATT of Birmingham was adjudged—

For the best Essay on the Discoveries in Galvanism, to

George Oswald Sym, A.M., East Kilpatrick.

Two Prizes for the best Latin Orations, in the Common Hall, were adjudged to

John Russel, jun., Glasgow.

Robert Stephenson, A.M., Ireland.

––––––

Two Prizes for excelling in the daily examinations, proposed to those Students of SCOTS LAW who chose to be examined, were adjudged to

Donald Cuthbertson, Glasgow.

Thomas Smith,   „

––––––

A Prize in the NATURAL HISTORY CLASS,

For the best Essay on the Faculties of the inferior Animals, to

William Fleming, Strathaven.

The Prizes of the *Senior* MATHEMATICAL CLASS were adjudged to

John Leech Moodie, Largs.

James Sym, Old Kilpatrick.

Those of the *Junior* MATHEMATICAL CLASS to

Seniores.

George Lang, Port-Glasgow.

William Wodrow, Ayrshire.

George Nisbett, Old Monkland.

John Hyndman, Antigua.

William Adair, Ireland.

Juniores.

Robert Mair, Ayrshire.

Alexander H. S. Rennie, Kilsyth.

––––––

The Prizes of the NATURAL PHILOSOPHY CLASS, for propriety of conduct, exemplary diligence, and display of eminent abilities, during the Session, were adjudged to

Samuel Eccles, A.M., Ireland.

John Leech Moodie, Largs.

Stair Macquhae, A.M., Ayrshire.

Robert Lyon, A.M., Lanark.

John Russell, jun., Glasgow.
David Davidson, A.M., Ireland.
Thomas B. Broadbent, A.M., Warrington.
Robert Stephenson, A.M., Ireland.

———

The Prizes of the ETHIC CLASS,

For the best Specimens of Composition on various Subjects in Moral Philosophy, prescribed to the Students, or selected by themselves; and for distinguished eminence in the business of the Class. were adjudged to

Seniores.

James Rennie, Sorn.
James Sym, East Kilpatrick.
Alexander Waugh, London.
Gabriel Alexander, Ayrshire.
William Wodrow,   „
John Couper, Glasgow.
James Glen, Lochwinnoch.

Juniores.

John Crosbie, Anderston.
Robert Thomson, Glasgow.
William Symington, Paisley.
James A. Steele, Dumbarton.
George Nisbett, Old Monkland.
James Gilfillan, Comrie.

———

The Prizes of the LOGIC CLASS,

For Exercises executed during the Vacation, were adjudged—

1. For the best Translation of Aristotle's Art of Poetry, to
George Nisbet, Old Monkland.

2. For the best Essay on Evidence, to
William Wodrow, Ayrshire.

3. For the best Essay on First Principles, particularly those of Dr. Reid, to
James Rennie, Sorn.

To the Students of the present Session, for the best Specimens of Analysis and Composition, on various Subjects of Reasoning

and Taste, connected with the Lectures, and for distinguished
eminence and proficiency in the whole business of the Class—

Seniores.

Joseph France, England.
William Moncrieff, Glasgow.
John French, Lanarkshire.
Charles Young, Glasgow.
Robert Dow, Cathcart.
Charles Grace, Glasgow.
Andrew Sym, East Kilpatrick.
John Clarke, Glasgow.
John Heywood, Liverpool.
John Marshall, Glasgow.

Juniores

George Miller, Glasgow.
Alexander Dick,   ,,
William Richard Young, Glasgow.
Alexander Monteath, Perthshire.
John Brown, Kilmalcolm.
Andrew Young, Paisley.
David Perrie, Glasgow.
William Couper, ,,
Mathew Stewart, Ayrshire.
James Davidson, Kilsyth.

For the best Essays on the Extension of the Sense of Sight, by
the discoveries of the Properties of Glass.

I. For the best Exercise in Prose, to
            Joseph France, England.

II. For the best Exercise in Verse, to
            John Heywood, Liverpool.
            Charles Young, Glasgow.

For the best Specimen of Recollection, to
            John Marshall, Glasgow.

For the best appearance at the Annual Black Stone Examination, to
            James Cousins, Ireland.

For the best Public Theme, to
> Alexander Dick, Glasgow.

The Prizes of the GREEK CLASS were adjudged—

I. For the best Critical Essay on the Medea of Euripides, to
> John Russell, Glasgow.

II. For the best Essay on the Versification of Homer, to
> Robert Bright, Bristol.

III. For the best Poetical Version of a Chorus from the Oedipus Tyrannus of Sophocles, to
> Robert Marshall, Glasgow.

IV. For the best Poetical Version of another Chorus from the same Play, to
> John Russell, Glasgow.

V. For the best Exemplifications of the Greek Verb, to
> Walter Rankine, East Monkland.
> Alexander Grahame, East Kilbride.

VI. For Propriety of Conduct, Diligence, and eminent abilities, displayed during the Session, to

> *Charles Grace*, Glasgow.
> Alexander Monteath, Perthshire.
> James Cousins, Ireland.
> Thomas Blain,   „
> Andrew Young, Paisley.

> *Matthew Young*, Loudon.
> Alexander H. S. Rennie, Kilsyth.
> James How, Glasgow.
> Andrew Kerr,   „
> William Russell, „

> *Reuben Bryce*, Ireland.
> Robert Fleming, Loudon.
> Andrew Buchanan, Glasgow.
> William Girdwood,   „
> Alexander Houstoun,   „
> Alexander Grahame, East Kilbride.

> *Hugh Lockhart*, Fenwick.
> Ebenezer Russell, Glasgow.
> James Muir,   „

The Prizes in the HUMANITY CLASS were adjudged—

I. For the best Critical Essay on the II. Book of Virgil's Georgic, to

Robert Thomson, Glasgow.

II. For the best Account of the Architecture of Roman Houses, and an Illustration of the Doric Order in the Hunterian Museum, to

Andrew Macneil, A.M., Renfrewshire.

III. For the best Translations from Terence, Livy, Tacitus, Cesar, and Ovid, to

Arthur Oughterson, Barbadoes.
James Thomson, A.M., Ireland.
Robert Monteath, Glasgow
Arthur Oughterson, Barbadoes.
William Macleroy, Glasgow.
John Macleroy,   ,,
John Macadam,
John Morrison,
Robert Monteath,   ,,

IV. For the best Translations from English into Latin, to

Alexander Rennie, Kilsyth.
Charles Grace, Glasgow.

V. For the best Latin Verses, to

James Ballantine, Glasgow.
James Mitchel, Ayrshire.

VI. For excelling at the Examination on Roman Antiquities, to

Andrew Fergus, Kirkintulloch.

VII. For excelling at the Black Stone Examination, to

William Russell, Glasgow.
James Stirling, Strathaven.
John Stevenson, Stirlingshire.
Henry Inglis, Glasgow.

VIII. For Exemplary Diligence, and Regularity of Attendance to

Alexr. Houston, Glasgow.
Andrew Simson, Strathaven.

Andrew Kerr, Glasgow.
William Hall,   ,,
Andrew Fergus, Kirkintulloch.
James Ewing, Dumbartonshire.
James Dennistoun, Glasgow.
Andrew Watt, Lanarkshire.
Robert Wilson, Glasgow.

GLASGOW COLLEGE, 2nd MAY, 1814.

This day, the Annual Distribution of Prizes was made in the Common Hall, by the Principal, Dean of Faculty, and Professors, in presence of a numerous meeting of the University, and of many Reverend and respectable Gentlemen of this City and neighbourhood.

Three Silver Medals, given by the UNIVERSITY, were adjudged—

I. For the best Account of the Jewish Sects and their Tenets, at the time of our Saviour's appearance, to
Stair Macquhae, A.M., Ayrshire.

II. For another Essay on the same Subject, to
David M'Gill, A.M., Port-Glasgow.

III. For the best Specimen of Elocution, to
Robert Kirkwood, Ayrshire.

The Prizes on Mr. COULTER's Donation were adjudged—

I. For the best Essay on the immortality of the Soul, to
John Buchanan, Perthshire.

II. For the best Translation of Cicero's Treatise de Amicitia, to
William Wodrow, Ayrshire.

A Prize on a Donation by Dr. WATT of Birmingham was adjudged—

For the best Account of Friction and its effects on machinery, to
James Sym, East Kilpatrick.

A Prize for the best Latin Oration, in the Common Hall, was adjudged to

James Sym, East Kilpatrick.

The Prizes of the HEBREW CLASS were adjudged—

I. For distinguished eminence and proficiency in the whole business of the Class, to

Seniores.

David M'Gill, A.M., Port-Glasgow.

Juniores.

David Brown, Kilmarnock.

II. For the best Paradigmas of the Hebrew Verb,

David Brown, Kilmarnock.
James Duncan, Glasgow.
Thomas Kirkwood, A.M., Falkirk.

Two Prizes for excelling in the daily Examinations, proposed to those Students of SCOTS LAW who chose to be examined, were adjudged to

William Gebbie, Galston, Ayrshire.
James Harvie, Garthamlock, Lanarkshire.

A Prize in the NATURAL HISTORY CLASS was adjudged—

For the best Account of the Gradations of the Kingdoms of Nature, to

William Fleming, Strathaven.

The Prizes of the *Senior* MATHEMATICAL CLASS were adjudged to

William Adair, A.M., Ireland.
James Rennie, Sorn.

Those of the *Junior* MATHEMATICAL CLASS, to

Seniores.

Thomas Kennedy, Ireland.
James Boyd, Paisley.
James Paterson, Glasgow.
Robert Carlisle, Ireland.

Juniores.

David Allison, Paisley.
Robert Buchanan, Glasgow.
John Stevenson, Stirlingshire.

The Prizes of the NATURAL PHILOSOPHY CLASS,
For propriety of conduct, exemplary diligence, and display of eminent abilities, during the Session, were adjudged to

James Sym, East Kilpatrick.
William Wodrow, Ayrshire.
John Couper, Glasgow.
William Hutton, A.M., Ireland.
James Rennie, Sorn.
William Anderson, Glasgow.
John Thomson, Renfrewshire.
William Adair, A.M., Ireland.

The Prizes in the ETHIC CLASS,
Given for general eminence in the duties and business of the Class, and for the best Specimens of Composition, on Subjects Metaphysical and Ethical, prescribed by the Professor, or chosen by the Students themselves, were adjudged to

Seniores.

Joseph France, England.
Andrew Sym, East Kilpatrick.
David Longmoore, Ireland.
John Brown, Kilmalcolm.
George Colville, Ochiltree.
Robert Dow, Cathcart.
William Smith, Loudoun, Ayrshire.

Juniores.

Andrew Young, Paisley.
Peter Buchanan, Callander.
Alexander M'Neil, Glasgow.
Robert Wylde, Paisley.
Robert Hogg, Blantyre.

The Prizes of the LOGIC CLASS,

For Exercises executed during the Vacation were adjudged—

For the best Analysis of the principles of Association, to

William Smith, Loudoun, Ayrshire.

To the Students of the present Session for the best specimens of Analysis and Composition on various subjects of Reasoning and Taste, connected with the Lectures ; and for distinguished eminence and proficiency in the whole business of the Class.

Seniores.

John Evans, Wales.
Right Hon. Viscount Glenorchy.
John B. Gray, Ayrshire.
Archd. Connell, Edinburgh.
Andrew Crawford, Lochwinnoch.
Thomas Heywood, Liverpool.
Robert Young, Avendale.
Theophilus Eastman, Hampshire.
George R. Hunter, Dorsetshire.
Samuel Wood, Liverpool.
James Ballantine, Glasgow.
Mathew Young, Loudon.

Juniores.

William Young, Falkirk.
William Shortridge, Glasgow.
Andrew Bannatyne,   .,
William Hall,   ,,
Reuben Bryce, Ireland.
Joseph Stuart, Luss.
Robert Buchanan, Glasgow.
Andrew Buchanan,   ,,
James How,   ,,
Alexander Rennie, Kilsyth.
David Connell, Glasgow.
Robert Hilton, Lancashire.

I. For the best Essay on the progress of Reason and of Language in Children.

Private Student—John Graham, Kilbride.
Public Students—Andrew Bannatyne, Glasgow.
                  Samuel Wood, Liverpool.

For the best Essays on the competition for Prizes, in Prose, to
> Andrew Crawford, Lochwinnoch.
> Right Hon. Viscount Glenorchy.
> James Duncan, Glasgow.

For the best Exercise in Verse, on the same subject, to
> Robert Young, Avendale.
> Robert M'Gill, Ireland.

For the best Specimen of Recollection, to
> Robert Kennedy, Perthshire.
> William Hall, Glasgow.

For the best Public Theme, to
> Robert Young, Avendale.

For the best Appearance at the Black Stone Examination, to
> Robert Carlisle, Ireland.
> George R. Hunter, Dorsetshire.

The Prizes of the GREEK CLASS were adjudged—

I. For the best Critical Essay on the Oedipus Tyrannus of Sophocles, to
> [1] Duncan Stewart, Glasgow.

II. For the best Essay on the Use of the Infinitive Mood of the Greek Verb for the Imperative, to
> William Symington, Paisley.

III. For the best Poetical Version of certain Choruses from the Clouds of Aristophanes, to
> John Crosbie, Glasgow.

IV. For the best Exemplifications of the Greek Verb, to
> *John Finlay*, Glasgow.
> William M'Queen, Ayrshire.

V. For Propriety of Conduct, Diligence, and Eminent Abilities, displayed during the Session, to
> *Robert Carlisle*, Ireland.
> David Kirkpatrick, Ireland.
> George Gordon M'Dougall, St. Croix.
> Alexander M'Ilwain, Ireland.
> Reuben J. Bryce,   ,,

[1] This young Gentleman having died after his Exercise was given in, the Prize was delivered to his Relations.

Alexander Graham, East Kilbride.
David Allison, Paisley.
John Gemmil, Cambuslang.
Gilbert Wardlaw, Glasgow.
James Muir, Glasgow.
Thomas Curr, Shotts.
Alexander Ewing, Glasgow.
Peter M'Bride, North Knapdale.
John Russell, Canada.
Charles Wallace, Worcestershire.
William Penney, Glasgow.
Charles Parker, Glasgow.
John M. Spooner, Demerara.
William Graham, East Kilbride.

The Prizes in the HUMANITY CLASS were adjudged—

I. For the best Account of the Rise, Progress, and Decline of Roman Poetry, to

[1] Duncan Stewart, Glasgow.

For another Essay on the same subject, to

Charles Young, Glasgow.

II. For the best Account of the Rise, Progress, and Termination of the Decemvirate at Rome, to

Charles Young, Glasgow.

III. For the best Translations into English, from Cicero, Livy, Plautus, and other Authors, to

James Steel, Dumbarton.
Andrew Fergus, Kirkintulloch.
Alexander Graham, Lanarkshire.
John Anderson, Paisley.
Alexander M'Ilwain, Ireland
Ebenezer Russel, Glasgow.
Robert Monteath,   ,,
Ebenezer Russel,   ,,

[1] This young Gentleman having died during the present Session of College, as has been mentioned above, the Prize was regularly claimed on the part of his Relations ; and was delivered with all the consideration due to his eminent abilities, good dispositions, literary ardour, and literary acquirements, which were particularly distinguished by his ingenuity in Classical and Philosophical Criticism.

IV. For the best Translations from English into Latin, to
   John Wallace Hozier, Glasgow.

V. For the best Latin Verses, to
   Thomas Rutherford, Glasgow.
   John Martin Spooner, Demerara.

VI. For excelling at the Examination in Roman Antiquities, to
   James Stirling, Strathaven.

VII. For excelling at the Black-stone Examination, to
   William Davidson, Glasgow.
   Robert Macnair Wilson, Glasgow.
   James Muir,   ,,
   Robert Wallace,   ,,
   Thomas Curr, Lanarkshire.

VIII. For Exemplary Diligence and Regularity, to
   Robert Macnair Wilson, Glasgow.
   Ebenezer Russel,   ,,
   John Gemmel, Lanarkshire.
   James Muir, Glasgow.
   Alexander Graham, Lanarkshire.
   George Gibb, Ayrshire.
   Alexander Ewing, Glasgow.
   William Muir, Kilmarnock.

GLASGOW COLLEGE, 1st MAY, 1815.

This day, the Annual Distribution of Prizes was made, in the Common Hall, by the Principal and Professors, in presence of a numerous meeting of the University, and of many Reverend and respectable Gentlemen of this City and neighbourhood.

Three Silver Medals, given by the UNIVERSITY, were adjudged:
I. For the best account of the Tenets of Arius, and of those who embraced his opinions in after ages, variously modified, to
   Stair Macquhae, A.M., Ayrshire.

II. For the best account of the recently discovered Planets, to
John Couper, Glasgow.

III. For the best specimen of Elocution, to
Gavin G. Dunn, A.M., Fintry.

The GARTⱯORE GOLD MEDAL,

For the best exercise on the probable effects of the extended
Conquests in the East on the British Constitution, was adjudged to
George Oswald Sym, A.M., East Kilpatrick.

A Prize on Mr. COULTER's DONATION was adjudged—
For the best translation of Xenophon's Agesilaus, to
Andrew Sym, East Kilpatrick.

A Prize on a DƆNATION by Dr. WATT of Birmingham was
adjudged—
For the best comparative view of the Huttonian and Wernerian
Systems of Geology, to
George Oswald Sym, A.M., East Kilpatrick.

A Second Prize, for an Essay on the same subject, was given,
on Mr. Coulter's Donation, to
James Rennie, Sorn.

A Prize was given by a private Gentleman, an alumnus of this
University,
For the best Essay on Bible Societies, to
James Rennie, Sorn.

Three Prizes for the best LATIN ORATIONS, in the Common
Hall, were adjudged to
Robert Wylde, Paisley.
Andrew Sym, East Kilpatrick.
Hugh Mayne, A.M., Ireland.

Prizes to Students of THEOLOGY of the first and second years.
I. Essay on the Qualifications for the Ministerial Office, to
Mr. Adam Forman, A M.
Mr. John Thomson.

II. Essay on the Character and Conduct of a Student in Divinity, to

Mr. James Glen.

III. Essay on Testimony, with a view to its application to the Evidence of Christianity, to

Mr. William Woodrow.
Mr. James Rennie.

IV. For general eminence, on the conclusion of his Theological Courses of Study, to

Richard Thomson.

———

The Prizes of the HEBREW CLASS were adjudged—

I. For distinguished eminence and proficiency in the whole business of the Class, to

Edward Gibb, Bothwell.
John Brown, Ayrshire.

II. For the best Paradigmas of the Hebrew Verb, to

James Forsyth, Glasgow.
John Steel, Quarrelton.
John Vicar, Beith.

———

Two Prizes for excelling in the daily examinations proposed to those Students of SCOTTISH LAW who chose to be examined, were adjudged to

Andrew Simson, Glasgow.
Robert Walkinshaw, jun., Paisley.

———

Prizes in the NATURAL HISTORY CLASS were adjudged.

I. On Petrefactions, to

James Rennie, Sorn.

II. On the Inducements to the Study of Entomology, to

John Campbell, Largs.

———

The Prizes of the *Senior* MATHEMATIC CLASS were adjudged to

Robert Watson, Glasgow.
John Dunmore Lang, Largs.
Alexander H. S. Rennie, Kilsyth
George Lang, Port-Glasgow.

Those of the *Junior* MATHEMATIC CLASS, to

Seniores.

David Kirkpatrick, Ireland.
Theophilus Eastman, Hampshire.
John Gallaway, Stirlingshire.
William Anderson, Ireland.
Samuel Neilson,   ,,
John Aiton, Strathaven.

Juniores.

William Anderson, Kilsyth.
Henry Dunlop, Glasgow.
Thomas Andrews, Ireland.

The Prizes of the NATURAL PHILOSOPHY CLASS were adjudged:
I. For the best Essay on the Thermometer, to

Alexander M'Lean, Rothesay.

II. For propriety of conduct, exemplary diligence, and display of eminent abilities, to

Andrew Sym, East Kilpatrick.
Hugh Mayne, A.M., Ireland.
John Orr, A.M.,   ,,
Robert Wylde, Paisley.
John Adamson, Peebles-shire.
Archibald Bennie, Anderston.
William Rintoul, Kincardine.
John Park, Hutcheson.
John D. Lang, Largs.

The Prizes in the ETHIC CLASS,

Given by the votes of the Students, for distinguished Eminence exhibited during the Session, in the composition of various Essays on subjects either prescribed to the Students, or chosen by themselves, and in all the other duties and business of the Class, were adjudged to

Seniores.

Andrew Crawford, Lochwinnoch.
Robert Magill, Ireland.
William Shortridge, Glasgow.

Robert Young, Avondale.
Theophilus Eastman, Portsmouth.
William Anderson, Coleraine.
Samuel Wood, Liverpool.

Juniores.

George G. M'Dowall, West Indies.
Reuben John Bryce, Coleraine.
Alexander H. S. Rennie, Kilsyth.
Joseph Stuart, Luss.
James Paterson, Glasgow.

A Prize given for the best Essay on Instinct was adjudged to
Andrew Sym, East Kilpatrick.

The Prizes of the LOGIC CLASS.

I. For the best Essays on the Evidence of the Senses, executed
during the Vacation, to
Andrew Crawford, Lochwinnoch.
Andrew Bannatyne, Glasgow.

II. For the best Analysis of the Rhetorical figure called
Prosopopeia, to
Robert Young, Avondale.
John Anderson, Paisley.

The Prizes of this Session,

III. For the best specimens of Analysis and Synthesis, on
various Subjects of Philosophy and of Taste, and for distinguished
eminence and proficiency in the whole business of the Class.

First Division.

James Brown, Paisley.
Charles Burton, Manchester.

Second Division.

Seniores.

David Bogue, Hampshire.
Charles Wallace, Worcester.
Gillian M'Laine, Argyllshire.
Thomas Cumming, Armagh.

Gilbert Wardlaw, Glasgow.
David Clarke, County of Down.
William Worsley, Plymouth.
Joseph Hay, Perthshire.
Duncan M'Lean, Rothesay.

Juniores.

Alexander Graham, East Kilbride.
David Allison, Glasgow.
Michael Willis, Stirling.
Ebenezer Russel, Glasgow.
James Gibson, Doune.
John M'Leod Campbell, Argyleshire.
William Penney, Glasgow.
John Thomson, Edinburgh.
Æneas M'Lean, Argyleshire.
Robert M'Nair Wilson, Glasgow.
Alexander Houston,   ,,

IV. During this Session, Prizes were proposed for the best account of the Socratic Dialogue, which have been adjudged to

David Kirkpatrick—Private Class.
David Bogue, Hampshire. }
Alex. Grahame, East Kilbride. } Public Class.

V. For the best specimen of Recollection, to
David Allison, Paisley.

VI. For the best appearance at the Black-stone Examination, to
David Clarke, Down, Ireland.

VII. For the best Public Theme, to
David Bogue, Hampshire.

————

The Prizes of the GREEK CLASS were adjudged—

I. For the best Critical Essays on the Clouds of Aristophanes, to
William Spiers, Paisley.
Thomas Heywood, B.A., Manchester.

II. For the best Translation of a Chorus from the Choephoroe of Æschylus, to
John Evans, B.A., Haverford West.

III. For the best Essays on the Mental Process, by which Conditional Particles (such as EI, AI, SI, AN, etc.) came to be estimated, in Language, as Symbols of Wish, Intreaty, Regret, Interrogation, etc., to

Samuel Wood, B.A., Liverpool.
Reuben J. Bryce, Ireland.

IV. For the best Essay on the Versification of Homer, to

Francis Pett, London.

V. For the best Exemplification of the Greek Verb, to

George Gibb, Ayrshire.
John Macintyre, Kincardine.

VI. For Propriety of Conduct, Diligence, and Eminent Abilities, displayed during the Session, to

David K. Clarke, Ireland.
Michael Willis, Stirling.
Joseph Hay, Alyth.
William Penney, Glasgow.
Alexander Ewing,   „

James Muir, Glasgow.
Thomas Curr, Shotts.
William Davidson, Glasgow.
Charles Parker,   „
James Mylne,   „

John Macintyre, Kincardine.
Thomas Williamson, Stirling.
William Bain, Paisley.
James Taylor, Foulis.
William Muir, Kilmarnock.
James Russell, Glassford.

David Macintosh, London.
William Chrystall, Glasgow.
James Hodgert, Paisley.

The Prizes in the HUMANITY CLASS were adjudged—

I. For an Essay on Figurative Language, to

Peter M'Funn, Glasgow.

II. For the best descriptions of the march and encampment of a Roman Army, to

   Alexander Graham, E. Kilbride
   William Muir, Kilmarnock.

III. For a Translation of Tacitus' Life of Agricola, to

   Alexander M'Neil, Glasgow.

IV. For the best Translations of the Andria of Terence, to

   Ebenezer Russel, Glasgow.
   William Davidson, ,,

V. For the best Translations of Cicero de Amicitia, to

   Thomas Curr, Shotts.
   William Denniston, Glasgow.

VI. For a Translation from Cæsar, to

   Duncan M'Intyre, Eastwood.

VII. For the best Translation into Latin Verse of Cowper's Poem on the loss of the Royal George, to

   David M'Intosh, London.

VIII. For the best Translation from English into Latin, to

   William Davidson, Glasgow.

IX. For excelling at the Black-stone examination, to

  1. James Mylne, Glasgow.
  2. Patrick Wilson, St. Martin's, West Indies.
  3. John Connel, Glasgow.
   James Laurie, Newmilns.
  4. William Muir, Kilmarnock.
   William Bain, Paisley.

X. For exemplary diligence, regularity and good behaviour, to

  1. Thomas Curr, Shotts.
   William Muir, Kilmarnock.
   Archibald Nisbet, Newmilns.
   Duncan M'Intyre, Eastwood.
   William Hamilton, Muiravonside.
  2. Thomas Aitken, Stirling.
   John M'Intyre, Kincardine.
   Thomas Williamson, Stirling.

3. John Peters, Glasgow.
4. John Dymock, ,,
   William Arnell, ,,
   John Hamilton Gray, Carntyne.

Prizes were adjudged at the close of Mr. Alexander's course of MATERIA MEDICA, by the votes of their fellow students, to the following Gentlemen, as the rewards of superior diligence and proficiency.

Seniors.

William Train, Dalry, Ayrshire.
Charles Kennedy, Ayr.
John Macfadzean, Kirkoswald.

Juniors.

[1] John Clarke, Glasgow. ·
Samuel M'Gee, Rady, Armagh.
Douglas Wills, New Cumnock, Ayrshire.
William M'Clure, Glasgow.
Thomas Craig, Neilston.
John Blackwood, Cathrine, Ayrshire.
William Ralston, Paisley.

GLASGOW COLLEGE, 1st MAY, 1816.

This day, the Annual Distribution of Prizes was made in the Common Hall, by the Principal and Professors, in presence of a numerous meeting of the University, and of many Reverend and respectable Gentlemen of this City and neighbourhood.

[1] This most promising young man, the friend and favourite of the poor, was cut off by an infectious fever, caught in the discharge of his duty, to an indigent female, two weeks before the prizes were adjudged. But his class-fellows, impressed with a sense of his unwearied and very successful diligence throughout the Session, unanimously voted this posthumous mark of their esteem and respect for his memory, which was accordingly presented to his father, Mr. Andrew Clarke, surgeon in this city

Two Silver Medals, given by the UNIVERSITY, were adjudged—

I. For the best Essay upon the Internal Evidence of Christianity, to

John Brown, Stewarton.

II. For the best Specimen of Elocution, to

John Crosbie, Glasgow.

————

Two Prizes on Mr. COULTER's Donation were adjudged—

I. For the best Lecture on the Parable of the Talents, Matthew xxv. 14, etc., to

Stair Macquhae, A.M., St. Quivox.

II. For the best Translation of Tacitus de Moribus Germanorum, to

David Bogue, Gosport.

————

A Prize on a Donation by Dr. WATT of Birmingham,

For the best Essay on the Improvements in the Art of Bleaching by the application of the Principles of Chemistry, was adjudged to

James Rennie, A.M., Sorn.

————

Two Prizes for the best LATIN ORATIONS in the Common Hall, were adjudged to

Andrew Crawford, Lochwinnoch.
Robert Graham, Aberfoyle.

————

Prizes of the THEOLOGICAL CLASS to Students of the first and second years, were adjudged—

For Essays—1. On the necessity of Revelation, evinced from the consideration of the general circumstances and character of mankind. 2. On the Imperfection of that Knowledge which the Light of Nature affords on the Pardon of Sin, and our condition after Death.

2nd Year, to

John Thomson, Houston.
Thomas Kirkwood, Strathaven.
John C. Jameson, Kilmarnock.

1st Year, to
John Marshall, Glasgow.
Robert Wylde, Paisley.
Archibald Bennie, Anderston.
John D. Lang, Largs.

For an abridged statement of the Lectures in Theology during the course of this Session, to
William Weir, Ireland.
John M'Dougal, Argyllshire.

For voluntary Exercises in Theology, to
James Marshall, Rothesay.

The Prizes of the HEBREW CLASSES were adjudged—

Senior Class.

I. For the best Analysis of a passage in Isaiah, chap. v. 1-7, to
David Bogue, Gosport.

Junior Class.

I. For distinguished eminence and proficiency in the whole business of the Class, to

Robert Gray, Ireland.
John D. Lang, Largs.

II. For the best Paradigmata of the Hebrew verb, to
Alexander Lochore, A.M., Glasgow.
James A. Steele, A.M., Dumbarton.
John Allan, Tarbolton.
Peter M'Laren, Comrie.
Robert Paterson, Camnethan.

Two Prizes for excelling in the daily examinations, proposed to those Students of SCOTTISH LAW, who chose to be examined, were adjudged to
John Fyfe, Glasgow.
James Burnside, Glasgow.

The Prizes of the MATHEMATIC CLASS, for excelling in Exercises prescribed during the Session, and for general propriety, diligence, and ability, were adjudged—

SENIOR CLASS, to

David Allison, Paisley.
Thomas Andrews, Ireland.
William Anderson, A.M., Ireland.

JUNIOR CLASS, to

Seniores.

Joseph Hay, Perthshire.
Michael Willis, Stirling.
James Reston, Lanarkshire.
Robert Wilson, Glasgow.
William Raphael, Ireland.

Juniores.

William Bain, Paisley.
John Dixon, Dumbarton.

The Prizes of the NATURAL PHILOSOPHY CLASS, given by the votes of the Students, for propriety of conduct, exemplary diligence, and display of eminent abilities, were adjudged to

William Anderson, A.M., Ireland.
Alexander H. S. Rennie, Kilsyth.
Archibald Armstrong, A.M., Ireland.
James Paterson, Glasgow.
John Stevenson, A.M., Campsie.
Thomas M'Vey, Polmont.
Charles Muirhead, Drymen.
James Bain, Row.

The Prizes in the ETHIC CLASS,

Given for eminence displayed during the Session, in the composition of Essays on Subjects prescribed to the Students, **or** chosen by themselves ; and in the other business and duties of the Class, were adjudged to

Seniores.

David Bogue, Gosport.
Gillian Maclaine, Argyllshire.
Charles Wallace, Worcestershire.
William Raphael, Ireland.
Duncan M'Lean, Perthshire.
Alexander Ewing, Glasgow.

Juniores.

Ebenezer Russell, Glasgow.
Michael Willis, Stirling.
William Hall, Glasgow.
John M'Leod Campbell, Argyllshire.
William Penney, Glasgow.

A Prize was given for an Essay on Habit, prescribed at the end of last Session, to

William J. Shortridge, A.M., Glasgow.

————

The Prizes of the LOGIC CLASS were adjudged—

I. For the best Essay on the influence of Attention on the other Powers of the Mind, executed during the Vacation, to

David Bogue, Gosport.

II. For the best Essay on the Standard of Taste, to

Charles Wallace, Worcester.

The Prizes for this Session were adjudged—

III. For the best specimens of Composition, on various subjects of Philosophy, and of Taste, and for distinguished Eminence and Proficiency in the whole business of the Class, during the Session to

Seniores.

John Macfarlane, Campbelton.
David Wyllie, Liverpool.
David Smith, London.
Samuel Bright, Bristol.
Cosmo Innes, Durris.
Henry Marsland, Bradbury.
William Davidson, Glasgow.

Alexander Stewart, Dingwall.
Edward Wakefield, Kendal.
James Cross, Glasgow.

Juniores.

James Mylne, Glasgow.
Charles Parker, Glasgow.
Robert Crawfurd, Dalry.
William Gordon, Edinburgh.
John Connell, Glasgow.
William Black, East Monkland.
Robert Leechman, Paisley.
Samuel Nelson, Downpatrick.
Thomas Buchanan, Callender.
David Logan, Glasgow.

IV. During the Christmas Holidays, Prizes were proposed,

1st. For the best Essay on the Happiness of Youth, executed in Prose or in Poetry. The Prize for the best Essay in Prose was adjudged to

Henry Marsland, Bradbury.

In *Poetry*, to

George Wood, Liverpool.

2nd. For the best Essay on the Comparison of Man with the Inferior Animals, to

Robert King, Johnston.

V. For the best specimen of Recollection, to

William Black, East Monkland.
Charles Parker, Glasgow.

VI. For the best Appearance at the Black Stone Examination, to

David Rees, Cardiganshire.

VII. For the best Public Theme, to

Samuel Nelson, Downpatrick.

————

The Prizes of the GREEK CLASS were adjudged—
I. For the best Essay on the Greek Middle Verb, to

Robert Young, Avondale.

II. For the best Critical Essay on the XXIV. Book of the Iliad, to

William Rankin, East Monkland.

III. For the best Criticism on the first Book of the Iliad, to
Ebenezer Russel, Glasgow.

IV. For the best Translation, in Verse, of a Chorus, from the Medea of Euripides, to

Robert Young, Avondale.

V. For the best Exemplifications of the Greek Verb, to
John Bell, Glasgow.
Robert Smith, maj., Kilwinning.

VI. For Propriety of Conduct, Diligence, and Eminent Abilities, displayed during the Session, to

Thomas Curr, Shotts.
David Wyllie, Liverpool.
William Davidson, Glasgow.
Samuel Nelson, Ireland.
William Thompson, Kilmarnock.

John Thompson, Glasgow.
William Graham, East Kilbride.
Archibald Jack, Glasgow.
James Lawrie, Loudon.
Walter M'Pherson, Cardross.

Robert Potter, Ayr.
David Bryden, „
John Dymock, Glasgow.
Jamieson Willis, Stirling.
John H. Gray, Carntyne.
James M'Lean, Glasgow.

James Dennistoun, Dumbartonshire.
John M'Brair, Newfoundland.
William Giffen, Paisley.

The Prizes of the HUMANITY CLASS were adjudged—

I. For a Historical Account of the Occupation of Rome and Siege of the Capitol by the Gauls under Brennus, to

William Hall, Glasgow.

II. For a Historical Account of the ten years' Siege of Veii and of its reduction by Camillus, to

William Muir, Kilmarnock.
Ebenezer Russell, Glasgow.

III. For a Translation of Cicero's first Oration against Catiline, to

William Muir, Kilmarnock.

IV. For a Translation of the Somnium Scipionis, to

William Muir, Kilmarnock.

V. For a Translation of the Trinummus of Plautus, to

Duncan M'Intyre, Eastwood.

VI. For a Translation of the 1st, 4th, and 8th Epistles of Ovid, to

David Macintosh, London.

VII. Map of the Roman Empire, distinguishing its extent, at the end of the 5th, 6th, and 7th Centuries, from the Building of the City, to

Thomas Bissland, Renfrewshire.

VIII. Latin Verses on the Battle of Waterloo, to

Robert Potter, Ayr.

IX. For a Translation into English Verse of the 16th Ode of the 2nd Book of Horace, to

Edmund Kell, Birmingham.

X. Public Theme, to

Robert Potter, Ayr.

XI. For Excelling at the Black Stone Examination, to

1. Robert Potter, Ayr.
2. John Dymock, Glasgow.
3. Thomas Bissland, Renfrewshire.
4. William Graham, East Kilbride.
5. Charles Rowatt, Kintyre.
6. John H. Gray, Carntyne.

XII. For exemplary diligence, regularity and talents displayed during the Session, to

1. John Dymock, Glasgow.
David Macintosh, London.

William Graham, East Kilbride.
Charles Rowatt, Kintyre.
James Hodgert, Johnston.
Joseph Yair, Glasgow.

2. Robert Potter, Ayr.
David Bryden, Ayr.
Edmund Kell, Birmingham.
Thomas Bissland, Renfrewshire.
James M'Lean, Gorbals.

3. Frederic Stuart, Glasgow.

4. William Laird, America.
James Dennistoun, Dumbartonshire.
John Connell, Glasgow.
James Donaldson, ,,

GLASGOW COLLEGE, 1st MAY, 1817.

This day, the Annual Distribution of Prizes was made in the Common Hall, by the Principal and Professors, in presence of a numerous meeting of the University, and of many Reverend and respectable Gentlemen of this City and neighbourhood.

Two Silver Medals, given by the UNIVERSITY, were adjudged—

I. For the best Essay on the necessity of Revelation, to
John Thomson, Houston.

II. For the best Specimen of Elocution, to
James Tait, Glasgow.

Prizes on Mr. COULTER'S DONATION.

I. For the best Sermon on St. Matthew xvi. 24, to
Archibald Bennie, Barony of Glasgow.

II. For the second best Sermon, to
James A. Steele, A.M., Dumbarton.

N

III. For the third, to
    John Marshall, Glasgow.

For the best Account of the Moral Faculty in Man, to
    Peter M'Phun, Glasgow.

For the best Translation into English of the **Penegyrical** Oration of Isocrates, to
    James Mylne, Glasgow.

The GARTMORE GOLD MEDAL.

For the best Essay on the rise of Bullion during the late War, and its great decline since the Peace, to
    Alexander M'Niel, Glasgow.

IV. On the FOUNDATION of Dr. WATT, of Birmingham.

For the best Essay on the application of Steam to the purposes of Navigation, to
    James Rennie, A.M., Sorn.

V. Two Prizes for the best Latin Orations were adjudged to
    Ebenezer Russell, Glasgow.
    Joseph Curry, A.M., Londonderry.

Prizes in the THEOLOGICAL CLASS to students of the second and first years, for the best Essays on the following subjects:—

1. On the Testimonies of Ancient Authors and Traditions of Nations which corroborate the Mosaic History—2. On the Internal Evidences for the Divine Authority of the Mosaic Dispensation —3. On the evidence for Christianity derived from the Character and Conduct of its great Author.

Of the 2nd Year.

Archibald Bennie, Barony of Glasgow.
John Macdougal, Argyllshire.
John Marshall, Glasgow.
John Dunmore Lang, Largs.
Archibald Connell, Islay.
John Russel, Gorbals.

1st Year.

Robert Young, Avondale.
Robert MacGill, Ireland.
John Birkmyre, Paisley.
James Miller, Glasgow.
Charles Grace,   „
John Macfarlane, Kilbarchan.

The Prizes to the Students of the HEBREW CLASSES were adjudged as follow,

Senior Hebrew Class.

For the best Essays on the Radical and Acquired Significations of the word Barak,

    1. To James A. Steele, A.M., Dumbarton.
    2. To John Dunmore Lang, Largs.

For the best Criticism on the Parable of the Vineyard, Isaiah v. 1-7.

    To James A. Steele, A.M., Dumbarton.

For the best Translation of the Sixth Chapter of Job, with Notes on the Original, Critical and Explanatory,

    To James A. Steele, A.M., Dumbarton.

Junior Hebrew Class.

Prizes given for General Eminence in the daily Examinations, throughout the Session,

    1st, To Mathew Brown, Kilmaurs.
    2nd, To William Anderson, Kilsyth.

Prizes given for the best Specimens of the Paradigma of the Hebrew verb,

    1st, To J. G. Crosbie, Dumfries.
    2nd, To John H. Tudehope, Cambuslang.
    3rd, To George Todd, Falkirk.

Prizes in the LAW CLASSES.

Three Prizes, for excelling in the examinations on ROMAN LAW, were adjudged to

    James Maxwell, Glasgow.

William Couper, Glasgow.
Patrick Shaw, Ayrshire.

Two Prizes for excelling in the daily examinations proposed to those Students of SCOTTISH LAW who chose to be examined, were adjudged to

Stuart Bell, Glasgow.
Patrick Shaw, Ayrshire.

––––––

The Prizes to the Students of the SURGERY CLASS were adjudged,

For the best Exercise on Concussion of the Brain, to
Robert Cowan, Glasgow.

For excelling in the daily examinations, to
Daniel Mackinlay, Paisley.

––––––

The Prizes of the MATHEMATICAL CLASS, for Excelling in exercises prescribed during the Session, and for general propriety, diligence, and ability, were adjudged—

SENIOR CLASS, to

Michael Willis, Stirling.
Reuben Bryce, Derry.
David Wylie, Liverpool.

JUNIOR CLASS, to

Seniores.

Samuel Neilson Craig, Down.
James Dick, Tyrone.
Samuel Cleland, Down.
James Taylor, Perthshire.
John Warnock, Antrim.
James Steele, Donegal.

Juniores.

Edmund Kell, Birmingham.
William Veitch, Dumfries-shire.

The Prizes of the NATURAL PHILOSOPHY CLASS, for propriety of conduct, exemplary diligence, and Specimens of Composition on Physical Subjects, prescribed by the Professor, or chosen by the Students themselves, were adjudged to

Andrew Buchanan, Glasgow.
Reuben John Bryce, A.M., Londonderry.
John Bleckley, A.M., Down.
William Penney, Glasgow.
Edward Wakefield, Kendal.
Michael Willis, A.M., Stirling.
Joseph Curry, A.M., Londonderry.
William Johnston, A.M., Biggar.
William Pinkerton, Glasgow.
Kenneth M'Kenzie, Gorbals.

———

The Prizes in the ETHIC CLASS,

For excellence in the Composition of Exercises on Subjects prescribed weekly to the Students, or occasionally chosen by themselves, and for general eminence in the business and duties of the Class, were adjudged to

Seniores.

John M'Farlane, Campbeltown.
David Wylie, Liverpool.
David Smith, Perthshire.
Andrew Rutherford, Peebleshire.
Matthew Adam, Kilmarnock.
Robert Gilchrist, Dumbartonshire.

Juniores.

Samuel Craig Neilson, Downpatrick.
Angus M'Laine, Argyllshire.
James Vary, Lanark.
Charles S. Parker, Glasgow.
James Candlish,   ,,
Robert Leishman, Paisley.

A Prize for the best Essay on Lord Bacon's Idyls was adjudged to

Ebenezer Russell, Glasgow.

The Prizes of the LOGIC CLASS were adjudged—

I. For the best Essay on the experimental method of studying Mind, executed in the Vacation, to

David Smith, Perthshire.

II. For the best Essay on the reflex sense of Ridicule, to
1. Henry Marsland, Bradbury, Cheshire.
2. William Davïdson, Glasgow.

III. For the best Specimens of Composition on various Subjects of Philosophy and of Taste, and for distinguished Eminence and Proficiency in the whole business of the Class, during the Session, to

1st DIVISION.

Robert Potter, Ayr.
Archibald Jack, Edinburgh.
Robert Craig, Eaglesham.

2nd DIVISION—*Seniores.*

Edmund Kell, Birmingham.
John Tayler, Nottingham.
David Bryden, Ayr.
Thomas Thomson, Glasgow.
Thomas Bissland, Renfrewshire.
Abel Peyton, Birmingham.
David M'Intosh, London.
John Hamilton Gray, Lanarkshire.
William Laird, North America.
James M'Cree, Perthshire.

3rd DIVISION—*Juniores.*

Peter Lang, Liverpool.
William Bain, Paisley.
Jamieson Willis, Stirling.
William Grahame, East Kilbryde.
David Strong, Glasgow.
John Miller,   ,,
William Wood, Liverpool.
John Thomson, Glasgow.
James King, Hamilton.
James Laurie, Ayrshire.

During the Christmas Holidays, prizes were proposed,
For the best Poetical Essays on the Advantages and Disadvantages of Holidays, these prizes were adjudged to
1. Edward Kell, Birmingham.
2. William Wood, Liverpool.

For the best Essays, in Prose, on the same subject, to
David M'Intosh, London.
Robert Johnston, Glasgow.
Thomas Young, Renfrewshire.

For the best Specimen of Recollection, to
William Bain, Paisley.

For the best appearance at the Blackstone Examination, to
Robert Potter, Ayr.
David Bryden, Ayr.

For the best Public Theme, to
Peter Lang, Liverpool.

———

The Prizes of the GREEK CLASS were adjudged—
I. For the best Critical Essay on the Medea of Euripides, to
Peter M'Phun, Glasgow.

II. For the best Essay on Homer's Catalogue of the Chiefs, and Forces, engaged in the Siege of Troy, to
James Mylne, Glasgow.

III. For the best Translation of a Chorus in the Oedipus Tyrannus of Sophocles, in Verse, to
William Muir, Kilmarnock.

IV. For the best Translation of another Chorus, in the same Tragedy, to
Alexander Graham, Kilbride.

V. For the best Essay on the Syntax of the Greek Language, compared with that of the Latin, to
Robert Young, Avondale.

VI. For the best Exemplification of the Greek Verb, to
James Ferguson, Blairlogie.
John Ferguson, Ayr.

VII. For Propriety of Conduct, Diligence, and Eminent Abilities, displayed during the Session, to

Robert Potter, Ayr.
Archibald Jack, Glasgow.
David Bryden, Ayr.
Walter M'Pherson, Cardross.
Peter Lang, Liverpool.

Thomas Burnside, Glasgow.
William Swan, Markinch.
William Chrystal, Glasgow.
Joachim Castillo, Mexico.
John Millar, Glasgow.

James M'Litchie, Dalrymple.
James Parker, Glasgow.
John Fergusson, Ayr.
Robert Stewart, Glasgow.
Alexander Cowan, „
John Bell, Paisley.

John Watt, Glasgow.
George Reid,   „
John Mitchell, Anderston.

Prizes in the HUMANITY CLASS.

I. For the best Original Composition in Latin Verse, to

Robert Potter, Ayr.

II. For the best Original Composition in Latin Prose, to

John Dymock, Glasgow.

III. For the best Translation into English Verse of the Episode of Nisus and Euryalus, in the 9th Æneid of Virgil, to

Thomas Bissland, Renfrewshire.

IV. For the best Chronological Tables of Events in Roman, Grecian, and Jewish History, from the 1st to the 749th year, U.G., to

Thomas Bissland, Renfrewshire.
William Graham, East Kilbride.

V. For the best Essay on the Personal and Literary Character of Horace, to

John Campbell, Roxburghshire.
John Birkmyre, Renfrewshire.

VI. For the best History of the second Punic War, to

Robert Potter, Ayr.
Thomas Bissland, Renfrewshire.

VII. For the best Translation of the Andria of Terence, to

Thomas Brown, Glasgow.
John Garven, Arran.

VIII. For the best Translation of Cicero de Senectute, to

Abel Peyton, Birmingham.

IX. For the best account of the political structure of the Roman Republic, to

Edmund Kell, Birmingham.

X. For the greatest portions of the Latin Poets, committed to memory, to

John Hall, Northumberland.
Thomas Dymock, Glasgow.

XI. For Excelling at the Black Stone Examination, to

1. James Dennistoun, Dumbartonshire.
2. William Veitch, Dumfries-shire.
3. William Tennant, Ayrshire.
4. James Hopkirk, Glasgow.
5. Mathew Turnbull, Dunipace.

XII. For Exemplary Diligence, Regularity, and Talents, displayed during the Session, to

1. Charles Rowatt, Campbelton.
Robert M'Lure, Glasgow.
William Mather, Renfrewshire.
John Cuthbertson, Gorbals.
Thomas Christie, Glasgow.

2. James M'Litchie, Ayrshire.
William Swan, Fifeshire.
John Fergusson, Ayr.
Alexander Cowan, Glasgow.
John Montgomery Bell, Paisley.

3. John Thomson, Dalry, Ayrshire.
4. John Watt, Glasgow.
   George Reid,   ,,
   James J. Wood, Northumberland.
   James Ferguson, Blairlogie.

For Excelling at the separate meeting of the Junior Students, to
   1. James R. Gibb, Ayrshire.
   2. John Watt, Glasgow.

GLASGOW COLLEGE, 1st MAY, 1818.

This day, the Annual Distribution of Prizes was made in the Common Hall, by the Principal and Professors, in presence of a numerous meeting of the University, and of many Reverend and respectable Gentlemen of this City and neighbourhood.

One Silver Medal, given by the UNIVERSITY, was adjudged—
I. For the best Illustration of the Prophecies in Support of the Mosaic Dispensation, to
      Archibald Bennie, Barony of Glasgow.

Prizes on Mr. COULTER's Donation.

I. In THEOLOGY.

For the best Lecture on the 110th Psalm, to
      James Miller, Glasgow.

II. For the best Translation into English of Tacitus' Life of Agricola, to
      James Mylne, Glasgow.

Three Prizes given by the JURISDICTIO ORDINARIA, for the best Latin Orations, were adjudged to
      William Muir, Kilmarnock.
      James Mylne, Glasgow.
      John M'Farlane, Campbeltown.

The Prizes in the DIVINITY CLASS were adjudged, for the best Essays,

I. On the Rapid and Extensive Propagation of Christianity :

II. On the Effects of Christianity on the Characters and Manners of Men :

Of the 2nd Year, to

Matthew Brown, A.M., Ayrshire.
Robert Young, Avondale.
John Birkmyre, A.M., Paisley.
James Miller, Glasgow.
William Mair,   ,,

Of the 1st Year, to

Peter M'Phun, Barony of Glasgow.
Matthew Dickie.
George Ritchie, A.M., Glasgow.
James Gibson, A.M., Crieff.
William Pinkerton, Barony of Glasgow.
Ebenezer Russel, Glasgow.

For general merit, to

Michael Willis, A.M., Stirling.

For the best Specimens of Public Reading among Students of the 2nd year, to

Alexander Lang, Paisley.
James Boyd, A.M., Glasgow.

The Prizes of the HEBREW CLASSES were adjudged—

Senior Class.

I. For the best Essays on certain peculiarities of Hebrew Syntax, in the use of the past and future tenses of the Verb, and more particularly as affected by the presence or absence of the particle Waw, to

John Geddes Crosbie, Glasgow.
William Swan, Kirkaldy.

II. For the best Translation and Critical Analysis of Isaiah xiv., 4-27.

John Geddes Crosbie, Glasgow.
William Swan, Kirkaldy.

Junior Class.

I. For general eminence in the daily examinations throughout the Session, to

> Robert Young, Avondale.
> James Gibson, A.M., Crief.

II. For the best Specimens of the Paradigma of the Hebrew Verb, to

> Michael Willis, A.M., Stirling.
> William Pinkerton, Glasgow.

———

Two Prizes for excelling in the daily examinations, proposed to those Students of SCOTTISH LAW, who chose to be examined, were adjudged to

> Robert Cowan, Glasgow.
> David Connell,   ,,

———

Prize in the NATURAL HISTORY CLASS.

A Prize for the best Essay on the Inducements to the Study of Natural History, was adjudged to

> Archibald Bennie, Barony of Glasgow.

———

MEDICAL CLASSES.

A Prize was given in the ANATOMY CLASS for the best Essay on the Motions of the Iris and the power of adapting the Eye to see objects at different distances, to

> Robert Marshall.

———

The Prizes in the SURGERY CLASS were adjudged—

I. For the best Essay on the Effect of Ligatures when applied to Arteries, to

> Thomas Patterson, Glasgow.

II. For the best Specification of those accidents which require and admit of the operation of amputation, to

> Mathew Nisbett, Glasgow.

The Prizes of the MATHEMATICAL CLASSES, for exemplary propriety, diligence, and ability, and for excelling in Exercises prescribed during the Session, were adjudged—

SENIOR CLASS, to

William Bain, Paisley.
Peter Lang, Liverpool.
Edmund Kell, Birmingham.
James Ferguson, Greenock.

JUNIOR CLASS, to

Seniores.

David Bryden, Ayr.
James Dennistoun, Glasgow.
John Morton, Down.
Donald M'Lachlan, Argyllshire.
William Somerville, Down.
William Mather, Renfrewshire.
Thomas Smyth, Donegal.

Juniores.

Jamieson Willis, Stirling.
John Montgomery Bell, Paisley.
James M'Whirter, Ayr.
William Johnson, Tyrone.

———

The Prizes of the NATURAL PHILOSOPHY CLASS, for general eminence and proficiency in the business of the Class, and for the best Specimens of Composition in Essays on Subjects in Natural Philosophy, were adjudged to

David Wyllie, A.M., Liverpool.
Alexander Stewart, Dingwall.
James Steele, A.M., Donegall.
James Mylne, Glasgow.
James Smith Candlish, Edinburgh.
John Stewart, A.M., Greenock.
Joseph Hay, A.M., Perthshire.
Thomas Curr, A.M., Shotts.

The Prizes in the ETHIC CLASS,

For Excellence in the Composition of Exercises on Subjects prescribed weekly to the Students, or occasionally chosen by themselves, and for distinguished eminence in the other business and duties of the Class, were adjudged to

Seniores.

Robert Potter, Ayr.
John James Tayler, Nottingham.
Archibald Jack, Edinburgh.
James Smith, Glasgow.
Edmund Kell, Birmingham.
Robert Craig, Eaglesham.
Donald M'Kellar, Argyllshire.

Juniores.

William Bain, Paisley.
Peter Lang, Liverpool.
James Adair Lawrie, Newmills.
Robert King, Paisley.
Jamieson Willis, Stirling.
James Ferguson, Greenock.

A Prize for the best Translation of the first Book of Cicero's Offices, with Critical Observations, was adjudged to

John Stewart, A.M., Greenock.

The Prizes of the LOGIC CLASS were adjudged—

I. For the best Essay on irregular Syllogisms, executed during the Vacation, to

William Bain, Paisley.
David Strong, Glasgow.

II. For the best Essays on Figurative Language, also executed during the Vacation, to

Robert Potter, Ayrshire.
Edmund Kell, Birmingham.

The Prizes of this Session were adjudged—

III. For the best Specimens of Composition on Various Subjects of Philosophy and Taste, and for distinguished eminence and proficiency in the business of the Class, to

Seniores.

Eugene Theodore Suliot, Paris.
John Barr, Lochwinnoch.
Theodore W. Rathbone, Liverpool.
Donald Maclachlan, Argyllshire.
George Drummond, Edinburgh.
James Weston, London.
Joseph Wallis, Loughborough.
Charles Rowat, Campbeltown.
George Hay, East Lothian.
Alexander Paterson, Leicester.

Juniores

Robert Robertson, Berwickshire.
John Miller, Glasgow.
James M'Letchie, Ayrshire.
George Dundas, Edinburgh.
Duncan Macfarlane, Stirlingshire.
George Gordon, Ayrshire.
Thomas Burnside, Glasgow.
William Meikleham,   ,,
Joachim Castillo, Mexico.
James Hamilton, Glasgow.
William Lockhart,   ,,
John Crooks,   ,,

For Essays executed during the Christmas Holidays, to
Eugene Theodore Suliot, Paris.
George Drummond, Edinburgh.
James Weston, London.

For a Poetical Essay, to
Robert Robertson, Berwickshire.

For the best specimen of Recollection, to
James Weston, London.

For excelling at the Black Stone Examination, to
James M'Letchie, Ayrshire.

For the best public Theme, to
James Weston, London.

The Prizes of the GREEK CLASS were adjudged—

I. For the best Critical Essay on the Oedipus Tyrannus of Sophocles, to

Peter M'Phunn, Glasgow.

II. For the best Account of the Diction of Homer, as illustrating General Principles of Grammar, and Particular Greek Idioms, to

William Moncrieff, Glasgow.

III. For the best Essay on the mode of connecting the Agent with the Passive Voice of a Transitive Verb in the Greek, compared with the modes adopted in other Languages, to

Alexander Logan, Eastwood.

IV. For the best Translation, in Verse, of a Chorus from the Clouds of Aristophanes, to

John Campbell, Ancrum.

V. For the best Exemplification of the Greek Verb, to

Alexander Burn, Stirling.
James Aitken, Borrowstounness.

VI. For Propriety of Conduct, Diligence, and Eminent Abilities displayed during the Session, to

James M'Letchie, Dalrymple.
Walter M'Pherson, Cardross.
James Weston, London.
Joseph Wallis, Loughborough.
Abraham Perry, Exeter.

James Bardsley, Nottingham.
George Reid, Glasgow.
Thomas Brown,   ,,
James Wood, Northumberland.
John M. Bell, Paisley.

James M'Kenzie, Campsie.
John M'Intyre, *maj.*, Greenock
James R. Gibb, Auchinleck.
Robert Sym, Glasgow.
Thomas Liddell, St. Ninians.
Andrew Sym, Glasgow.

{ *John W. Semple*, Glasgow.
James M'Callum,   ,,
David Douie,

Prizes in the HUMANITY CLASS.

I. For the best Original Composition in Latin Verse, to
George Reid, Glasgow.

II. For the best Original Composition in Latin Prose, to
William Chrystal, Glasgow.

III. For the best Translation into Verse of Juvenal's 8th Satyre, to
John Campbell, Ancrum, Roxburghshire.

IV. For the best Account of the levying, organization and array of a Roman Army, to
William D. Veitch, Edinburgh.

V. For the best Translation of Cicero de Amicitia, to
George Buchanan, Glasgow.
Thomas Christie,   ,,

VI. For the best Translation from English into Latin, to
James Dennistoun, Dumbartonshire.

VII. For the best History of the Sedition of the Gracchi, to
John Watt, Glasgow.

VIII. For the best Translation into Verse of a Satire of Horace, to
Thomas Brown, Glasgow.

IX. For the best Translation, into Verse, of the Epistle of Medea to Jason from Ovid, to
James Wood, Glasgow.

X. For the same into Prose, to
William Haggart, Glasgow.

XI. For the greatest portion of the Latin Poets, committed to Memory, to
Thomas Dymock, Glasgow.
John Russell,   ,,

XII. For the best Specimens of Elocution, in delivering Latin Orations, to

> James Wood, Glasgow.
> John W. Semple,   ,,

XIII. For the best Public Theme, to

> George Napier, Edinburgh.

XIV. For Excelling at the Black Stone examination, to

> 1. James Bardsley, Nottingham.
> 2. Gavin Lochore, Glasgow.
> 3. George Reid,   ,,
> 4. John Bell,   ,,
> 5. George M. Young,   ,,
> 6. James Smith, Paisley.

XV. For exemplary diligence, regularity, and talents, displayed throughout the Session, to

> 1.—1. James Wood, Glasgow.
>   2. John M. Bell, Paisley.
>   3. George Reid, Glasgow.
>   4. James Aitken,   ,,
>   5. John Watt,   ,,

> 2.—1. John Bell, Glasgow.
>   2. James Bardsley, Nottingham.
>   3. James Smith, Paisley.
>   4. Gavin Lochore, Glasgow.
>   5. John Bell, Ayr.
>   6. James M'Kenzie, Campsie.

> 3.—1. James M'Callum, Glasgow.
>   2. John W. Semple,   ,,
>   3. Thomas Buchanan,   ,,
>   4. Charles Stewart, Campbelton.

XVI. For excelling at the separate meeting of the Junior Students, to

> 1. David Douie, Glasgow.
> 2. James M'Callum,   ,,
> 3. John W. Semple,   ,,

GLASGOW COLLEGE, 1st May, 1819.

This day, the Annual Distribution of Prizes was made in the Common Hall, by the Principal and Professors, in presence of a numerous meeting of the University, and of many Reverend and respectable Gentlemen of this City and neighbourhood.

Prizes on Mr. Coulter's Donation.

I. In Theology.

For the best Sermon on Isaiah xxviii. 22. Be ye not mockers, lest your bonds be made strong, to
Archibald Bennie, Barony of Glasgow.

II. In Philosophy.

On the External Senses, as affording evidence of the existence of external objects, to
William Bain, A.M., Paisley.

III. For the best Translation of Plato's Defence of Socrates, to
James Weston, A.B., London.

The Gartmore Gold Medal,

For the best Essay on the effects produced on the Literature and Science of Europe by the Reformation, was adjudged to
Archibald Bennie, Barony of Glasgow.

Prizes on Dr. James Watt's Foundation.

I. For the best Essay on the history and principles of the application of Gas to the lighting of streets and public and private buildings, and on the best means of rendering the residuum useful or inoffensive, to
Archibald Bennie, Barony of Glasgow.

II. For the best Essay on the most accurate methods of determining Specific Gravities, to
Gilbert Wardlaw, Glasgow.

Two Prizes given by the JURISDICTIO ORDINARIA for the best Latin Orations, were adjudged to

Thomas Henderson Wightman, A.M., Ireland.
David Bryden, A.M., Ayrshire.

The Prizes in the DIVINITY CLASS were adjudged, for the best Essays,

I. On the Justice of God :

II. On Providence :

Of the 2nd Year, to

Michael Willis, A.M., Stirling.
Peter M'Phun, Barony of Glasgow.
John M'Leod Campbell, Kilninver.
George Ritchie, A.M., Glasgow.
James Gibson, A.M., Crieff.
William Pinkerton, Barony of Glasgow.

Of the 1st Year, to

John Stewart, A.M., Greenock.
Alexander Stewart, Dingwall.
Thomas Curr, A.M., Shotts.
James Steele, A.M., Raphoe, Ireland.

For the best Specimen of Public Reading, among Students of the 2nd year, to

Fergus Jardine, Portpatrick.

The Prizes in the HEBREW CLASS were adjudged—

Senior Class.

1. For the best Critical Analysis of Isaiah ix. 1-6, to
Archibald Jack, Edinburgh.
Robert Sellers, Glasgow.

2. For the best Essay on the two Hebrew words,
Elohim and Berith, to
Archibald Jack, Edinburgh.

Junior Class.

1. For general eminence in the daily examination throughout the Session, to

> John Stewart, Greenock.
> Robert M'Nair Wilson, Gorbals.

2. For the best Specimens of the Paradigma of the Hebrew Verb, to

> Thomas Aitken, Stirling.
> John Stewart, Greenock.
> Ebenezer Russel, Glasgow.

Two Prizes for excelling in the daily examinations proposed to those Students of SCOTTISH LAW who chose to be examined, were adjudged to

> Archibald Grahame, Glasgow.
> James Mylne, Glasgow College.

NATURAL HISTORY.

For the best Essay on the Siliceous Substances which occur in Great Britain, and the uses to which they may be rendered subservient, to

> Archibald Bennie, Barony of Glasgow.

The Prizes of the MATHEMATICAL CLASSES, for general eminence and proficiency during the Session, were adjudged—

SENIOR CLASS, to

> John Morton, Down, Ireland.
> Donald Maclachlan, Argyleshire.
> William Sommerville, Down.
> Eugene Theodore Suliot, Paris.
> James M'Whirter, Ayr.

JUNIOR CLASS, to

1st Division.

> James M'Letchie, Ayrshire.
> Peter M'Dowall. Stranraer.
> Andrew Kippis Watson, Bath.
> George Dundas, Edinburgh.
> Samuel Moore, Down.
> George Drummond, Edinburgh.
> Duncan Macfarlan, Stirlingshire.

2nd Division.

John William Semple, Glasgow.
Thomas Burnside,   „
Thomas S. Gladstone, Liverpool.

The Prizes of the NATURAL PHILOSOPHY CLASS,

For general eminence and proficiency in the business of the Class, and for the best Specimens of Composition in Essays on subjects in Natural Philosophy, were adjudged to

David Bryden, A.M., Ayrshire.
William Bain, A.M., Paisley.
Dugald M'Kichan, Argyllshire.
James Smith, Glasgow.
John Barnett, A.M., Belfast.
William Somerville, A.M., Ireland.
James Ferguson, A.M., Greenock.
John Dymock, A.M., Glasgow.
James Laurie, Loudoun.
George Cullen, Glasgow.
John Morton, A.M., Ireland.

The Prizes in the ETHIC CLASS,

Given for distinguished eminence displayed in Examinations, and in the Composition of weekly Exercises on subjects prescribed by the Professor, or of voluntary Exercises on subjects chosen by the Students themselves, were adjudged, to

John Phillip Malleson, A.B., Chelsea.
Eugene Theodore Suliot, Paris.
Theodore W. Rathbone, Liverpool.
George Maurice Drummond, Edinburgh.
James Weston, A.B., London.
James Strang, Stirlingshire.
George Dundas, Edinburgh.
Donald Maclachlan, Argyllshire.

A Prize given for the best Illustration of the 49th Aphorism of Bacon's Novum Organum, was adjudged to
James Ewing.

The Prizes of the LOGIC CLASS were adjudged—

I. For the best Essay on Association, to

> John Millar, Glasgow.
> Thomas Burnside, Glasgow.

II. For the best Essay on Description, Direct or Indirect, to

> James Weston, London.
> Eugene Theodore Suliot, Paris.

The Prizes of this Session,

III. For Habitual Industry combined with talent—for eminence and superiority in the whole business of the Class, combined with regular and uninterrupted diligence through the whole Session, were adjudged to

Seniores.

> Andrew Kippis Watson, London.
> Alexander Murray, Edinburgh.
> James Wood, Northumberland.
> James Bardsley, Nottingham.
> William M'Dowell, Downshire.
> Erskine Neale, Exeter.
> John Bell, Glasgow.
> Mark Philips, Manchester.
> William Mather, Renfrewshire.

Juniores.

> John Montgomerie Bell, Paisley.
> Thomas Brown, Glasgow.
> James Parker,   „
> George Patton, Perth.
> George Reid, Glasgow.
> William Lindsay, Carluke.
> James Mitchell, Anderston.
> George Lang, Largs.
> John Bell, *secundus*, Ayrshire.
> Thomas Gladstone, Liverpool.
> Andrew Lambie, Auchinleck.

Prizes were proposed this Session for the best Essay on Emulation, and adjudged to

> James Hopkirk, Dalbeth.
> John Bell, *tertius*, Glasgow.
> John Dill, *major*, Ireland.

For the best Poetical Descriptive Exercises, to
         George Lang, Largs.
         Erskine Neale, Exeter.

For the best Specimens of Recollection, to
         William Lindsay, Carluke.
         John Glass, Greenock.

For Excelling at the Blackstone Examination, to
         Alexander Murray, Edinburgh.

For the best Public Themes, to
         Samuel Moore, Ireland.
         George Napier, Edinburgh.

———

The Prizes of the GREEK CLASS were adjudged—

I. For the best Essays on the Rhetorical Character of Isocrates, to
        {Alexander Logan, Eastwood.
        {James Mylne, Glasgow.

II. For the best Account of the Clouds of Aristophanes, to
         John Campbell, Ancrum.

III. For the best Essay on the Greek Prepositions, considered as Adjectives, and as regulated by the Grammatical Laws incident to those parts of Speech, to
         Alexander Logan, Eastwood.

IV. For the best Metrical Translation of a Chorus of Æschylus, to
         William Muir, Kilmarnock.

V. For the best Translation of another Chorus, to
         George Muir, A.M., Glasgow.

VI. For the best Translation of another Chorus, to
         Edmund Kell, A.M., Birmingham.

VII. For the best Exemplification of the Greek Verb, to
         Robert Neill, Dunnipace.
         David Meikleham, Glasgow.

VIII. For Propriety of Conduct, Diligence, and Eminent Abilities, displayed during the Session, to

Alexander Murray, Edinburgh.
John M. Bell, Paisley.
Andrew Lambie, Tarbolton.
William Lindsay, Carluke.
George Patton, Perth.

William Giffin, Paisley.
Thomas Bell, Queensferry.
David Douie, Glasgow.
John W. Semple, ,,
William Durant, Dorsetshire.

James Brydon, Ayr.
James Russell, Avondale.
Andrew Wilson, Carluke.
David Meikleham, Glasgow.
Thomas Russell, Slamannan.
Thomas Brackenridge, Cambusnethan

William G. Glen, Glasgow.
Archibald Gordon, ,,
William Steele, ,,

Prizes in the HUMANITY CLASS.

I. For the best original Composition in Latin Verse, to

Thomas Russell, Slamannan.
Thomas Bell, Queensferry.

II. For the best original Composition in Latin Prose, to

Thomas Brown, Glasgow.
George Dundas, Edinburgh.
Robert Hagart, Glasgow.

III. For the best Table of the different Classes of Latin Verbs, :to

James Wood, Northumberland.

IV. For the best Essays on Didactic Poetry, to

William Hagart, Glasgow.
William Davidson, ,,
William Laird, America.

V. For the best Translations of Terence's Eunuch, to
>   John M. Bell, Paisley.
>   James Wood, Northumberland.

VI. For the best Translations of Cicero's Oration for Archias, to
>   Archibald Campbell, Ancrum.
>   George Reid, Glasgow.

VII. For the best Translation from Latin into English, to
>   John M. Bell, Paisley.

VIII. For the best Abridgements of Cicero on Old Age, in Latin, to
>   William Giffen, Paisley.
>   William Durant, Dorsetshire.

For the same, in English, to
>   William Motherwell, Paisley.

IX. For the best Public Theme, of Students ranking in the Greek Class, to
>   David Douie, Glasgow.

Of those ranking in the Latin Class, to
>   Archibald Gordon, Ayrshire.

X. For the best Elocution in delivering Latin Orations, to
>   John Simmons, Lancashire.
>   John Semple, Glasgow.
>   James Smith, Paisley.
>   George Yuille, Glasgow.

XI. For committing to Memory the greatest number of Latin Verses, to
>   Walter Nicol, Stirlingshire.
>   John Gordon, Edinburgh.
>   John Mitchell, Glasgow.

XII. For excelling at the Black Stone Examination, as Competitors.
>   1. William Durant, Dorsetshire.
>   2. David Douie, Glasgow.
>   3. John Semple,   „

4. James Buchanan, Paisley.
5. James M'Callum, Glasgow.
6. (Without competing)—William Giffen, Paisley.
7. John Gordon, Edinburgh.

XIII. For exemplary diligence and talents, displayed through-out the Session, to

1.—1. William Giffen, Paisley.
    2. James Smith,   ,,
    3. William Pettigrew, Glasgow
    4. John Park, East Kilbride.
    5. David Douie, Glasgow.

2.—1. William Durant, Dorsetshire.
    2. John Gordon, Edinburgh.
    3 James Buchanan, Paisley.
    4. Thomas Russel, Slamannan.
    5. George Gordon, Edinburgh.

3.—   John Simmons, Lancashire.

4.—1. William G. Glen, Glasgow.
    2. John Wingate,   ,,
    3. William Steel,   ,,
    4. Thomas Miller,   ,,
    5. Archibald Gordon, Ayrshire.
    6. Robert Candlish, Glasgow.
    7. Robert Lamond,   ,,

GLASGOW COLLEGE, 1st MAY, 1820.

This day, the Annual Distribution of Prizes was made in the Common Hall, by the Principal and Professors, in presence of a numerous meeting of the University, and of many Reverend and respectable Gentlemen of this City and neighbourhood.

TWO SILVER MEDALS.
I. IN THEOLOGY.

For the best illustration of the Prophecies in proof of the Christian Dispensation, adjudged to

James Miller, Glasgow.

II. In Philosophy.

For the best Essay on the use of the Barometer in the measurement of Heights, adjudged to

John Dymock, A.M., Glasgow.

———————

On Mr. Coulter's Donation.

1. For the best Lecture on the Parable of the Sower in the 13th Chapter of Matthew, adjudged to

William Anderson, Kilsyth.

2. For the best Essay on the Relation of Cause and Effect, with Remarks on the late writers on that subject, adjudged to

William Muir, Kilmarnock.

3. For the best Translation of Cicero's Somnium Scipionis, adjudged to

John Sandford, Edinburgh.

———————

On Dr. Watt's Foundation.

Two Prizes given for the best Essays on the Specific Gravity of the Gases, were adjudged to

1. Alexander Harvey, Stirlingshire.
2. Arch. Bennie, A.M., Barony of Glasgow.

———————

Two Prizes given by the Jurisdictio Ordinaria, for the best Latin Orations, were adjudged to

Theodore Eugene Suliot, A.M., Paris.
Daniel Thomson, Lanark.

———————

Prizes in the Divinity Class were adjudged—

I. For Exercises written during the Summer Vacation :

1. For an account of the Lectures in Divinity, delivered during the preceding Session, to

John Stewart, A.M., Greenock.

2. For an Essay on a special Providence, to

James Miller, Glasgow.

3. For an Essay on the depravity and fallen condition of Man, to

John Stewart, A.M., Greenock.

II. For an Essay executed during the present Session, on the effect of depraved disposition and habits on the religious knowledge and opinions of mankind :

Of the 2nd Year, to

John Stewart, A.M., Greenock.
James Ferguson, Inch, Galloway.
Alexander Stewart, Dingwall.
John M'Farlane, Argyllshire.

Of the 1st Year, to

Robert Potter, Ayrshire.
Thomas H. Wightman, A.M., Ireland.
James Smith, A.M., Glasgow.
David Bryden, A.M., Ayrshire.
Robert Craig, A.M.,   ,,

III. For the best Specimen of Public Reading, among competitors of the 2nd year, to

Robert Crawfurd, Dalry, Ayrshire.

———

Prizes in the SENIOR HEBREW CLASS were adjudged—
I. For the best Essays on Hebrew Poetry, to

John M'Leod Campbell, Argyllshire.
John Stewart, Greenock.

For the best Critical Analysis and Exposition of the Forty-ninth Psalm, to

1 William Anderson, Kilsyth.
2. John Stewart, Greenock.

Prizes in the JUNIOR HEBREW CLASS were adjudged—
For General Eminence, in the daily examinations throughout the Session, to

1. James Finlay, Barony, Glasgow.
2. John Dymock, A.M.,   ,,

For the best Exemplification of the Hebrew Verb, to

1. Robert Blackburn, Johnstone.
2. John Dymock, A.M., Glasgow.

Two Prizes for excelling in the daily examinations in the
SCOTTISH LAW CLASS proposed to those Students whose chose to
be examined, were adjudged to

> Thomas Duncan, Glasgow.
> Robert Goodwin,   ,,

The Prizes in the SURGERY CLASS were adjudged—
For the best Essays on Injuries of the Head, to

> 1. Robert Hunter, Glasgow.
> 2. Robert King, Glasgow.

NATURAL HISTORY CLASS.
For the best Essay on the Natural History of Man, to

> Gilbert Wardlaw, Glasgow.

The Prizes of the MATHEMATICAL CLASSES, for general eminence and proficiency during the Session, were adjudged—

SENIOR CLASS, to

> Samuel Cleland, Down, Ireland.
> John William Semple, Glasgow.
> William Mather, Renfrewshire.
> John Davidson, Maybole.
> John Montgomerie Bell, Paisley.

JUNIOR CLASS, to

1st Division.

> John M'Gregor, Perth.
> William Giffen, Paisley.
> George Reid, Glasgow.
> James Wood, Northumberland.
> Heywood Birch, Liverpool.

2nd Division.

> James M'Callum, Glasgow.
> James Mitchell, Anderston.
> George Patton, B.A., Perth.

The Prizes of the NATURAL PHILOSOPHY CLASS, for propriety of conduct, exemplary diligence, and Specimens of Composition on Physical Subjects, prescribed by the Professor, or chosen by the Students themselves, were adjudged to

> Peter Lang, A.M., Liverpool.
> Theodore Eugene Suliot, A.M., Paris.
> Samuel Cleland, A.M., County of Down, Ireland.
> John Miller, Glasgow.
> John M'Millan, Argyllshire.
> George Dundas, Edinburgh.
> James Walker Aitken, Falkirk.
> John King, A.M., Monaghan.
> John Davidson, Maybole.

The Students of the Public Class gave a Prize for eminent talent and exemplary diligence, in performing voluntarily the various exercises, to a Student of the Private Class,

> John Angus, Port-Glasgow.

––––––––

The Prizes in the ETHIC CLASS, for the best Specimens of Composition on various Subjects connected with the business of the Class, and either prescribed weekly by the Professor or chosen by the Students themselves; and for exemplary good conduct and distinguished eminence, were adjudged to

Seniores.

> 1. Solomon Leonard, A.M., Bristol.
> 2. William Henry M'Dowall, Donaghadee.
> . James Bardsley, Nottingham.
> 3. Henry M'Connel, Manchester.
> . John Bell, Glasgow.
> 6. William Mather, Renfrewshire.

And to

Juniores.

> 1. John Montgomery Bell, Paisley.
> 2. Thomas Brown, Glasgow.
> 3. Andrew Lambie, Auchinleck.
> 4. George Patton, A.B., Perth.
> 5. James Mitchell, Anderston.

A Prize for the best Exercise on the History and Doctrines of the Epicurean Philosophy, prescribed at the close of last Session,. was adjudged to

Theodore Eugene Suliot, A.M., Paris.

———————

The Prizes of the Logic Class, for Essays executed during the last vacation, were adjudged—

I. For the best Essay on the Standard of Taste, to

 1. George Napier, Edinburgh.
 2. John Montgomery Bell, Paisley.

II. The Prizes of this Session, for Eminence combined with Industry and Proficiency in the Examinations and Exercises of the Class, during the Session, to

Seniores.

William Durant, Dorsetshire.
William Giffen, Paisley.
Haywood Birch, Liverpool.
Thomas Winslow, London.
John Simmons, Wigan.
Charles Hope M'Lean, East Lothian.
James Richey, Ireland.
Thomas Hamilton, Staffordshire.
Franklin Baker, Birmingham.
Edmund Clark, ,,
Andrew O'Beirne, Ireland.
Donald M'Farlane, Aberfoil.
Joseph Wickstead, Shrewsbury,

Juniores.

John William Semple, Glasgow.
David Douie, Glasgow.
Thomas Longman, London.
Thomas Bell, Queensferry.
Thomas Carson, Liverpool.
James Buchanan, Paisley.
Robert Aspland, London.
James Patton, Greenock.
Thomas Buchanan, Glasgow.
Wilmer Gossip, Yorkshire.

A Prize was proposed and executed for the best specimen of an Address to Students, after the Distribution on the 1st May,

In Prose, to

      1. Robert Wellbeloved, York.

      2. David Meikleham, Glasgow.

Poetry,

      1. Thomas Hamilton, Staffordshire.

      2. Robert Pollock, Eaglesham.

For the best Specimen of Recollection, to

      William M'Coll, Glasgow.

For excelling in the Black Stone Examination, to

      1. Andrew O'Beirne, Ireland.

      2. Robert Scott, Lanarkshire.

For the best Public Theme, to

      Wilmer Gossip, York.

———

The Prizes of the GREEK CLASS were adjudged—

I. For the best Essay on the Rhetorical Character of Lysias, to

      Alexander Logan, Eastwood.

II. For the best Translation in Verse of the Choephorae of Æschylus, to

      John Montgomery Bell, Paisley.

III. For the best Translation in Verse of a Chorus of Euripides, to

      Archibald Blair Campbell, Ancrum.

IV. For the best Translation in Verse of another Chorus, to

      William Moncrieff, Glasgow.

V. For the best Essays on the Interior Syntax of the Fractional Portions of Compounded words; and the influence which the Different Arrangements of those fractional portions have on the Amount of the Signification of the Composite, to

      {Alexander Logan, Eastwood.

      {William Penney, Glasgow.

VI. For the best Exemplification of the Greek Verb, to

      Thomas Ainsworth, Lancashire.

      Allan John M'Kenzie, Glasgow.

VII. For Propriety of Conduct, Diligence, and Eminent Abilities, displayed during the Session, to

John W. Semple, Glasgow.
Andrew O'Beirne, Ireland.
William Durant, Dorsetshire.
David Douie, Glasgow.
Charles Hope M'Lean, East Lothian.

James M'Kenzie, Campsie.
James Johnston, Kilmarnock.
Archibald C. Gordon, Glasgow.
Robert S. Candlish,   ,,
Matthew B. Pollock, Govan.

William Rennie, Glasgow.
Thomas Muter,   ,,
Andrew Urquhart, Kilbirnie.
William Mitchell, Perthshire.
John Bryden, Ayr.
John Watson, Montrose.

Robert Wilson, Glasgow.
Adam Bogle,   ,,
Thomas Ainsworth, Lancashire.

Prizes in the HUMANITY CLASS.

I. For the best original Composition in Latin Verse, to
Thomas Russell, Slamannan.
John Cowan, Hutchesontown.

II. For the best original Composition in Latin Prose, to
John Cowan, Hutchesontown.
Robert S. Candlish, Glasgow.

III. For the best Table of the different classes of Latin Verbs, to
Tho. Miller, Glasgow.

IV. For the best Essay on the Tribunitian Power, to
William Durant, Dorsetshire.

V. For the best Translation of the Trinummus of Plautus, to
James Smith, Paisley.
William Durant, Dorsetshire.

VI. For the best Translation of Cicero's Treatise on Old Age, to
>David Douie, Glasgow.
>James Buchanan, Paisley.

VII. For the best Translation into English verse of Horace, Book I., Satire 9.
>Joseph Wicksteed, Shrewsbury.
>Thomas Thomson, Glasgow.

VIII. For the best Translation into Latin verse of one of Gay's Fables, to
>Tho. Ainsworth, Lancashire.

IX. For the best Translation from English into Latin Prose, to
>Archibald C. Gordon, Ayrshire.
>Robert S. Candlish, Glasgow.

X. For the best Elocution in delivering Latin Orations, to
>John Browning, Lanarkshire.
>Robert Lamond, Glasgow.
>Thomas Miller,   ,,
>William M'Lauren, Middlesex.

XI. For the best Public Theme of Students ranking in the Greek Class, to
>Matthew B. Pollock, Govan.

Of those ranking in the Latin Class, to
>Adam Bogle, Glasgow.

For excelling at the Blackstone Examination (as Competitors),
>William H. Steel, Glasgow.
>Archibald C. Gordon, Ayrshire.
>William G. Glen, Glasgow.
>Thomas Miller,   ,,

>*(Without Competing.)*
>John Wingate, Glasgow.
>Josiah Walker,   ,,

For exemplary diligence and talents, displayed throughout the Session,
>I.—1. William G. Glen, Glasgow.
>2. William H. Steel, Glasgow.
>3. John Wingate,   ,,
>4. Archibald C. Gordon, Ayrshire.
>5. Robert S. Candlish, Glasgow.

2.—1. John Watson, Montrose.
   2. John Cowan, Hutchesontown.
   3. Alexander Scott, Greenock.
   4. William C. M'Lauren, Middlesex.
   5. James Johnston, Kilmarnock.

3.— Thomas Grahame, Annan.

4.—1. Adam Bogle, Glasgow.
   2. Robert Wilson, Glasgow.
   3. William Park, Hutchesontown.
   4. William M'Lean, Glasgow.
   5. Thomas Ainsworth, Lancashire.
   6. James Stirling, Craigie.
   7. John M'Lean, Glasgow.

GLASGOW COLLEGE, 1st MAY, 1821.

This day, the Annual Distribution of Prizes was made in the Common Hall, by the Principal and Professors, in presence of a numerous meeting of the University, and of many Reverend and respectable Gentlemen of this City and neighbourhood.

ONE SILVER MEDAL.
In THEOLOGY.

For the best Essay on the evidence for Christianity, arising from the character of its Author, adjudged to

Robert Blackburn, Johnstone.

On Mr. COULTER's Donation.

1. For the best Sermon on John iii, 19—"This is the Condemnation," etc., to

John Whitson, A.M., Perth.

2. For the best Essay on the Nature and Theory of Sound, to

James Julius Wood, A.M., Northumberland.

3. For the best translation of Theophrastas's Characters, to

John Montgomerie Bell, Paisley

Gartmore Gold Medal.

For the best Essay on the History of International Commerce and the principles on which it should be conducted, to

Ebenezer Russell, Glasgow.

On Dr. Watt's Donation.

For the best Essay on the Rapidity of the Current, and the quantity of Water which the Clyde discharges at the New Bridge, to

John G. Dymock, A.M., Glasgow.

The following Prizes are given from a sum granted by the Earl of Glasgow, late Lord Rector :

For the best Essay on the importance of Classical Learning, to

1. Ebenezer Russell, Glasgow.
2. William Frend Durant, Dorsetshire.

For the best Essay on the communication of Infection, and the means of preventing it, to

George Brown, A.M., Ayrshire.

Two Prizes given by the Jurisdictio Ordinaria, for the best Latin Orations in the Common Hall, were adjudged to

Robert Young, Stonehouse.
James Julius Wood, A M., Northumberland.

The Prizes of the Theological Class were adjudged—

I. For the best Specimen of Public Reading, among Students of the 2nd year, to

John Thomson, Barony of Glasgow.
Robert Craig, A.M., Eaglesham.

II. For a voluntary Essay, written during the Summer, "On objections against the lateness of the period assigned in the Mosaic writings to the formation of the Earth," to

William Muir, Kilmarnock.

III. For Exercises prescribed during the Session, to Students of of the 1st and 2nd year :

1. "On the ignorance and false notions of mankind, when unassisted by Revelation, respecting a Future State," to

        Robert Craig, A.M., Eaglesham.
        William Nixon, Glasgow.

2. "On the Corroborations afforded by the Histories, Traditions, and Customs of Ancient Nations, to the Mosaic Record," to

        Thomas Thomson, Gorbals.
        John M'Millan, Fortwilliam.

IV. For exemplary diligence and regularity of attendance during the Session, to

        James Ewing, Ardrossan.

———

Prizes in the SENIOR HEBREW CLASS were adjudged—

I. For the best Essay on the various significations of the word Shama, to

        David Bryden, A.M., Ayrshire.

For the best critical Analysis and Exposition of Isaiah ix. 1-12, to

        David Bryden, A.M , Ayrshire.

Prizes in the JUNIOR HEBREW CLASS were adjudged—

For General Eminence in the daily examinations throughout the Session, to

        1. Andrew M'Lean, Glasgow.
        2. William Robb, Barony Parish.
        3. James C. Ewing, Ayrshire.

For the best exemplification of the Hebrew Verb, to

        1. James M'Lean, A.M., Gorbals.
        2. George Muir, A.M., Glasgow.

———

Two Prizes for excelling in the daily examinations in the SCOTTISH LAW CLASS proposed to those Students who chose to be examined, were adjudged to

        John Kennedy, Glasgow.
        David Rentoul,   ,,

The Prizes in the SURGERY CLASS were adjudged—

For an Essay on the best absorbable material for Ligatures on the Arteries, to

Robert Marshall, Glasgow.

For an Essay on Injuries and Diseases of the Spine, to

James Smith Candlish, A.M., Glasgow.

NATURAL HISTORY CLASS.

1. For the best Sketch of the Life and Writings of Linnæus, to

James Maclean, A.M., Gorbals.

2. For the best Essay on the Structure and Physiology of Birds, to

Alexander Leitch, A.M., Barony of Glasgow.

The Prizes of the MATHEMATICAL CLASSES, for exemplary propriety, diligence, and ability, and for excelling in Exercises prescribed during the Session, were adjudged—

SENIOR CLASS, to

William Giffin, Paisley.
James M'Callum, Glasgow.
James Buchanan, Paisley.
James Smith, Paisley.
John Stevenson, Cadder.

JUNIOR CLASS, to

Senior Division.

James Brownlee, Falkirk.
Thomas Miller, Glasgow.
Thomas Thomson, Hamilton.
John Ramsay, Kilwinning.
John Park, East Kilbryde.

Junior Division.

Thomas Hargreaves, Oakhill, Lancashire.
Francis Hamilton, Hamilton.
Laurence Hargreaves, Oakhill, Lancashire.

The Prizes of the NATURAL PHILOSOPHY CLASS, for propriety of conduct, exemplary diligence, and Specimens of Composition on Physical Subjects, prescribed by the Professor or chosen by the Students themselves, were adjudged to

James Parker, Glasgow.
John Montgomerie Bell, Paisley.
Robert Wallace, A.M., Glasgow.
William Mather, A.M., Mearns, Renfrewshire.
Robert Smith, Kilwinning, Ayrshire.
Gavin Rowatt, A.M., Penpont.

The Prizes in the ETHIC CLASS, for the best specimens of Composition on the various subjects connected with the business of the Class, and either prescribed weekly by the Professor, or chosen by the Students themselves. And for exemplary conduct and distinguished eminence, were adjudged to,

Seniores.

1. John Hoppus, A.B., Northamptonshire.
2. William Frend Durant, Poole, Dorsetshire.
3. Thos. Hamilton, Staffordshire.
4. Edmund Clark, Birmingham.
5. Franklin Baker,   ,,
6. Christopher Muston, A.B., London.
7. Robert Pollock, Eaglesham.

Juniores.

1. James Buchanan, Paisley.
2. John William Semple, Glasgow.
3. Hugh Colquhoun,   ,,
4. James M'Callum,
5. David Dowie,   ,,
6. James Robison,   ,,

Prizes for superior excellence in the Public Theme were adjudged to

1. John Hoppus, A.B., Northamptonshire.
2. William Frend Durant, Dorsetshire.

Prizes for a Latin Poem on the Immortality of the Soul were adjudged to,

1. Thos. Hamilton, Staffordshire.
2. Wilmer Gossip, Yorkshire.

The Prizes of the LOGIC CLASS, for Essays executed during the last Vacation, were adjudged—

I. For the best Essay on the External Senses and the means of their improvement, to

Robert Pollock, Eaglesham.

II. For the best Essay on the Faculty of Imagination, and the means of improving it, to

Thomas Riddell, London.

The Prizes of this Session,

III. For Eminence, combined with Industry and Proficiency in the whole business of the Class during this Session, to

Seniores.

James Acworth, Chatham.
James Johnston, Kilmarnock.
James M'Kenzie, Campsie.
Mathew Kirkland, Colmonell.
John Bryden, Ayr.
William Fraser, Colmonell.
Archibald Gordon, Ayrshire.
John Clapham, Leeds.
John Gilmore, Glasgow.
William Glen,　　,,

Juniores.

Alfred Cookman, Hull.
Robert Brown,　　,,
James Crawford, Ardmillan.
James Lewis, Glasgow.
Robert Candlish,　,,
William Steel,　　,,
William M'Laurin, Middlesex.
Josias Walker, Glasgow.
John Moore, London.
James Nicol, Kincardineshire.

IV. For the best Translation of the Speeches of Julius Cæsar and Cato, from Sallust, with Critical Remarks, to

James Johnston, Kilmarnock.
James Acworth, Chatham.
Allan M'Kenzie, Glasgow.

V. For the best Specimen of Recollection, to
   Robert Candlish, Glasgow.
   James Stirling,   „

VI. For Excelling in the Black Stone Examination, to
   John Ramsay, Kilmarnock.
   Robert Candlish, Glasgow.
   James MacKenzie, Campsie.
   William Steel, Glasgow.

VII. For the best Public Theme, to
   Campbell Stirling, Campsie.

Prizes of the GREEK CLASS.

For the best poetical translation of the Medea of Euripides, to
   John M. Bell, Paisley.

For the best critical Essay on the poetical character of Euripides, to
   John M. Bell, Paisley.

For the best account of the mode of education which prevailed among the Ancient Greeks, to

   William Williamson, Paisley.
   James Buchanan, „

For the best poetical translation of a Chorus in the Oedipus Tyrannus of Sophocles, to
   Joseph Wicksteed, Shrewsbury.

For the best translation into Greek Hexameter Verse of the Song of Moses, contained in the Book of Exodus, Chap. xv., to
   John Moore, London.

For Good Conduct, Diligence, and Talent, shewn during the Session, to

Senior Class.

LOGIC.   *James Acworth*, Chatham.
   James Johnstone, Kilmarnock.
   William Steel, Glasgow.
   Robert Candlish, „
   Matthew Kirkland, Carmunnock.

GREEK.	*Robert Wilson*, Glasgow. James Fairlie, Fenwick, Ayrshire. Adam Bogle, Glasgow. James Bryce, Coleraine. Thomas Ainsworth, Preston.

Junior Class.

GREEK.	*William Park*, Hutchesontown. William Lindsay, Irvine. John Robson, Cupar in Fife. Thomas Neilson, Kirkowen. John Ferguson, Denny. John Muir, Ardrossan.

LATIN.	Robert M'Corkle, Port-Dundas. John W. Ferguson, Glasgow. Peter Maccallum, united Parishes of Kilmore and Kilbride.

For the best Paradigmas of the Greek verb, to

George Baird, Old Kilpatrick.
John Ferguson, Denny.

———

Prizes in the HUMANITY CLASS.

I. For the best original Compositions in Latin Verse, Vacation Exercise, to

Thomas Russell, Slamannan.
James J. Wood, A.M., Northumberland.

Written during the Session, to

Adam Bogle, Glasgow.
Thomas Ainsworth, Preston.

II. For the best original Composition in Latin Prose, Vacation Exercise, to

Robert Candlish, Glasgow.
Andrew Urquhart, Kilbirnie.

Written during the Session, to

John Reddie, Glasgow.
Adam Bogle,   ,,
James M'Farlane, ,,

III. For the best Table of the different Classes of Latin Verbs to
> Adam Bogle, Glasgow.

IV. For the best Essay on the literary Character of Livy, to
> James J. Wood, A.M., Northumberland.

V. For the best Translation of Terence's Andrian, to
> James Nicol, Kincardineshire.
> William M'Laurin, Middlesex.

VI. For the best Translation of Cicero de Amicitia, to
> Robert Candlish, Glasgow.

VII. For the best Poetical Translation of Horace, Book 3, Ode 29, to
> Joseph Wicksteed, Shrewsbury.
> Robert Scott, Lanark.

VIII. For the best Translation of an English Poem into Latin Verse, to
> William Taylor, Glasgow.

IX. For the best Translation from English into Latin Prose, to
> James Stirling, Craigie.
> Adam Bogle, Glasgow.

X. For the best Elocution in delivering Latin Orations, to
> John Muir, Muirkirk.
> William Blair, Balfron.
> Andrew Bryson, Mearns.
> John Spittal, Glasgow.

XI. For the best Public Theme of Students ranking in the Greek Class, to
> John Reddie, Glasgow.

Of those ranking in the Latin Class, to
> James Reddie, Glasgow.

XII. For accuracy in correcting the Exercises of other Students, to
> Edward Hawkes, Lincoln.
> John M'Ewen, Ayr.

XIII. For excelling at the Blackstone Examination, to

COMPETITORS. { 1. Adam Bogle, Glasgow.
2. James Fairlie, Fenwick.
3. Robert Wilson, Glasgow.

NON-
COMPETITORS. { 1. Andrew Bryson, Mearns.
2. William Lindsay, Irvine.
3. Thomas Dove, Glasgow.

XIV. For exemplary Diligence and Talents displayed throughout the Session, to

I.—1. Adam Bogle, Glasgow.
2. William Park, Hutchisontown.
3. James Fairlie, Fenwick.
4. Robert Wilson, Glasgow.
5. Andrew Bryson, Mearns.
6. Breadie Dalglish, Glasgow.
7. Thomas Ainsworth Preston.

II.—1. Thomas Dove, Glasgow.
2. William Lindsay, Irvine.
.. William Mylne, Glasgow.
4. Duncan Smith, Glenorchy.
5. John Robson, Fife.
6. John Reddie, Glasgow.

III.— Thomas Brydson, Eastwood.

IV.—1. Robert M'Corkle, Port-Dundas.
2. John Willison Ferguson, Glasgow.
3. James Chrystal,   ,,
4. William Taylor,   ..
5. James M'Farlane,   ,,
6. John Buchanan, Dowanhill.
7. James Reddie, Glasgow.
8. James Newlands, ,,

GLASGOW COLLEGE, 1st MAY, 1822.

This day, the Annual Distribution of Prizes was made, in the
Common Hall, by the Principal and Professors, in presence of a
numerous meeting of the University, and of many Reverend and
respectable Gentlemen of this City and neighbourhood.

ONE SILVER MEDAL.
IN PHILOSOPHY.

For the best Account of the recent Discoveries regarding the Polarization of Light, adjudged to

John William Semple, A.M., Glasgow.

On Mr. COULTER'S DONATION.

I. For the best Lecture on the First Psalm, to

John Park, A.M., Hutchesontown, Glasgow.

II. For the best Essay on the Standard of Taste, to

James Buchanan, Paisley.

III. For the best translation of Cicero's Oration for the Manilian Law, to

Henry Renton, A.B., Edinburgh.

On Dr. WATT'S DONATION.

For the best Essay on the Practice and Theory of Calico Printing, to

Hugh Colquhoun, Glasgow.

On the DONATION of FRANCIS JEFFREY, Esq., present Lord Rector of this University.

For the best Specimens of Elocution, by Students in the Greek and Latin Classes, alternately, adjudged by the Students themselves, First Prize, a Gold Medal, to

Thomas M'Mayne, Paisley, Greek Class.

Second Prize, to

William Blair, Glasgow, Greek Class.

Two Prizes given by the JURISDICTIO ORDINARIA, for the best Latin Orations in the Common Hall, were adjudged to

John Hoppus, A.M., Northamptonshire.
Charles Hope M'Lean, Ardgower, Argyllshire.

The Prizes of the DIVINITY CLASSES were adjudged—

I. To Students of the JUNIOR Class—

1. For eminence at the weekly Examinations, to
> William Mather, A.M., Mearns.
> - James Julius Wood, A.M., Northumberland.

2. For eminence in all the Exercises prescribed during the Session, to
> Andrew Glen, Lochwinnoch.
> David John Walker, A.M., Londonderry.
> John M'Intyre, Greenock.
> John Dill, A.M., Londonderry.
> James Julius Wood, A.M., Northumberland.
> John Ramsay, A.M., Donegal.

3. For meritorious Exercises during the Session, though having been necessarily prevented from writing one of those prescribed, he was not included in the general Competition, to
> William Mather, A.M., Mearns.

4. For exemplary diligence and regularity of attendance during the Session, to
> William Gilchrist, A.M., Glasgow.

II. To Students of the SENIOR Class.

1. For the best Specimen of Public Reading, among Students of the second year, to
> William Nixon, Glasgow.
> John Clugston,   „

2. For eminence in Exercises prescribed during the Session, among Students of the second year, to
> John Clugston, Glasgow.
> Thomas Thomson, Gorbals.

3. For exemplary diligence and regularity of attendance during the Session, to
> John Turner, A.M., Glasgow.

Prizes in the *Senior* HEBREW CLASS were adjudged—

1. For the best Essay on the principal terms employed in the Hebrew Scriptures to denote the Divine Being, to
> Duncan Macfarlane, Cardross.

For the best Critical Analysis and Exposition of the 49th Psalm, to

    1. Duncan Macfarlane, Cardross.
    2. James M'Lean, A.M., Gorbals.

Prizes in the *Junior* HEBREW CLASS were adjudged—

For General Eminence in the daily examinations throughout the Session, to

    1. James Allan, Lesmahagow.
    2. John MacIntyre, Greenock.
    3. Archibald Connel, Islay, Argyllshire.

For the best exemplification of the Hebrew Verb, to

    1. John Harvie, Stirling.
    2. William Gilchrist, A.M., Glasgow.
    3. Thomas Riddell, London.

———

Two Prizes for excelling in the daily examinations in the SCOTTISH LAW CLASS, proposed to those Students who chose to be examined, were adjudged to

    Robert Knox, Larbert, Stirlingshire.
    John Buchanan, Slatefield, near Glasgow.

———

The Prize in the ANATOMY CLASS,

For the best Essay on the Circulation of the Blood, was given to

    Robert Marshall, Glasgow.

———

The Prizes of the MATHEMATICAL CLASSES, for exemplary propriety, diligence, and ability, and for excelling in Exercises prescribed during the Session, were adjudged—

SENIOR CLASS, to

    John Hoppus, A.M., Northampton.
    John Park, East Kilbride.
    John Ramsay, Kilwinning.
    Christopher Muston, A.M., London.
    Samuel Moore, County Down, Ireland.

JUNIOR CLASS, to

Senior Division.

James Johnston, Kilmarnock.
Andrew Urquhart, Kilbirnie.
William M'Kerrow, Kilmarnock.
Mathew B. Pollock, Govan.
Hugh Moore, County Down, Ireland.
Robert Laing, East Monkland.
James Jo. Knox, Larbert.

Junior Division.

John Moore, London.
William Walker, Irvine.
David Buchan Dowie, Glasgow.

The Prizes of the NATURAL PHILOSOPHY CLASS, for propriety of conduct, exemplary diligence, and Specimens of Composition on Physical Subjects, prescribed by the Professor or chosen by the Students themselves, were adjudged to

John Hoppus, A.M., Northamptonshire.
James Smith, Paisley.
James Bryden, Ayr.
John Stevenson, Cadder.
John W. Semple, A.M., Glasgow.
James Buchanan, Paisley.
James Robison, Glasgow.
James M'Callum, ,,

The Prizes in the ETHIC CLASS, for the best specimens of Composition on the various subjects connected with the business of the Class, and either prescribed by the Professor, or chosen by the Students themselves; and for exemplary conduct and distinguished eminence, were adjudged to,

Seniores.

1. James R. Mackenzie, Campsie.
2. James Acworth, Chatham.
3 and 4. (the votes for the gentlemen being equal)
   James Johnstone, Kilmarnock, and
   John Bryden, Ayr.
5. Matthew Kirkland, Carmunnock.

Juniores.

1. Robert Smith Candlish, Glasgow.
2. Alex. John Scott, Greenock.
3. Alfred Cookman, Hull.
4. Henry Renton, Edinburgh.
5. Thomas Henderson, Stirling.

Prizes for superior excellence in the Latin Theme, were adjudged to

1. Robert Smith Candlish, Glasgow.
2. James Johnston, Kilmarnock.

A Prize for Excellence in various Essays in Verse, read in the Class, was adjudged to

John Peele Clapham, Leeds.

———

The Prizes of the LOGIC CLASS, executed during the Vacation,

I. For the best Essay on the Causes of Diversity of Style in Composition, to

James Johnston, Glasgow.

II. For the best Essay on the Controversy between the Nominalists and Realists, to

Robert Smith Candlish, Glasgow.
James Lewis, Glasgow.

The Prizes of this Session were adjudged—

III. For General Eminence, to

Seniores.

Theyre Smith, Fulham, London.
James Johnston, Alva.
Charles Marshal, Paisley.
Alexander Thomson, Paisley.
Thomas Dalrymple, Cleland.
Thomas Dove, Glasgow.
Matthew Miller, ,,
George Lewis, London.
John Greig, ,,
Duncan M'Lean, Irvine.
William Lindsay, Rothesay.
John Robson, Cupar, Fife.
Thomas Nelson, Galloway.

Juniores.

William Park, Hutchesontown, Glasgow.
James Stirling, Craigie.
James Fairlie, Fenwick.
Thomas Ainsworth, Preston.
Dugald Bannatyne, Glasgow.
Adam Bogle,   ,,
Robert Wilson,   ,,
Thomas Grahame,   ,,
John Stodhart, London.
Geddes Scott,   ,,
William Mackay, Glasgow.
John Lumgeur, Arbroath.
William Gardner, Edinburgh.

IV. For the best Essay on the Influence of Habits of Attention on Imagination and Genius, executed during Holidays, to

Theyre Smith, Fulham, London.
William F. Gardner, Edinburgh.
George Lewis, London.

V. For a Poetical Essay on the same subject, to

Thomas Dalrymple, Cleland.

VI. For the best Specimens of Recollection of Sermons preached in the Chapel, to

James Stirling, Craigie.
Dugald Bannatyne, Glasgow.
Adam Bogle,   ,,
William Park, Hutchesontown, Glasgow.

———

Prizes of the GREEK CLASS.

For the best Critique on the Sixth Book of Homer's Iliad, to

Alfred Cookman, Hull.

For the best poetical translation of the Œdipus Tyrannus of Sophocles, to

James Fairlie, Fenwick, Ayrshire.

For the best translation of the Sixth Book of the Iliad, to

William M'Kerrow, Kilmarnock.

For the best translation of the "Sale of Lives" by Lucian. to

Alexander Mitchell, Glasgow.

For the best translation of 40 Odes of Anacreon, to

Andw. Buchanan, Ardenconnel, Dumbartonshire.

For the best translation of Three Chapters from each of the Evangelists, to

John Buchanan, Dowanhill.

For the best Analysis of Verbs in Anacreon, to

James Buchanan, Dowanhill.

For the best translation of the Fifth Book of Xenophon's Anabasis, to

Josias Walker, Glasgow.

For Good Conduct, Diligence, and Talent, shewn during the Session, to

Senior Class.

LOGIC.
- *James Fairlie*, Fenwick, Ayrshire.
- Robert Wilson, Glasgow.
- William Park, Hutchesontown, Glasgow.
- Adam Bogle, Glasgow.
- Duncan Smith, Glenorchy.
- Thomas Dove, Glasgow.

GREEK.
- *James Macfarlane*, Glasgow.
- John W. Ferguson, ,,
- James Chrystal, ,,
- William Rennie, ,,
- Peter M'Callum, Oban, Argyleshire.
- Alexander Munro, Paisley.

For excelling in the Black Stone Examination, to

COMPETITORS.
- Adam Bogle, Glasgow.
- James Fairlie, Fenwick.
- Alfred Pitt, England.

NON-COMPETITORS.
- Samuel M'Cosh, Ayrshire.
- Duncan Smith, Glenorchy.
- Geddes Scott, London.

For excelling in the Greek Exercises in Verse and Prose, prescribed weekly during Session, to

Adam Bogle, Glasgow.
William Park, Hutchesontown, Glasgow.
Robert Wilson, Glasgow.
Duncan Smith, Glenorchy.

For the best translation into Greek Hexameter Verse of some lines from the Epithalamium of Catullus, to

John Cowan, Glasgow.
William Park, Hutchesontown, Glasgow.
William Rennie, Glasgow.

For the best poetical translation of a Chorus in "the Clouds" of Aristophanes, to

Alexander Munro, Paisley.

For the best account of the Laws of Iambic, Trochaic, and Dactylic Metres, to

Adam Bogle, Glasgow.
John Reddie,   ,,

Junior Class.

For Good Conduct, Diligence, and Talent, shewn during the Session, to

PROVECTIORES.
{
Robert Paisley, Glasgow.
James Clason, Dunblane.
Richard Lockhart, Germiston.
John Downie, Kippen.
William Ainsworth, Preston.
Peter Campbell, Argyleshire.
John Chamberlain, York.
John M.tchell, Glasgow.
}

TYRONES.
{
Allan King, Govan.
John M'Isaac, Argyleshire.
Moses Steven, Glasgow.
James M'Ewan, Glasgow.
Hugh Kennedy, Denny.
Alexander M'Naught, Kilmarnock.
}

For the best Paradigmas of the Greek verb, to

Adam Pearson, Glasgow.
Johnston Thomson, ,,

———

Prizes in the HUMANITY CLASS.

I. For the best Latin Verses, written during the Vacation, to

Robert M'Corkle, Port-Dundas.

Written during the Session, to
> Anthony C. Stirling, London.
> Adam Bogle, Glasgow.

II. For the best Essay in Latin Prose, written during the Vacation, to
> Adam Bogle, Glasgow.

Written during the Session, to
> Robert M'Corkle, Port-Dundas.

III. For the best Essay on the Roman Dictatorship, to
> Robert Candlish, Glasgow.

IV. For the best Translation of Plautus's Aulularia, to
> Adam Bogle, Glasgow.

V. For the best Translation of Cicero's Oration against Catiline, to
> Alexander Mitchell, Glasgow.
> Andrew Buchanan, Ardenconnel.

VI. For the best Translation of the 2nd Epode of Horace, to
> Joseph Wicksteed, Shrewsbury.
> John Reddie, Glasgow.

VII. For the best Translation of English into Latin, to
> Robert M'Corkle, Port-Dundas.

VIII. For the best Translation of an English Poem into Latin Verse, to
> Peter Miller, Stirling.

IX. For the best Table of the different Classes of Latin Verbs, to
> Hugh Ferguson, Glasgow.
> James R. Grant,   ,,

X. For the best Public Theme of the Greek Students, to
> James C. Reddie, Glasgow.

Of the Latin,

> Richard D. Lockhart, Glasgow.
> John Stirling, Dunblane.

XI. For the best Elocution, to
> David Ritchie, Glasgow.
> Robert Miller, Dalry, Ayrshire..

XII. For excelling in Correcting Exercises, to
> Robert M'Corkle, Port-Dundas.
> Alexander M'Haffie, Glasgow.

XIII. For excelling at the Blackstone Examination, to

COMPETITORS.
1. Robert M'Corkle, Port-Dundas.
2. Hugh Ferguson, Glasgow.
{ James M'Farlane, ,,
{ James C. Reddie, ,,

NON-COMPETITORS.
1. Alexander Munro, Paisley.
2. Jo. Willison Ferguson, Glasgow.
3. James Chrystal, ,,

XIV. For exemplary Eminence throughout the Session, to

I.—1. Robert M'Corkle, Port-Dundas.
2. Jo. Willison Ferguson, Glasgow.
3. Alexander M'Haffie, ,,
4. John Ferguson, Denny.
5. James Chrystal, Glasgow.
6. James M'Farlane, ,,

II.—1. Alexander Munro, Paisley.
2. John Easton, Glasgow.
3. Anthony C. Stirling, London.
4. George Parker, Glasgow.
5. Alexander M'Naught, Kilmarnock.
6. Adam Haldane, Gallashiels.

III.— James Ralston, Glasgow.

IV.—1. Robert Paisley, Glasgow.
2. Peter Miller, Stirling.
3. John Downie, Kippen.
4. William Ainsworth, Preston.
5. William Buchanan, Dalmarnock.
6. John Stirling, Dunblane.
7. Richard D. Lockhart, Glasgow.

GLASGOW COLLEGE, 1st May, 1823.

This day, the Annual Distribution of Prizes was made in the Common Hall, by the Principal and Professors, in presence of a numerous meeting of the University, and of many Reverend and respectable Gentlemen of this City and neighbourhood.

Two Silver Medals.
I.—In Theology.

For the best Account of the State of the Heathen at the time of the coming of our Saviour, adjudged to

Thomas Thomson, Hutchesontown.

II.—In Philosophy.

For the best account of the Discoveries of Roemer and Bradley relating to the Motion of Light, to

James Mitchell, Glasgow.

On Mr. Coulter's Donation.

I. For the best Sermon on Heb. x. 25, to

Thomas Thomson, Hutchesontown.

II. For the best Essay on the principle of Sympathy, to

William Park, Hutchesontown, Glasgow.

III. For the best Translation of Demosthenes's Oration De Corona, to

George Lewis, London.

Gartmore Gold Medal.

For the best Essay on the Effects which would result to the commercial interests of Great Britain from throwing open the Trade of the East Indies, to

James Buchanan, Paisley.

Mr. Jeffrey's Gold Medal.

For the best specimens of Elocution by Students in the Humanity Class, to

William Steel.

Two Prizes given by the JURISDICTIO ORDINARIA for the best Latin Orations in the Common Hall, to

Samuel Craig Neilson, A.M., Downpatrick.
Josiah Walker, Glasgow.

The Prizes of the DIVINITY CLASSES were adjudged—

I. To Students of the SENIOR Class,

1. For the best specimen of Public Reading among Students of the second year, to

James Julius Wood, A.M., Northumberland.

2. For the best Abstract of the Lectures on the Evidences for Divine Revelation, written during the summer, to

George Boag, Glasgow.

3. For the best Essay on the Prophecies respecting the Dispersion and Restoration of the Jewish people, to

John Dill, A.M., Londonderry.

4. For Eminence in the Weekly Examinations and Exercises prescribed during the Session, to

James Julius Wood, A.M., Northumberland.
John Dill, A.M., Londonderry.

II. To Students of the JUNIOR Class,

1. For Eminence in the Weekly Examinations and Exercises, prescribed during the Session, to

James Buchanan, Paisley.
Charles M'Intosh, Tain.
James Buchanan Hamilton, Glasgow.

2. For General Eminence, though, from particular circumstances, not included in the Competition of the Class, to

Thomas Henderson Wightman, A.M., Ireland.

Prizes in the *Senior* HEBREW CLASS were adjudged—

I. For the best Dissertation on the meaning and application of the Hebrew word Sheol, to

James C. Ewing, Saltcoats.

II. For the next best Dissertation on the same subject, to

John M'Intyre, Greenock.

III. For the best critical Analysis on the fifth chapter of Isaiah, to

John Dill, A.M., Ireland.

IV. For the next best Analysis on the same subject, to

Duncan M'Dougall, Lanarkshire.

Prizes in the *Junior* HEBREW CLASS were adjudged—

For General Eminence in the daily examinations throughout the Session, to

1. Archibald Nisbet, Ayrshire.
2. James B. Hamilton, Glasgow.

For the best exemplification of the Hebrew Verb, to

1. William Eason, Larbert.
2. Thomas Turnbull, Airth.

For a well executed exemplification of the Persian Verb, to

James M'Callum, Glasgow.

Two Prizes for excelling in the daily examinations in the SCOTTISH LAW CLASS, proposed to those Students who chose to be examined, were adjudged to

Alexander Thomson, Glasgow.
James Hamilton,   ,,

The Prize in the ANATOMY CLASS,

For the best Essay on Respiration, to

John Dill, Ireland.

NATURAL HISTORY.

For the best Essay on the Physiology and Habits of Fishes, to

Mr. James Macrie, Ayrshire.

The Prizes of the MATHEMATICAL CLASSES, for exemplary propriety, diligence, and ability, and for excelling in Exercises prescribed during the Session, were adjudged,

Senior Class, to

Robert Laing, Airdrie.
Geddes M. Scott, London.
Robert Smith Candlish, Glasgow.
Robert Houston, Girvan.

Junior Class, to,

Senior Division.

Samuel M'Cosh, Dalrymple, Ayrshire.
William Park, Hutchesontown, Glasgow.
William Lindsay, Irvine.
John Robb, Roberton, Lanarkshire.
George Boucher, Cumbernauld
James Fairlay, Fenwick, Ayrshire.

Junior Division.

Campbell M'Kinnon, Ayr.
William Mackie, Glasgow.
Thomas Dove,   „
Thomas Ainsworth, B.A., Preston, Lancashire.

The Prizes of the Natural Philosophy Class, for propriety of conduct, exemplary diligence, and Specimens of Composition on Physical subjects, prescribed by the Professor, or chosen by the Students themselves, were adjudged to

James Johnston, Kilmarnock.
Robert Smith Candlish, A.M., Glasgow.
John Ramsay, Kilwinning.
James Mitchell, A.M., Glasgow.
Josiah Walker, Glasgow.
John Bryden, Ayr.
Samuel Craig Neilson, A.M., Downpatrick.
Robert Houston, Girvan.

The Prizes in the Ethic Class, for the best specimens of Composition on various subjects connected with the business of the Class, and either prescribed weekly by the Professor, or chosen by the Students themselves ; and for exemplary good conduct and distinguished eminence, were adjudged to

Seniors

1. Theyre Smith, London.
2. John M'Ewen, Ayr.
3. George Lewis, London.
4. Thomas Neilson, Galloway.
5. Alexr. Thomson, Paisley.
6. John Cowan, Old Monkland.

Juniors.

1. William Park, Hutchesontown, Glasgow.
2. James Fairlie, Fenwick.
3. Thomas Ainsworth, Preston.
4. Willm. Mackey, Glasgow.
5. John Frederick Stoddart, Malta.
6. Dugald Bannatyne, Jun., Glasgow.

A Prize for distinguished eminence, and particularly for the superior merit of various Poetical Essays read in the Class, was adjudged to

William Fullarton Gardner, Edinburgh.

Prizes were given for the best Public Theme.

1. To Adam Bogle, Glasgow.
2. To Robert Wilson,   „

And for the best Theme executed in Latin Verse, to

Alfred Pett, London.

———

The Prizes of the LOGIC CLASS, executed during the Vacation.

I. For the best Essay on Perception, as modified by the External Senses, to

1. John Stodart, London.
2. Adam Bogle, Glasgow.

II. For the best Essay on the difference betwixt Poetry and Prose, to

1. Adam Bogle, Glasgow.
2. George Lewis, London.

III. For the best Essay " On the Pleasures of the Country, and of Study during the Vacation," in Prose, to

1. James Cairns, Edinburgh.
2. John Hill, Dundee.

In Poetry.

1. Alex. Munro, Paisley.
2. William M'Lean, Glasgow.
3. Henry Green, Kent.

To render the Competition equal, Prizes were given for General Eminence to the more advanced Students, to

1. Alexander Monro, Paisley.
2. James Sprigg, Birmingham.
3. Samuel Allard, Bury, Lancashire.
4. Henry Green, Kent.

The Class was next divided into the Seniores and Juniores.

Seniores.

Prizes for General Eminence were adjudged to

1. James Cairns, Edinburgh.
2. Archd. Davidson,   ,,
3. John Stirling, London.
4. John Blythe, Kent.
5. John Brown, Kilmarnock.
6. Ninian Bannatyne, Rothesay.
7. Adam Sim, Glasgow.
8. John Mitchel, Johnstone.
9. William M'Lean, Glasgow.

Juniores.

1. James Buchanan, Glasgow.
2. Henry Berry, London.
3. Moses Steven, Glasgow.
4. John Willison Ferguson, Glasgow.
5. Robert M'Corkle, Port Dundas.
6. Charles Baird, Canal Basin, Glasgow.
7. William Rennie, Garnet-hill.
8. William Blair, Balfron.
9. James Macfarlane, Glasgow.

For the best specimens of Recollection of Sermons preached in the Chapel, to

James Buchanan, Glasgow.
William Orr, Saltcoats.

GREEK CLASS.

Private.

For the best Essay on the Poetical Character of Aristophanes, as it is displayed in the conception and execution of "the Clouds," to

Robert Smith Candlish, Glasgow.

For the best Poetical version of Chorusses in "the Frogs" of Aristophanes, to

Joseph Wicksteed, England.

For the best Paraphrase of Aristotle's Poetics, cap. 10, to

James Sprigg, England.

Public.

For the best Translation into English Prose of the first Book of the Iliad, to

Allan King, Govan.

For the best Poetical version of some odes of Anacreon, and two War-songs of Tyrtæus, to

Richard Lockhart, Germiston.

For the best translation of Extracts from Xenophon's Cyropedeia, to

William Ainsworth, England.

For the best translation into Greek Iambics of Horace, Epod. xvii. v. 1-24, to

Logic Side—Wm. Park, Hutchesontown, Glasgow.
Greek Side—Wm. Rennie, Garnethill.

For the best translation of "the choice of Hercules" from Xenophon, to

William M'Lean, Glasgow.

For the best translation of the Hippolytus of Euripides, to

.   Wm. Rennie, Garnethill.

For the best Translation of Xenophon's Memorabilia, Book IV., to

Andrew Buchanan, Ardenconnell.

Prizes for Eminence at the Black-stone Examination,

Competitors.

1. John Willison Ferguson, Glasgow.
2. John Ferguson, *minor*, Denny, Stirlingshire.
3. Henry Berry, England.

Non-Competitors.

1. Wm. Gaskell, England.
2. Wm. Auld, Greenock.
3. Wm. Blair, Balfron, Stirlingshire ; and
    Wm. Scott, Ireland.

For General Eminence in Scholarship, Conduct and Attendance, throughout the Session.

SENIOR CLASS.

Logic Side.

1. James Chrystal, Glasgow.
2. James Macfarlane,   ,,
3. Wm Rennie, Garnethill, Glasgow.
4. Henry Berrie, England.
5. Robert M'Corkle, Port-Dundas, and
    J. Willison Ferguson, Glasgow.
6. James Playfair, Dalmarnock.
7. Wm. M'Lean, Glasgow.

Greek Class.

1. Wm. Jacobson, Great Yarmouth, England.
2. John M'Isaac, Campbeltown.
3. Allan King, Govan.
4. Wm. Ford, Stockton, England.
5. Hugh Ferguson, Glasgow.
6. John Easton,   ,,
7. Joseph Hoskins, England.

For Eminence in the Exercises, in Greek, Verse and Prose prescribed weekly during Session :

1 James Macfarlane, Glasgow.
2. Wm. Rennie, Garnethill, Glasgow.
3. James Chrystal,   ,,
4. Robert M'Corkle, Port-Dundas.

For the best Version, in Greek Hexameters, of some lines from Catullus :

Wm. Rennie, Garnethill.

JUNIOR CLASS.

For General Eminence, in Scholarship, Conduct and Attendance, during Session:

Provectiores.

1. Wm. Kidston, Glasgow.
2. Mathew Barclay, Paisley.
3. Wm. Govan, Dumbarton.
4. Wm. Wingate, Glasgow.
5. James Robertson, Paisley.
6. Alex. Moody, 	,,
7. Mungo Parker, Kilmarnock.
8. John Adam, Paisley.
9. Robert Baird, Glasgow, and
   Malcolm Ellis, Saltcoats.
10. Alex. Bell, Paisley.
11. James Syme, Glasgow.
12. George Barbour, 	,,
13. James Graham, 	,,

Tyrones.

1. Richard Tucker, England.
2. James Bannatyne, Rothesay.
3. James Reid, Stevenston, Ayrshire.
4. Patrick Edgar, Renfrew.
5. Alex. Mackintosh, Ross-shire.
6. Wm. Jamieson, Kilbirnie, Ayrshire.
7. Wm. Lambert, Neilston, Renfrew.
8 Archibald Campbell (Jura), Glasgow.
9. Charles Martin, Argyllshire.
10. Adam Lillie, Bridgetown.
11. James Ralston, Glasgow.
12. James Blythe, England.
13. Wm. Cunninghame, North Berwick.

For the Paradigma of the Greek verb :

1. Micaiah Smith, Glasgow.
2. John Boyle, 	,,
3. A. Moody, Paisley, and Robert Stiven, Glasgow.

Prizes in the HUMANITY CLASS.

I. For the best Latin Verses, written during the Vacation, to
Walter M'Farlane, Port, Stirlingshire.

Written during the Session, to
Hugh Fergusson, Glasgow.

II. For the best Essay in Latin Prose, written during the Vacation, to
James M'Farlane, Glasgow.
John W. Fergusson, „

Written during the Session, to
James Robertson, Paisley.
William Nimmo, Glasgow.

III. For the best Essay on the Roman Censorship, to
Robert Smith Candlish, Glasgow.

IV. For the best Translation of Terrence's Andria, to
John Ferguson, Denny.

V. For the best Translations of Cicero's Third Oration against Cataline, to
John Buchanan, Glasgow.
John Ferguson, Denny.

VI. For the best Translation into English Verse of a Passage of Virgil, to
William D. F. Gardner, Edinburgh.
William Jacobson, Great Yarmouth.

VII. For the best Translation of English into Latin Prose, to
Will. Wardlaw, Glasgow.

VIII. For the best Translation of an English Poem into Latin Verse, to
William M'Lean, Gorbals.
William M'Donald, Glasgow.

IX. For the best Public Theme, to
William Nimmo, Glasgow.

X. The Second Prize for Elocution, to
John Easton, Glasgow.

Q

XI. For excelling in the Weekly Exercises, to

1st Division.—William Jacobson, Great Yarmouth.
William Ford, Stockton.
Jos. Hoskins, London.

2nd Division.—James Burns, Brechin.
Pat. Edgar, Erskine.

XII. For Excelling at the Black-stone Examination, to

COMPETITORS, { William Ford, Stockton.
Pat. Edgar, Erskine.
James Robertson, Paisley.

NON-COMPETITORS, { William Kidston, Glasgow.
Mungo Parker, Kilmarnock.
Robert Whyte,   „

XIII. For exemplary eminence throughout the Session, to

I.—1. H. Fergusson, Glasgow.
2. John Easton,   „
3. John M'Isaac, Argyllshire.
4. William Ainsworth, Preston.
5. John Roxburgh, Glasgow.
6. John Stirling, Dumblane.

II.—1. William Jacobson, Great Yarmouth.
2. William Ford, Stockton.
3 James Robertson, Paisley.
4. Jos. Hoskins, London.
5. Matthew Barclay, Paisley.
6. William Kidston, Glasgow.

III.—1. Pat. Edgar, Erskine.
2. James Bannatyne, Rothesay.
3. James Reid, Stevenston.
4. Laurence Craigie, Perth.

IV.—1. James Laurie, Glasgow.
2. William Steel,   „

V.—1. William Wingate, Glasgow.
2. James Syme,   „
3. James Colquhoun, Stirling.
4. Alexander Moody, Paisley.
5. James Graham, Glasgow.
6. Alexander Bell, Paisley.
7. Robert Horn, Glasgow.

GLASGOW COLLEGE, 1st MAY, 1824.

This day, the Annual Distribution of Prizes was made in the Common Hall, by the Principal and Professors, in presence of a numerous meeting of the University, and of many Reverend and respectable Gentlemen of this City and neighbourhood.

TWO SILVER MEDALS.

I. IN THEOLOGY.

For the best view of the Evidence from Miracles for the Truth of Christianity, adjudged to

Robert Smith Candlish, A.M., Glasgow.

II.—IN PHILOSOPHY.

For the best Essay on the most practicable methods of Lessening the Aberrations of Form, and of Refrangibility in the Telescope, to

Adam Bogle, Glasgow.

On Mr. COULTER'S Donation.

I. For the best Lecture on the 24th Psalm, to

James Buchanan, Paisley.

II. For the best Essay on the use of the Categories and Predicables, to

William Park, A.M., Hutchesontown, Glasgow.

III. For the best Translation of the first Book of Cicero de Officiis, to

John Cameron, Glasgow.

On Mr. WATT'S Donation.

I. For the best Essay on the Properties of Steam as a Moving Power, to

James Walker Aitkin, Falkirk.

II. For the best Essay on the quantity of Moisture in the Atmosphere, to

Hugh Colquhoun, Glasgow.

Mr. Jeffrey's Gold Medal.

For the best specimens of Elocution by Students in the Greek Class, to

William Halbert, Glasgow.

Two Prizes given by the Jurisdictio Ordinaria, for the best Latin Orations in the Common Hall, to

William Park, A.M., Hutchesontown, Glasgow.
Adam Bogle, Glasgow.

The Prizes of the Divinity Classes were adjudged,
To Students of the 2nd year in the Senior Class,

1. For a written account of the Lectures of the preceding Session, to

James Buchanan, Paisley.

2. For the best Specimen of Public Reading, to

Duncan Lennie, Glasgow.

3. For general Eminence in the Exercises and Examinations of the Class, to

James Buchanan, Paisley.
Charles Macintosh, Tain.
James B. Hamilton ⎱ Equal, both of Glasgow.
Gavin Lochore ⎰

4. For the best Essay "On the Inspiration of the New Testament," to

James Buchanan, Paisley.
Gavin Lochore, Glasgow.

5. For the best Essay on the universal obligation, and advantages of the Sabbath, to

James Buchanan, Paisley.
Charles Macintosh, Tain.
David Horne, Kirkintilloch.

To Students of the Junior Class, the Prizes were adjudged for

1. General Eminence in the Exercises and Examinations of the Class, to

Matthew Kirkland, Carmunnock.
John Bryden, Ayr.
Robert Smith Candlish, A.M., Glasgow.

2. For the best Essay on the Knowledge afforded by the Light of Nature respecting a future state, to

Matthew Kirkland, Carmunnock.
John Simpson, Glasgow.

3. For the best Essay "On the Internal Evidence for the Mosaic Dispensation, arising from the Nature of its Doctrines and Laws," to

Matthew Kirkland, Carmunnock.
John Bryden, Ayr.

Oriental Languages.

Prizes in the Senior Class.

1. For the best exemplification of the Arabic Verb, to

John Smith, Gorbals, Glasgow.

2. For the best Analysis of the first ten verses of the 21st Chapter of Isaiah, to

James Buchanan Hamilton, Glasgow.

Prizes in the Junior Class.

1. For General Eminence in the daily examinations throughout the Session, to

1. Geddes Scott, A.M., London.
2. Thomas Findlay, Strathaven.

2. For the best exemplifications of the Hebrew Verb, to

1. James Pearson, Glasgow.
2. Robert Laing, New Monkland.

3. For the best exemplification of the Persiac Verb, to

William Cooper Thomson, A.M., Balfron.

Two Prizes for excelling in the daily examinations proposed to those Students of Scottish Law who chose to be examined, were adjudged to

James Dunlop, Glasgow.
William Gray, Glasgow.

The Prize in the Anatomy Class,
For the best Essay on Absorption, to

Mr. Charles Bryce.

Natural History.

1. For the best Essay on the External Characters of Minerals, to
John Dill, A.M., Ireland.

For the best Essay on the Migration of Birds, to
Richard Dill, A.M., Ireland.

Prizes in the Chemistry Class.

1. For the best appearances in the public examinations during the Session, to
William Bromefield, Windsor.

2. For the best Essay on the Thermometer, to
Thomas Thomson, Hamilton.

3. For the Second Best Essay on the Thermometer, to
William Bromefield, Windsor.

The Prizes of the Mathematical Classes, for general eminence and proficiency during the Session, were adjudged,

Senior Class, to

John Robb, A.M., Roberton, Lanarkshire.
Henry Lee Berry, A.B., London.
Thomas Miller, A.M., Glasgow.
Robert Wilson,   ,,
John Greig, A.M., London.

Junior Class, to,

Seniores.

George Baird, West Kilpatrick.
John Cameron, Glasgow.
James Playfair,   ,,
William Gaskell, Warrington, Lancashire.
Ninian Bannatyne, Rothesay.

Juniores.

Robert Henderson, Stirling.
William Blair, Balfron.
Robert Elder, Campbelton.
James Chrystal, Glasgow.

The Prizes of the NATURAL PHILOSOPHY CLASS, for propriety of conduct, exemplary diligence, and Specimens of Composition on Subjects in Natural Philosophy, presented by the Professor, or chosen by the Students themselves, were adjudged to

Samuel Walker M'Cosh, Dalrymple, Ayrshire.
William Lindsay, Irvine.
William Park, A.M., Hutchesontown, Glasgow.
Thomas Miller, A.M., Glasgow.
Thomas Graham, A.M., „
John Robb, A.M., Roberton, Lanarkshire.
Adam Bogle, Glasgow.
Thomas Dove, A.M., Glasgow.
John M'Ewen, Ayr.
James Fairlie, A.M., Fenwick.

The Prizes in the ETHIC CLASS,

I. For superior merit in the Composition of Essays, on subjects prescribed weekly to the Students, or chosen by themselves ; and for distinguished eminence in the different parts of the business of the Class, were adjudged to

Seniors.

1. Alex. Monro, Paisley.
2. Henry Green, Kent.
3. James Sprigg, Birmingham.
4. John Edwards, Campsie.
5. Will. Gaskell, Warrington.
6. Will. Rennie, Garnethill, Glasgow.

Juniors.

1. Henry Lee Berry, A.B., London.
2. Will. M. James, Glamorganshire.
3. Will. Blair, Balfron.
4. James M'Farlane, Glasgow.
5. Robt. Henderson, Stirling.

II. For superior merit in Poetical Compositions, were adjudged to

Alex. Monro, Paisley.
Robert M'Corkle, Glasgow.

JII. For Exercises performed during the Summer Vacation.

1. For the best Translations of the Enchiridion of Epictetus, adjudged to

James Fairlie, A.M., Fenwick.

2. For the best Translation of, and Commentary on the First ten Aphorisms of Bacon's Novum Organum, adjudged to

Will. Park, A.M., Hutchesontown, Glasgow.

3. For the best Essay on the Origin and Nature of the Emotions excited by Beauty, adjudged to

Henry Lee Berry, A.B., London.

————

The Prizes of the LOGIC CLASS for Essays executed during the last Vacation.

I. For the best Essay on the Influence of Sympathy and the Moral Sense on the Powers of Taste, to

William Orr, Saltcoats.

II. For the best Essays on the Difficulties of Acquiring Habits of Attention, and on the Means of Removing them, executed during the Christmas holidays, to

1. Quintin M'Adam, Craigingellan.
2. William Ainsworth, Preston.
3. Henry Sandbach, Liverpool.

III. For the best Poetical Account of the Distribution of Prizes, and the business of the first of May in this University, to

1. Thomas Hudson, London.
2. Thomas Stevenson, Johnston.

IV. To render the Competition as equal as possible, Prizes are given for general eminence and superiority in the whole business of the Class, and supported during the whole Session, to Students farthest advanced in age, etc., to

1. Mathew Barclay, Paisley.
2. Thomas Hudson, London.
3. William Ford, Yorkshire.
4 Thomas Stevenson, Johnston.

V. The Class is then divided into the Seniores and Juniores.

Seniores.

1. John Roxburgh, Glasgow.
2. Henry Sandbach, Liverpool.
3. William Govan, Dumbarton.
4. Weatherby Phipson, Birmingham.
5. Mackenzie Wilson, Liverpool.
6. John M'Gill, Glasgow.
7. John Bruce, Newcastle.
8. John M'Isaac, Campbelton.
9. John Cropper, Warrington.
10. Robert M'Indoe, Partick.
11. Hugh Kennedy, Denny.

Juniores.

1. William Ainsworth, Preston.
2. Hugh Ferguson, Glasgow.
3. Allan King, Govan.
4. Thomas Muir, Muirpark.
5. John M'Farlane, Fifeshire.
6. William Gladstone, Liverpool.
7. Andrew Greig, Glasgow.
8. Mungo Parker, Kilmarnock.
9. John Stirling, Dunblane.
10. Alexander Ure, Glasgow.
11. John Adam, Paisley.

VI. For the best specimens of Recollection of a Sermon preached in the College Chapel, and done without Notes or assistance of any kind, to

John Roxburgh, Glasgow.

———

Prizes of the GREEK CLASS.

Private—Vacation Exercises.

1. Essay on the character of Aristotle as a Critic, as it is to be deduced from the Plan and Principles of the Poets, to

James Fairlie, Fenwick, Ayrshire.

2. Essay on the Comparative Merits of Epic and Dramatic Poetry, to

William Gardiner, Edinburgh.

Written during Session.

1. Commentary on the 35th and 36th chapters of Longinus, to
John Pringle, Tranent, Haddingtonshire.

2. Translation of Sappho's Ode preserved by Longinus, to
James Fairlie, Fenwick, Ayrshire.

Senior—Vacation Exercises.

1. Translation into Greek Iambic Trimeters of 30 Lines from
Milton's Samson Agonistes, to

    1. James Macfarlane, Glasgow, Logic side.
    2. William Ford, England, Greek side.

2. Translation of the Contest between Æschylus and Euripides
in the Frogs of Aristophanes, to
John Ferguson, *major*, Denny.

3. Translation of Books I. and II. of Xenophon's Anabasis, to
John Ferguson, major, Denny.

4. Translation of the Alcestis of Euripides, to
Hugh Ferguson, Glasgow.

Written during Session :—

1. Translation into Greek Hexameters of 20 lines from
Catullus, to
Matthew Barclay, Paisley.

2. Essay on Origin and Meaning of Homeric Particles, to
Matthew Barclay, Paisley.

For excelling at the Black Stone Examination, to

COMPETITORS, { 1. James Bryce, Coleraine, Ireland.
              2. William Ford, England.
              3. Allan King, Govan.

NON-COMPETITORS, { 1. Henry Everett, England.
                  2. William Govan, Dumbarton.
                  3. Hugh Ferguson, Glasgow.

Second Prize for Elocution, to
John Jardine, Glasgow.

For Eminent Talent, Scholarship, Diligence and Conduct, throughout the Session.

Logic Side.

1. Wm. Ford, England.
2. Wm. Govan, Dumbarton.
3. James Bryce, Coleraine, Ireland.
4. Matthew Barclay, Paisley.
5. Allan King, Govan.
6. John M'Isaac, Campbelton.
7. Hugh Ferguson, Glasgow.

Greek Side.

1. Wm. Ramsay, Perthshire.
2. James Robertson, Paisley.
3. John Taylor, Argyllshire.
4. Wm. Wingate, Glasgow.
5. Quintin Stewart, Maybole.
6. Alexander Moodie, Paisley.
7. Malcolm Ellis, Saltcoats.

For Excelling in the Weekly Exercises in Greek Verse, throughout the Session, to

1. William Ford, England.
2. William Govan, Dumbarton.
3. Allan King, Govan.

In Greek Prose, to

John Wilson, Glasgow.

Junior Class—Vacation Exercises.

1. Translation into English Verse of some Odes of Anacreon, and War Songs of Tyrtæus, to

Malcolm Ellis, Saltcoats.

2. Translation into English Prose of the First Book of Homer's Iliad, to

James Robertson, Paisley.

3. Translations of Lucian's Dialogues of the Dead, to

Archibald Campbell, Jura (Glasgow).

For Eminent Talent, Scholarship, Diligence, and Conduct, throughout the Session ;

Provectiores.

1. Jonathan Anderson, Paisley.
2. John Tennent, Glasgow.
3. John Stewart, Paisley.
4. Edward Gordon, Jamaica.
5. Henry Provand, Glasgow.
6. Andrew Kerr, Kerrsland, Dalry.
7. John M'Nab, Irvine.
8. Gideon Colquhoun, Stirling.
9. James Heron, Kilwinning.
10. Samuel Tomkins, Virginia.
11. George Duncan, Perthshire.
12. William Jamieson, Kilbirnie Place, Ayrshire.
13. David M'Murtrie, Stranraer.

Tyrones.

1. William Robb, Roberton.
2. John Neilson, Paisley.
3. Samuel Cowan, Moffat.
4. Joseph Duncan, Rothesay.
5. Adam Stewart, Laurieston, Glasgow.
6. Alexander Davidson, Calder.
7. Andrew Niel, Dalry.
8. John Macfarlane, Glasgow.
9. Hugh Brown, Beith.
10. William Cooper, Ballindalloch, Stirlingshire.
11. David Ralston, Old Monkland.
12. James Orr, Dalry.
13. Alexander M'Glashan, Millburn ; and
    Thomas Burns, Cambusnethan.

Prizes in the HUMANITY CLASS—

I. For the best Latin Verses, written during the Vacation, to

James M'Farlane.

Written during the Session, to

Henry J. Provand, Glasgow.

II. For the best Essay in Latin Prose, written during the Vacation, to

James Robertson, Paisley.

Written during the Session, to.
John Muir, Glasgow.
William Lamond, Glasgow.

III. For the best Translation of the Aulularia of Plautus, to
William M'Donald, Glasgow.
John D. Campbell, Roseneath.

IV. For the best Essay on the Origin of the Political Parties in Rome, to

James M'Farlane.

V. For the best Poetical Translation of a Satire of Horace, to
Jamieson Willis, Stirling.

VI. For the best Poetical Translation of Ovid's Epistle from Hermione to Orestes, to

James Robertson, Paisley.

VII. For the best Alteration of an Epistle of Ovid into Hexameters, to

William MacDonald, Glasgow.

VIII. For the best Translation of English into Latin Prose, to

James Burns, Brechin.

IX. For the best Translation of the 46th Psalm into Latin Verse, to

Samuel Cowan, Moffat.

X. For the best Public Theme, to

Gideon Colquhoun, Stirling.

XI. For Excelling in the Weekly Exercises, to
1st Division. Quintin Stewart, Maybole.
William Wingate, Glasgow.
John Bogle,   ,,

2nd Division. John Tennent, Glasgow.
William Cunningham, North Berwick.

XII. For excelling at the Blackstone Examination, to

COMPETITORS. {William Wingate, Glasgow.
{John Bogle,   ,,

Non-Competitors.
{
James Graham, Glasgow.
James Sym, ,,
William Cooper, Ballindalloch.
William M'Intyre, Argyllshire.
}

For Exemplary Eminence throughout the Session, to

I.—1. James Robertson, Paisley.
2. William Wingate, Glasgow.
3. James Colquhoun, Stirling.
4. Alexander M. Bell, Paisley.
5. Alexander Moody, ,,
6. James Graham, Glasgow.
7. William M'Donald, ,,

II.—1. William Ramsay, Perthshire.
2. Quintin Stewart, Maybole.
3. Jonathan Anderson, Paisley.
4. David M'Murtrie, Stranraer.
5. William Baird, Glasgow.
6. John M'Nab, Irvine.

III.—1. Andrew Neil, Dalry.
2. William Cunningham, North Berwick.
3. Andrew Kerr, Kerrsland, Dalry.
4. Edward Gordon, Jamaica.
5. Samuel Tomkins, America.
6. James Orr, Dalry.
7. Joseph Duncan, Rothsay.

IV.—1. John Tennent, Glasgow.
2. John Stewart, Paisley.
3. Gideon Colquhoun, Stirling.
4. Henry J. Provand, Glasgow.
5. John Pollock, Paisley.
6. William R. Cameron, Glasgow.
7. William Lamond, ,,
8. James Sym, ,,
9. Alexander Thomson, ,,

GLASGOW COLLEGE, 30TH APRIL, 1825.

This day, the Annual Distribution of Prizes was made in the Common Hall, by the Principal and Professors, in presence of a numerous meeting of the University, and of many Reverend and respectable Gentlemen of this City and neighbourhood.

A SILVER MEDAL.

IN THEOLOGY.

For the best Essay on the rapid Propagation of Christianity, considered as a proof of its Divine origin, was adjudged to
William Park, A.M., Hutchesontown, Glasgow.

On Mr. COULTER'S DONATION.

I. For the best Sermon on Matthew, chap. 6. v. 33, to
William Park, A.M., Hutchesontown, Glasgow.

II. For the best Account of the Experiments which have been made respecting Friction, to
William Park, A.M., Hutchesontown, Glasgow.

III. For the best Translation of the Phœdon of Plato, to
Henry Green, A.M., Kent.

On Mr. WATT'S DONATION.

For the best Essay on the Theory of the Common Balance, to
James F. W. Johnston, Kilmarnock.

The GARTMORE GOLD MEDAL.

For the best Essay on the Policy of Repealing the Laws restraining the Emigration of Artificers, and the carrying abroad of Machinery, to
James Julius Wood, A.M., Northumberland.

Mr. JEFFREY'S GOLD MEDAL.

For the best Specimen of Elocution, by Students in the Humanity Class, to
Thomas Mackay.

Two Prizes given by the JURISDICTIO ORDINARIA, for the best Latin Orations, in the Common Hall, to
James Macfarlane, A.M., Glasgow.
Robert M'Corkle, A.M.,   „

The Prizes of the DIVINITY CLASS were adjudged—

I.

For the best Specimen of Public Reading, to
James Young, Kilbride.

II.

1. For the best Written Account of the Lectures of the First Course, executed during the Summer, to
Matthew Kirkland, Carmunnock.

2. For a voluntary Essay "On the Necessity and Evidence of a Divine Revelation," to
John Bryden, Ayr.

III.

For the best Essay executed during the Session "On Geological objections to the Mosaic Account of the Creation," to
Duncan Macdougal, A.M., Barony, Glasgow.

IV.

For Eminence in the Exercises of the Students in the second year, to
Matthew Kirkland, Carmunnock.
Alexander Scott, A.M., Greenock.
John Simpson, Glasgow.

V.

For Eminence in the Exercises of the Students of the first year, to
William Park, A.M., Hutchesontown, Glasgow.
David Thorburn, Leith.
Robert Wilson, Glasgow.
Geddes M. Scott, A.M , London.

VI.

For the best Essays "On the Mosaic Institutions," written by Students of the first year, to
David Thorburn, Leith.
William Park, A.M., Hutchesontown, Glasgow.} Both equal.

SENIOR HEBREW CLASS.

For the best Critical Analysis of the 45th Psalm, the Prize was adjudged to

Geddes Scott, London.

JUNIOR HEBREW CLASS.

For close attention and distinguished proficiency, Prizes were adjudged to

1. Wm. Park, A.M., Hutchesontown, Glasgow.
2. Robert Wilson, Glasgow.

For the best Exemplification of the Hebrew Verb, to

John Greig, London.

On the Exemplification of the Persian Verb, two exercises of very high and equal merit were given in, and a Prize adjudged to each, viz., to

John Greig, London, and
Robert Neill, Denovan, Stirlingshire.

Prizes in the CHURCH HISTORY CLASS were adjudged, for the best Essay on the Mosaic Account of the Deluge,

1. *To the Senior Students.*

Duncan Macdougal, Lanarkshire.

2. *To the Junior Students.*

William Park, A.M., Hutchesontown, Glasgow.
John Greig, London.

LAW.

Two Prizes for excelling in the Daily Examinations proposed to those Students of SCOTTISH LAW who chose to be examined, were adjudged to

John Park, Newbank, near Glasgow.
Charles Baird, Canal Basin, near Glasgow.

R

The Prize in the ANATOMY CLASS,
For the best Essay on the Anatomy of the Brain and Doctrine of
Phrenology, adjudged to

A. G. Campbell Stirling, A.M

N.B. The subject of the Prize Essay in the Anatomy Class for
next Session is, Do the red veins absorb?

CHEMISTRY.

For acquitting himself best during the public examinations
throughout the Session, to

Peter Maccallum, Argyllshire.

For the best Essay on Water, to

Andrew Steel, London.

The Prizes of the MATHEMATICAL CLASSES, for general eminence and proficiency during the Session, were adjudged—

SENIOR CLASS, to

James Playfair, Glasgow.
William Rennie, A.M., Garnethill, Glasgow.
Robert Henderson, Stirling.
Robert Cuthbertson, Paisley.
Robert Elder, Campbelton.

JUNIOR CLASS, to

Seniores.

James Gray, Ayr.
Archibald Mylne, Glasgow.
Matthew Barclay, Paisley.
James Symington,   ,,
William Thorburn, Blantyre.

Juniores.

John Thomson, Stirling.
Alan King, Govan.
William Hamilton, Kilmarnock.
Francis Menteath, Edinburgh.

The Prizes of the NATURAL PHILOSOPHY CLASS, for propriety of conduct, exemplary diligence, and eminent ability, displayed not only in the public examinations, but also in numerous Exercises involving the application of the principles of Mechanical Science, prescribed chiefly by the Professor, were adjudged to

James Playfair, A.M., Dalmarnock.
James Sprent, A.M., Manchester.
Henry Everett, Hampshire.
William Rennie, A.M., Garnethill, Glasgow.
William M. James, A.M., Glamorganshire.
Robert Henderson, A.M., Stirling.
Robert Elder, A.M., Campbeltown.
Robert Cuthbertson, Paisley.
James Chrystal, A.M., Glasgow.
John Russell, A.M., Errol.

The Prizes in the ETHIC CLASS, for superior merit in the Composition of the Essays weekly presented to the Students, or written on subjects chosen by themselves ; and for distinguished eminence in the various duties and business of the Class, were adjudged—

In the *Senior Division*, to

1. Matthew Barclay, Paisley.
2. John Roxburgh, Glasgow.
3. John C. Bruce, A.B., Newcastle.
4. John M'Isaac, Campbelton.
5. Weatherly Phipson, Birmingham.

In the *Junior Division*, to

1. William Ainsworth, Preston, Lancashire.
2. Allan King, Govan.
3. Hugh Ferguson, Glasgow.
4. Alex. Ure,   ,,

For superior merit in Poetical Compositions, a Prize was adjudged by the Class to

John Williams Hill, Pembrokeshire.

For the best Translation of the Table of Cebes, a Prize was adjudged to

Henry Green, A.M., Kent.

For the best Essay on the origin and nature of the emotions
excited by the Sublime, to

John Roxburgh, Glasgow.

———

The Prizes given in the LOGIC CLASS are of two kinds :—

I. For general eminence and superiority in the customary
exercises and examinations of the Class during the whole Session
—and II. For the best Essays on certain prescribed subjects,
executed either during the Summer vacation or during the
Christmas holidays of the present Session.

I.

Seniores.

1. George Samuel Evans, London.
2. James Robertson, Paisley.
3. Hugh Shield, Newcastle-upon-Tyne.
4. Alfred Day, Bristol.
5. John Ainslie, Edinburgh.
6. Archibald Mylne, Glasgow.
7. { Cathcart Kay, Daily, Ayrshire.
     { John Read, London.
8. Joseph Duncan, Rothesay.
9. Robert Archibald, Clackmananshire.
10. Archibald M'Kerrell, Paisley.
11. John Neilson,   ,,

Juniores.

1. Jonathan Blackburn, Liverpool.
2. George F. Barbour, Glasgow.
3. Robert M. Craig, Edinburgh.
4. James Blythe, Northumberland.
5. James Bruce Jardine, Glasgow.
6. Alexander Moodie, Paisley.
7. Robert Baird, Glasgow.
8. Henry M. Bowles, Yarmouth.
9. Alexander M. Bell, Paisley.
10. John Muir, Kilmarnock.
11. John Bogle, Glasgow.
12. Malcolm J. Ellis, Ayrshire.

II.

For Essays on prescribed subjects, composed during the Summer Vacation, prizes have been adjudged—

1st, For the best Essay on the Internal sense of Novelty, to
John Roxburgh, Glasgow.

2nd, For the best Analysis of the Faculty of Imagination, to
William Ainsworth, Lancashire.

Two Prizes have also been adjudged for Essays composed during the Christmas holidays by Students attending the Logic Class during this Session, the one in Prose, the other in Verse.

For the best Essay, in Prose, on the Horatian maxim, *Doctrina sed vim promovet insitam*, to
Hugh Shield, Newcastle-upon Tyne.

For the best Poem on the Liberation of Greece, to
James Robertson, Paisley.

And lastly, the Prize annually given for the best abstract, written down from memory, of a Sermon preached in the College Chapel towards the close of the Session, was adjudged to
Hugh Shield, Newcastle-upon-Tyne.

Prizes of the GREEK CLASS.

Private—Exercises written during Vacation.

1. Essay on the principles and character of the Treatise of Longinus on the Sublime,
Matthew Barclay, Paisley.

2. Essay on the Poetical merits of Aristophanes, as deducible from a perusal of his Knights,
James Macfarlane, Glasgow.

3. Translation into Tragic Iambic Trimeters of 23 lines from Shakespeare's Timon of Athens,
Matthew Barclay, Paisley.

WRITTEN DURING SESSION.

1. Translation into English Verse of the 14th Olympic Ode of Pindar,
John Gemmel, Port-Glasgow.

2. Essay on the object of the Dionysian Criticism, and how far it may be useful to Modern Writers,

Henry Green, England.

Public—Senior—Exercises written during Vacation.

1. Translation into Tragic Iambic Trimeters of 33 lines from the Tempest of Shakespeare,

William Ramsay, Banff,. Perthshire.

2. Translation of the Medea of Euripides,

James Robertson, Paisley.

3. Translation of the 6th book of Herodotus,

Allan King, Govan.

4. Translation of v. 415 to v. 620 of the Plutus of Aristophanes,

Allan King, Govan.

WRITTEN DURING SESSION.

1. Translation into Homeric Hexameters of Verses on the Tombs of Platæa,

Robert Paisley, Glasgow.

2. For excelling at the Black Stone Examination :—

COMPETITORS.
- 1. George Evans, England.
- 2. Alexander Bell, Paisley.
- 3. Alexander Moody, Paisley, and
- 4. John Ainslie, Edinburgh.

NON-COMPETITORS.
- 1. John Muir, *major*, Kilmarnock.
- 2. William Bell M'Donald, Glasgow.
- 3. Geo. Lowther Hamilton,   ,,
- 4. D. Mackintosh, Dumbartonshire.

3. For general eminence of Conduct, Scholarship, and Talent, throughout the Session—

LOGIC SIDE.

1. Alexander Bell, Paisley.
2. James Robertson, ,,
3. Hugh Shield, Newcastle-upon-Tyne.
4. John Muir, *major*, Kilmarnock.
5. John M'Nab, Irvine.
6. William Bell Macdonald, Glasgow, and
   William Lambert, Neilston.
7. John Ainslie, Edinburgh.

GREEK SIDE.

1. Robert Paisley, Glasgow.
2. John Tennent,　　,,
3. John Stewart,　　　,,
4. James Hill, Pembrokeshire.
5. Robert Whyte, Kilmarnock.
6. Henry Provand, Edinburgh, and
   Mungo Parker, Kilmarnock.
7. Quintin Stewart, Maybole.

For excelling in the Weekly Exercises in Greek Versification, prescribed throughout the Session.

1. William Ramsay, Banff, Perthshire.
2. Robert Paisley, Glasgow.
3. John Tennent,　　,,

For excelling in the Prose Exercises,

1. John Dewhurst, Santa Cruz, and
   James Gardiner, Bothwell.

Public—Junior.

Exercises written during Vacation.

Translation of Extracts from Homer and Herodotus,
    John Tennent, Glasgow.

Translation into English Verse of Extracts from Tyrtæus and Anacreon,
    Henry Provand, Edinburgh.

Translation of Extracts from the Dialogues of Lucian,
    William Cooper, Ballindalloch, Stirlingshire.

For general eminence of conduct, scholarship, and Talent through the Session—

PROVECTIORES.

1. John Macfarlane, *major*, Glasgow.
2. James Salmond, Irvine.
3. Robert Brown, Maryport.
4. Alexander Davidson, Cadder.
5. David Ralston, Tollcross.
6. William Baird, Paisley.

7. Hugh Brown, Beith.
8. Archibald Sconce, Stirling.
9. James Barnhill, Glasgow.
10. Alex. Willison Anderson, Campbelton, and
    James Barclay, Glasgow.
11. Andrew Dunlop,   ,,
12. William Smith, *minor*, Glasgow.

TYRONES.

1. John Aitken Dunlop, *minor*, Beith.
2. John Robertson, Glasgow.
3. John Martin, Paisley.
4. Archibald Buchanan, East Kilpatrick.
5. John Gilmour, Stewarton.
6. George Beveridge,   ,,
7. George Moodie, Paisley.
8. Andrew Robertson, Lochhead, Lochwinnoch.
9. James Swan, Neilston.
10. Andrew Ramsay, Shettleston, Glasgow.
11. John Dunlop, *major*, East Kilpatrick.
12. John Whiteford, Kilburnie.

Prizes in the HUMANITY CLASS.

I. For the best Original Latin Verses, written during the Session, to

      1st Division—Joseph Reade, Bristol.
      2nd   ,,   —John Dunlop, East Kilpatrick.

II. For the best Essay in Latin Prose, written during the Vacation, to

      James Robertson, Paisley.

Written during the Session, to

      1st Division—Quintin Stewart, Maybole.
      2nd   ,,   —William Gibb, Stirling.

III. For the best Translation of Cicero pro Archia, to
      Hugh Brown, Beith.

IV. For the best Essay on the Life and Writings of Tacitus, to
      William Logie, Glasgow.

V. For the best Essay on the Roman Dictatorship, to
William Lamond, Glasgow.

VI. For the best Translation into English Verse of an Ode of Horace, to
Hugh Brown, Beith.

VII. For the best Translation into English Verse of a passage of Ovid's Metamorphoses, to
John Dunlop, East Kilpatrick.
William M'Call, Lancashire.

VIII. For the best Translation into English Verse of an Epistle of Ovid, to
John Tennent, Glasgow.

IX. For the best Voluntary Exercise, to
John Tennent, Glasgow.

X. For the best Public Theme, to
Archibald Sconce, Stirling.

XI. For Excelling in the Weekly Exercises, to

1st Division—1. John Tennent, Glasgow.
2. { Gideon Colquhoun, Stirling. / Quintin Stewart, Maybole. } equal. / Robert Paisley, Glasgow.

2nd Division—William Wilson, Rutherglen.
Archibald Buchanan, East Kilpatrick.

XII. For excelling at the Black Stone Examination, to

COMPETITORS. { William Ramsay, Perthshire. / John Stewart, Glasgow. / John Tennent, „ / William Nimmo, „

NON-COMPETITORS. { Gideon Colquhoun, Stirling. / Robert Paisley, Glasgow. / Quintin Stewart, Maybole.

XIII. The Second Prize for Elocution, to
William Cameron, Glasgow.

XIV. For Exemplary Eminence throughout the Session,

I.—1. John Tennent, Glasgow.
  2. Robert Paisley,   ,,
  3. John Stewart,   ,,
  4. Gideon Colquhoun, Stirling.
  5. Quintin Stewart, Maybole.
  6. William Cameron, Glasgow.
  7. Henry J. Provand, Edinburgh.

II.—1. Augustus Yearwood, Demerary.
  2. John Dewhurst, St. Croix.
  3. Basil Bell, Cockburnspath.
  4. James Gardiner, Bothwell.
  5. James Hill, Pembrokeshire.
  6. William Dewhurst, St. Croix.

III.—1. George Beveridge, Stewarton.
  2. John Gilmour,   ,,
  3. Archibald Buchanan, East Kilpatrick.
  4 John A. Dunlop, Beith, Ayrshire.
  5. John Brown, Stewarton.
  6. William Wilson, Rutherglen.

IV.—1. John M'Farlane, Glasgow.
  2. William Baird, Paisley.
  3. Archibald Sconce, Stirling.
  4. James Barnhill, Glasgow.
  5. James Barclay,   ,,
  6. John Dunlop, East Kilpatrick.
  7. William Gibb, Stirling.
  8. William Lawrie, Glasgow.
  9. Archibald Currie,   ,,

GLASGOW COLLEGE, 1st MAY, 1826

ANNUAL PRIZES.

On the 1st of May, 1826, the Annual Distribution of Prizes was made in the Common Hall, by the Principal and Professors, in presence of a numerous meeting of the University, and of many Reverend and respectable Gentlemen of the City and neighbourhood

---

A Silver Medal.

I.—In Theology.

For the best Essay on the Argument for the Truth of Christianity, derived from the beneficial effects which its promulgation has produced on the character and happiness of mankind, was adjudged to

William Park, A.M., Hutchesontown, Glasgow.

II.—In Philosophy.

For the best Essay on the Question whether the Hypothesis of Franklin, or that of Du Faye, on Electricity is the most probable, to

James Finlay Weir Johnston, Kilmarnock.

On Mr. Coulter's Donation.

I. For the best Lecture on Luke, Chap. xi. v. 5-13, to
William Park, A.M., Hutchesontown, Glasgow.

II. For the best account of the nature and injurious effects of the four classes of Idols or Prejudices enumerated in the first book of Bacon's Novum Organum, to
James R. Miles.

III. For the best Translation of the Treatise generally ascribed to Tacitus, and entitled De Oratoribus, sive de causis corruptæ eloquentiæ Dialogus, to
Allan King, Govan, and
James Robertson, Paisley.

On Mr. Watt's Donation.

For the best Essay on the Theory and practice of Tanning, to
William Park, A.M., Hutchesontown, Glasgow.

Mr. Jeffrey's Gold Medal.

For the best Specimen of Elocution, by Students in the Greek
Class, to

William Norval, Glasgow.

Two Prizes given by the Jurisdictio Ordinaria, for the best
Latin Orations in the Common Hall, to

Allan King, A.M., Govan.
Hugh Ferguson, A.M., Glasgow.

The Prizes of the Divinity Class were adjudged to

Students of the 1st Year.

For General Eminence in the Exercises of the Class, to

. Alexander Munro, Paisley.
James Graham Campbell, Petershill, Glasgow.
James Macfarlane, A.M., Glasgow.

For the best Essay on the kindness and compassion of the
Mosaic Law, to

John Ferguson, Denny, Stirlingshire

For the best Essay on the question " Whether a public provision
for the poor was enjoined by the Law of Moses, " to

William Jackson, A.M., Mearns.

To Students of the Second Year.

For general Eminence in the Exercises of the Class, to

William Park, A.M., Hutchesontown, Glasgow.
Robert Wilson, A.M., Glasgow.

For the best Statement of Observations Preliminary to the consideration of the Atonement and Mediation of Christ, to

Peter Hay Keith, Glasgow.

For the best account of the Lectures of the preceding Session,
of the Evidences for Divine Revelation, to

William Park, A.M., Hutchesontown, Glasgow.

For the best Essay on the Prophecies respecting the Jewish
People, to

James Fairlie, A.M., Fenwick, Ayrshire.

For the best Essay on the Character of Christ, to
William Park, A.M., Hutchesontown, Glasgow.

For the best Specimens of Public Reading, to
John Cowan, A.M., Old Monkland.
Hugh Moore, A.M., Ireland.
James Clowe, A.M., Downe.

Senior HEBREW CLASS.

I. For the best Critical Analysis of the 6th Chap. of Isaiah, to
John Gemmel, A.M., Port-Glasgow.

II. For two Essays of great and equal merit on the Hebrew Verb, to
John Gemmell, A.M., Port-Glasgow, and
William Park, A.M., Hutchesontown, Glasgow.

Junior HEBREW CLASS.

I. For distinguished proficiency in the business of the Class, to
1. Robert M'Corkle, Glasgow.
2. John Brown, Galston, Ayrshire.

II. For the best Exemplification of the Paradigma of the Hebrew Verb, to
James Clason, Dunblane.

III. For the Exemplification of the Persian Verb, to
1. James Clason, Dunblane.
2. John Ferguson, Ayr.

Prizes in the CHURCH HISTORY CLASS were adjudged, for the best Account of the Christian Fathers of the first Century.

1 *To the Senior Students.*

Walter Taylor, A.M., Cromarty.

2. *To the Junior Students.*

James Robison, Leddrie Green, Strathblane.
Robert Neill, Crofthead, Neilston.

Law.

Two Prizes for excelling in the Daily Examination proposed to those Students of Scottish Law who chose to be examined, were adjudged to

John Jamieson, Glasgow.
Peter Ferrie,   ,,

The Prize in the Anatomy Class,

For the best Essay on the question, "Do the Red Veins Absorb?" was adjudged to

William Craig, Glasgow.

A Prize was given to
Campbell Stirling, Campsie,
for another Essay on the same subject, and of nearly equal merit.

The Prizes in the Theory and Practice of Medicine Classes for the greatest number of the best Exercises given in during the Session, were adjudged to

1. John Cowan, Ireland.
2. Alex. White, Girvan.

The Prize for the best Exercise on Digestion was adjudged to
John Thomson, Hamilton.

Two Prizes for the two best Exercises on Dysentery were adjudged to

1. John Cowan, Ireland.
2. James Bankier, Gorbals.

Prizes in the Chemistry Class.

For acquitting himself best during the Public Examinations throughout the Session, to
John Thomson, Hamilton.

For the best Essay on the Theory of Vapour, to
John Stevenson, Cadder.

The Prizes of the MATHEMATICAL CLASSES, for general eminence and proficiency during the Session, were adjudged—

SENIOR CLASS, to

William Stevenson, Lochwinnoch.
James Gray, Ayr.
John Thomson, Stirling.
Alexander Ure, Glasgow.

JUNIOR CLASS, to

Seniores.

William Ramsay, Perthshire.
Allan M'Nab, Glasgow.
John M'Nab, Irvine.
James Heron, Kilwinning.
John Reid, London.
Allan Henderson, Kinross shire.

Juniores.

James Salmond, Irvine.
William Cooper, Stirlingshire.
William Baird, Fintry.
James Rankine, Falkirk.

The Prizes of the NATURAL PHILOSOPHY CLASS, for propriety of conduct, exemplary diligence, and eminent ability, displayed not only in numerous Exercises involving the application of the principles of Mechanical Science, prescribed chiefly by the Professor, were adjudged to

William Wood, Glasgow.
Hugh Ferguson, A.M , Glasgow.
John Robson, A.M., Cupar-Fife.
William Stevenson, A M., Lochwinnoch.
John Macnaughton, A.M., Greenock.
Matthew Barclay, Paisley.
James Gray, Ayr.
John Thomson, Stirling.

The Prizes in the ETHIC CLASS, for general eminence in the business of the Class, and for excellence in the Composition of the Exercises weekly prescribed to the Students, or written on subjects chosen by themselves, were adjudged to

Seniores.

1. James Robertson, Paisley.
2. James Keyden, Dumfries-shire.
3. John R. Miles, Glasgow.
4. James Blair, Glasgow.
5. Cathcart Kaye, Daily, Ayrshire.

Juniores.

1. Jonathan Mercer Blackburn, Liverpool.
2. Robert Craig, Edinburgh.
3. James Blythe, Northumberland.
4. Robert Baird, Canal Basin, Glasgow.
5. Alexander Moody,   ,,

A Prize for superior merit in Poetical Composition was
adjudged to

James Robertson, Paisley.

———

The Prizes in the LOGIC CLASS for this Session, were adjudged
as follows :—

I. For general eminence and superiority in the various Exercises
and Examinations of the Class throughout the Session, to

Seniores.

1. Richard Alliott, Nottingham.
2. William Acworth, Chatham, Kent.
3. Jonathan Anderson, Paisley.
4. David Thomas, Port of Monteath, Perthshire.
5. Robert Paisley, Glasgow.
6. John Esdaile, London.
7. George Moody, Paisley.
8. James Jarvie, Glasgow.
9. John Taylor, *major*, Dunoon, Argyleshire.
10. Thomas Myles, Perth.

Juniores.

1. John Tennent, Glasgow.
2. William Lamond, ,,
3. Henry J. Provand, Edinburgh.
4. James Macbeth, Dalrymple, Ayrshire.

5. James Barnhill, Glasgow.
6. Dugald B. Stark, ,,
7. William Nimmo, ⎱ equal ⎰ Glasgow.
   John Taylor, jun. ⎰   ⎱ Renfrewshire.
8. Gideon Colquhoun, Stirling.
9. Samuel M. Greer, Londonderry, Ireland.
10. Samuel Horsley, Dundee.
11. Francis Garden, Glasgow.
12. Alexander W. Anderson, Campbeltown.

II. For Essays on the following subjects :—

1. For the best Essay on Intuitive Evidence (executed during the summer vacation), to
Jonathan Blackburn, Liverpool.

2. For the best Critical Analysis of Cicero's Second Oration against Anthony, pointing out the presence and influence of the Laws of Association, primary or secondary, as suggesting or modifying the train of argument or illustration (executed duirng the Christmas holidays), to
Richard Alliott, Nottingham.

3. For the best Essay showing by examples from the Poets and Orators that what we call Fancy, consists in a peculiar aptitude to associate, and a peculiar power of associating objects and ideas according to the relation of resemblance or analogy (also composed during the Christmas holidays), to
William Lamond, Glasgow.

4. For the most Accurate Report (written down wholly from memory) of a Sermon preached in the College Chapel in the course of the Session, to
Hugh Brown, Beith, Ayrshire.

————

Prizes in the GREEK CLASS.

I.

Private—VACATION EXERCISES.

Essay on the characteristic qualities and merits of Pindar,
Robert M'Corkle, Glasgow.

EXERCISES DURING THE SESSION.

1. Essay on the Aristotelian Definition of Tragedy,
Richard Alliott, Nottingham.

2. Translation into English Verse from "The Frogs" of
Aristophanes,
John Williams Hill, South Wales.

II.

Public, Senior—VACATION EXERCISES.

1. Translation into Greek Iambic and Anapæstic verse from the
" Comus " of Milton,
Robert Paisley, Glasgow.

2. Translation into English Verse of the " Prometheus Bound "
of Æschylus,
John Tennent, Glasgow.

3. Translation into English Prose of the Ninth Book of
Herodotus,
James Robertson, Paisley.

4. Translation into English Prose of the Corcyræn and
Corinthian Speeches in the First Book of Thucydides,
James Gardiner, Bothwell.

EXERCISES DURING SESSION.

Translation into Greek Hexameters of the Conclusion of "Lara,"
Canto I.
John Tennent, Glasgow.

For eminence in Scholarship, Conduct, and General Ability,
throughout the Session,

LOGIC SIDE.

1. Robert Paisley, Glasgow.
2. John Tennent,   ,,
3. John Stewart,   ,,
4. John Taylor, Dunoon, Argyllshire.
5. Richard Alliott, Nottingham.
6. James Barnhill, Glasgow.

GREEK SIDE.

1. Alexander Thomson, Glasgow.
2. James Gardiner, Bothwell.
3. John M'Farlane, *major*, Glasgow.
4. Alexander Brown, Campsie.
5. George Jamieson, Kincardine.
6. Alexander Davidson, Cadder.

For eminence in the Weekly Exercises prescribed during Session.

VERSE.

1. Robert Paisley, Glasgow.
2. John Tennent,   ,,
3. John Stewart,   ,,
4. John Taylor, Dunoon, Argyllshire.

PROSE.

1. Alex. Anderson, Campbeltown, and
   Archibald Buchanan, East Kilpatrick.
2. George Morton, Galston, Ayrshire.

For excelling at the Black-stone examination,

COMPETITORS.
{ 1. Robert Paisley, Glasgow.
{ 2. John Tennent,   ,,
{ 3. Samuel Greer, Londonderry.

NON-COMPETITORS.
{ 1. Richard Alliott, Nottingham.
{ 2. Basil Bell, Cockburn's-path, Berw.
{ 3. John Stewart, Glasgow.

III.

Public, Junior—VACATION EXERCISES.

1. Translation into Grammatical Greek of the Book of Exercises,
   John Aiken Dunlop, *minor*, Beith, Ayrshire.

2. Translation into English Verse of Extracts from Anacreon and Homer,
   Robert Walker, East Kilpatrick.

3. Translation into English Prose of Lucian's "Sale of Lives,"
   John Macfarlane, *major*, Glasgow.

PROVECTIORES.

For eminence in Scholarship, Conduct, and General Ability, throughout the Session,

1. Andrew Tennent, Glasgow.
2. John M'Kinlay,   ,,
3. John Aiken Dunlop, *minor*, Beith, Ayrshire.
4. George Beveridge, Stewarton,   ,,
5. John Dunlop, *major*, East Kilpatrick.
6. John Gilmour, Stewarton, Ayrshire.
7. Colin Young, Port-Glasgow.
8. Andrew Parker, Ayr.
9. William Moore, ,,
10. William Ritchie, ,,

For eminence in Voluntary Exercises, weekly performed,

1. Andrew Tennent, Glasgow.
2. John M'Kinlay,   ,,
3. Colin Young, Port-Glasgow, and
   John Aiken Dunlop, *minor*, Beith, Ayrshire.

TYRONES.

For eminence in Scholarship, Conduct, and General Ability, throughout the Session,

1. James Reid, Nether-Cambushinnie, Dunblane.
2. Robert Symington, Carmichael, Lanark.
3. Robert Erskine Macmurdo, Edinburgh.
4. John Macdonald, *major*, Dalbeith, Lanark.
5. Francis Macgregor, Callander, Perthshire.
6. Archibald MacGillvray, Greenock.
7. George Gilfillan, Comrie, Perthshire.
8. Alexander Fleck, Glasgow.
9. Peter Smith, Cowal, Argyll.
10. John Weir.   ,,   ,,

Second Prize for Recitation,

James Hume, London.

Prizes in the HUMANITY CLASS.

I. For the best Original Latin Verses, written during the Vacation, to

James D. Hill, South Wales.

Written during the Session, to

1st Division—James Barclay, Glasgow.
            John Dunlop, East Kilpatrick.
2nd   „   —William Galloway, Glasgow.

II. For the best Exercise in Latin Prose, written during the Vacation, to

William Gibb, Stirling.

Written during the Session, to

1st Division—Matthew King, Rothsay.
2nd   „   —William Reid, West Kincardine.
            Andrew Tennent, Glasgow.

III. For a Translation of Cicero's 1st Tusculan Question, to

John Stenhouse, Glasgow.
Robert Walker, East Kilpatrick.

IV. For a Translation into English Verse of Virgil's Episode of "Nisus and Euryalus," to

John Tennent, Glasgow.

V. For the best Exercise on the Tribunician Power, to

John M'Farlane, Glasgow.

VI. For the best Exercise on the arrangement of words in a Latin Sentence, to

John Tennent, Glasgow.

VII. For the best Translation into English Verse of the "Fasti ' of Ovid, Book I. from line 719 to line 852, to

Thomas Keir, Glasgow.

VIII. For the best Translation into English Verse of an Ode of Horace, to

Adam Roxburgh, Kilmaurs.

IX. For the best Tabular arrangement of the different Classes of Latin Verbs, to

John M'Kinlay, Glasgow.

X. For the best Voluntary Exercise, to

John M'Farlane, Glasgow.

XI. For the best Public Theme, to
William Reid, West Kincardine.

XII. For excelling in the Weekly Exercises, to

1ST DIVISION.
{ William Boyd, Largs.
{ Alexander Thomson, Glasgow.
{ William Gibb, Stirling.

2ND DIVISION.
{ Andrew Tennent, Glasgow.
{ John M'Kinlay,   ,,

XIII. For excelling in the Examination on Roman Antiquities,
to
Andrew Parker, Ayr.

XIV. For excelling at the Black Stone Examination, to
COMPETITOR,   John Inglis, Edinburgh.

NON-
COMPETITORS,
{ John M'Farlane, Glasgow.
{ Alexander Brown, Campsie.
{ William Boyd, Largs.
{ James Barclay, Glasgow.
{ Robert Ranken, Paisley.

XV. For Exemplary Eminence through the Session, to

I.—1. John M'Farlane, Glasgow.
2 Alexander Thomson, ,,
3. William Gibb, Stirling.
4. David Munro, Carron.
5. William Boyd, Largs.
6. James Barclay, Glasgow.
7. { Andrew Chrystal,   ,,   } equal.
   { William Dunn, Doune. }

II.—1. Andrew Parker, Ayr.
2. William Moore, ,,
3. John Inglis, Edinburgh.
4. Alexander Brown, Campsie.
5. Adam Roxburgh, Kilmaurs.
6. John Baillie, Jerviswood.

III —1. Ronald Young, Kelvin Dock.
2. Francis M'Gregor, Callender.
3. Walter M'Lay, East Kilpatrick.
4. Robert Ranken, Paisley.

5. Archibald Bannatyne, Rothsay.
6. { John Campbell, Balquhidder. } equal.
{ William Maxwell, Thornhill. }

IV.—1. Andrew Tennent, Glasgow.
2. John M'Kinlay,   „
3. William Reid, Kincardine.
4. Hugh Smith, Glasgow.
5. George Paterson, Middlefrew.
6. David M'Lean, Paisley.
7. William Watt, Glasgow.
8. Joseph Lamond, East Kilpatrick.
9. William Lyall, Paisley.

GLASGOW COLLEGE, 1st MAY, 1827.

This day, the Annual Distribution of Prizes was made, in the Common Hall, by the Lord Rector, Principal and Professors, in presence of a numerous meeting of the University, and of many Reverend and respectable Gentlemen of the City and neighbourhood.

A SILVER MEDAL.
IN THEOLOGY.

For the best Essay on the corroborations afforded to the principal facts of the Mosaic Record, was adjudged to
James Fairlie.

A SILVER MEDAL

For the best account of the Methods which have been suggested for correcting the local attractions of a Ship's Guns, and other Iron, on the Compass, and of the principles on which these Methods depend, to
James Fairlie.

On Mr. COULTER'S Donation.

For the best Sermon on Romans ch. xii., v. 21.—Be not overcome, etc., to
James Lewis, Glasgow.

For the best Essay on the Question, Is the train of thought in the Mind determined wholly by the Laws of Association ; or is it subject in whole or in part to the controuling power of the Will? to

Richard Alliot, Nottingham.

For the best Translation of the 7th Book of Thucydides, to

Alfred Day, B.A., Bristol.

On Mr. WATT's Donation.

For the best Account of the Method of Rectangular Co-ordinates applied to the Composition and Resolution of Mechanical Forces, to

William Park, A.M., Hutchesontown.

The GARTMORE GOLD MEDAL.

For the best Essay on the probable effects of the Introduction of a Metallic Currency into Scotland, to

John Ralston Wood.

Mr. JEFFREY's Gold Medal.

For the best Specimen of Elocution, to

Archd. Currie.

DEGREES IN ARTS

Were announced to have been conferred with the highest honour in, Languages, Logic, and Moral Philosophy, on

Geo. Saml. Evans, A.M., London.
Alfred Day, A.B., Bristol.

With second honours in the same departments,

Wm. Cooper, A.M., Ballindalloch, Stirlingshire.

Two Prizes given by the JURISDICTIO ORDINARIA, for the best Latin Orations in the Common Hall, to

Peter Millar, Stirling.
Samuel Paterson, Wigtonshire.

The Prizes of the DIVINITY CLASS were adjudged to Students of the 1st year,

For eminence in the " Examinations of the Class," to

Matthew Barclay, Paisley.
James Law, Lanark.

1. For the best Essay "On the Nature of Internal Evidence," to

James Lewis, Glasgow.

2. "On the Ignorance of Man, without Revelation, respecting our condition in a future state of being," to

James Lewis, Glasgow.

3. "On the character of Christ, as a proof of his Divine mission," to

John Roxburgh, Glasgow.
John Calder, Barony, Glasgow.

To Students of the 2nd year.

1. For the best Essay " On the Canon of the New Testament," to

William Jackson, A.M., Mearns.

2. "On the Inspiration of the Writings of the New Testament," and "On the Nature and Universal Obligation of the Sabbath," to

Oswald Hunter, Edinburgh.
James Clason, Dunblane.
James Chrystal, A.M., Glasgow.

3. For the best account " Of the Lectures of the preceding Session, on the Evidences for Divine Revelation," to

James Clason, Dunblane.

4. "On Miracles and Prophecy," to

James Macfarlane, A.M., Glasgow.

5. "For the best Specimen of Public Reading," to

James Macfarlane, A.M., Glasgow.

The Prizes of the HEBREW CLASS were adjudged—

SENIOR CLASS.

I. For the best Critical Analysis of part of the 9th ch. of Isaiah, to

    1. Robert M'Corkle, A.M., Glasgow.
    2. James Begg, A.M., New Monkland.

II. For the best Philological Dissertation on the Hebrew words Nephesh and Sheol, to

    Robert M'Corkle, A.M., Glasgow.

———

JUNIOR CLASS, *Old Side.*

For regular attendance, exemplary conduct, and eminent proficiency, to

    James Law, Lanark.

JUNIOR CLASS, *Young Side.*

I. For regular attendance, exemplary conduct, and eminent proficiency, to

    1. John Willison Ferguson, Glasgow.
    2. John Collingwood Bruce, Newcastle.

II. For the best written specimen of the Hebrew verb, to

    1. James Smith, Glasgow.
    2. John Collingwood Bruce, Newcastle.

———

Prizes in the CHURCH HISTORY CLASS were adjudged, for the best Essays on the Origin and Progress of the Reformation, with Reflections on the causes and consequences of that Event.

  1. *To the Students of the Third Year.*

    John Reid, A.M., Perthshire.

  2. *To the Students of the Second Year.*

    Robert Wilson, A.M., Glasgow.
    James Chrystal, A.M.,   ,,

  3. *To the Students of the First Year.*

    James Macfarlane, A.M., Glasgow.

LAW.

Two Prizes for excelling in the Daily Examination proposed to those Students of SCOTTISH LAW who chose to be examined, were adjudged to

William Steel, Glasgow.
Alex. Mitchell,　　,,

NATURAL HISTORY CLASS.

A Prize for the best Essay on the Natural History of the Dog, was adjudged to

Robert Neill, Renfrewshire.

Practice of MEDICINE CLASS.

The Prize for the greatest number of the best voluntary exercises, was adjudged to

Daniel M'Lachlan, Glasgow.

The Prize for the best exercise on Intermittent Fever, was adjudged to

Wm. Shirreff, Glasgow.

The Prize for the best exercise on Cholera Morbus, written during the Christmas Holidays, was adjudged to

Wm. Shirreff, Glasgow.

The first Prize for answering best in the Public Examinations of the Class during the Session was adjudged by the votes of the Class to

Wm. Shirreff, Glasgow.

And the second to

Daniel M'Lachlan, Glasgow.

The Prize for the best exercise on Jaundice, was adjudged to

Jas. M'C. Aitken, Ayrshire.

Prizes in the CHEMISTRY CLASS.

I. For acquitting himself best in the Public Examinations during the Session, to

Thomas Muir, Glasgow.

II. For the best Essay on Respiration, to
           John Taylor, Glasgow.
           Alexander Robb, ,,

The Prizes of the MATHEMATICAL CLASSES for general eminence and proficiency during the Session were adjudged to,

SENIOR CLASS.

James Ewing, Concraig, Crieff.
James Rankin, ⎫ Equal. Falkirk.
John Reid, ⎩ London.
John Boswell, Ayr.

JUNIOR CLASS.

Senior Division.

Richard Alliott, Nottingham.
Peter Morrison, Auchterarder.
Thomas Dymock, Glasgow.
John Reid, Paisley.
Quintin Stewart, Maybole.
John Alexander, Lochwinnoch.

Junior Division.

Robert Baird, Bellfield, Glasgow.
Adam Roxburgh, Kilmaurs.
James Wilson, Cockburnspath, Berwickshire.
James Barnhill, Glasgow.

The Prizes of the NATURAL PHILOSOPHY CLASS for propriety of conduct, exemplary diligence, and eminent ability, displayed not only in the public examinations, but also in numerous exercises involving the application of the principles of Mechanical Science, prescribed chiefly by the Professor, were adjudged to
           James Reid, Glasgow.
           William Gibb, Stirling.
           John Reid, London.
           James M'Gowan, Kincardine, Perthshire.
           Alexander Ure, Glasgow.
           James Heron, A.M., Kilwinning.
           William Moffat, Kirkintilloch.
           John Tudhope, Glasgow.

The Prizes in the ETHIC CLASS, for general eminence in the business of the Class, and for excellence in the Composition of the Exercises weekly prescribed to the Students, or written on Subjects chosen by themselves, were adjudged to

Seniores.

1. Richard Alliott, Nottingham.
2. David Thomas, Port of Monteith.
3. Robert Paisley, Glasgow.
4. James Munro,   ,,
5. James Jarvie,   ,,

Juniores.

1. John Tennent, Glasgow.
2. William Lamond,   ,,
3. James Barnhill,   ,,
4. Dugald B. Stark,   ,,
5. William Nimmo,   ,,

Two Prizes for superior merit of Poetical Exercises during the Session, were adjudged to

Henry J. Provand, Edinburgh.
Dugald D. Stark, Glasgow.

———

The Prizes in the LOGIC CLASS, for this Session, were adjudged as follows :—

I. For general eminence and superiority in the various exercises and examinations of the Class throughout the Session, to

Seniores.

FIRST DIVISION.—1. James Bankes, Saltcoats.
2. John Lamont, Glasgow.
3. William Heron, Greenock.
4. John Davidson, Lanark.

SECOND DIVISION.—1. Archd. Buchanan, East Kilpatrick.
2. William Gillespie, Glasgow.
3. John M'Farlane,   ,,
4. Hugh Wishart, Milnport.
5. William Mack, Glasgow.
6. Ebenezer Muirhead, Glasgow.
7. John S. Knox, Coleraine.
8. John Gilmour, Stewarton.
9. Archibald Bannatyne, Rothesay.

Juniores.

1. Henry J. S. Page, Worcester.
2. John Tait, Glasgow.
3. Francis J. Gardner, Edinburgh.
4. Archibald Gilkison, Glasgow.
5. Andrew B. Parker, Ayr.
6. Ralph Wardlaw, Glasgow.
7. Robert Brown, Paisley.
8. James Ogilvie, Dundee.
9. William Dunn, Doune.

II.

For Essays on the following Subjects :—

1. For the best Essay on Imagination ;—embracing a particular examination of the question whether Imagination ought or ought not to be regarded as a simple original faculty of the mind (executed during the Summer Vacation), to

Richard Alliott, Nottingham.

2. For the best Essay on the difference betwixt Wit and Humour (also executed during the Summer Vacation), to

John Tennent, Glasgow.

3. For the best Essay on Dreams, as exemplifying the laws of association, primary and secondary (written during the Christmas holidays of the present Session), to

William Heron, Greenock.

4. For the best Poem on Sleep (written during the Christmas holidays), to

William Henderson, Greenock.

5. For the most Accurate Report (written down wholly from memory) of a Sermon Preached in the College Chapel, in the course of the Session, to

John Maclean, Kilmarnock.

Prizes of the GREEK CLASS.

I.

Private—Vacation Exercises.

1. Essay on the comparative excellence of Epic and Dramatic Poetry :

Robert Paisley, Glasgow.

2. Essay on the Comparative merits of Æschylus and Euripides in Dramatic Composition :

Alfred Day, A.B., Bristol.

3. Translation into Greek Iambic Trimiters of Lines from Shakespeare, Henry v., Act III., Sc. 3.

John Tennent, Glasgow.

Exercises during the Session.

Essay on Passion as a source of the Sublime in Composition :

Mungo Parker, Kilmarnock.

II.

Public—Senior—Vacation Exercises.

1. Translation into Greek Iambic Trimiters of 30 lines from Shakespeare, King John, Act III., Sc. 3.

John Tennent, Glasgow.

2. Translation into English Verse of the "Hippolytus" of Euripides :

Adam Roxburgh, Kilmaurs.

3. Translation into English Prose of the Fifth Book of Herodotus :

Robert Paisley, Glasgow.

4. Translation into English Prose of the Corinthian and Athenian Speeches in the first Book of Thucydides :

Robert Paisley, Glasgow.

Exercises during Session.

1. Translation into Homeric Hexameters of lines from " Aikenside's Pleasures of Imagination : "

John Dewhurst, Santa Cruz.

2. For excelling in the weekly exercises prescribed during Session.

GREEK VERSE.

1. John Dewhurst, Santa Cruz.
2. John M'Kinlay, Glasgow.
3. John Macfarlane,   ,,.

GREEK PROSE.

James Muir, Kilmarnock.

For excelling at the Black Stone Examination.

COMPETITORS.

1. Alex. Thomson, Glasgow.
2. John Macfarlane,   ,,

NON-COMPETITORS.

1. Archd. Buchanan, East Kilpatrick.
2. John Martin, Paisley.

For eminence in conduct, scholarship, and talent, throughout the Session.

LOGIC SIDE.

1. John Macfarlane, Glasgow.
2. John Martin, Paisley.
3. Archibald Buchanan, East Kilpatrick.
4. Henry Page, Worcester.
5. Andrew Borland Parker, Ayr.

GREEK SIDE.

1. John M'Kinlay, Glasgow.
2. Andrew Tennent,   ,,
3. John Dewhurst, Santa Cruz.
4. Ronald Young, Kelvin-dock.
5. Jonathan Anderson, Paisley.

III.

PUBLIC—JUNIOR.

Vacation Exercises.

1. Translation into Homeric Hexameters of lines from Goldsmith's Deserted Village.

Andrew Tennent, Glasgow.

2. Translation into English Verse of Extracts from Homer and Theocritus.

Andrew Borland Parker, Ayr.

3. Translation into English Prose of Extracts from Herodotus.

John M'Kinlay, Glasgow.

4. Translation into Grammatical Greek of the " Introduction to the Writing of Greek, Parts II. and IV."

Joseph King, Stewarton.

5. Translation into English Prose of Lucian's Dialogues.

John Campbell, Balquhidder.

Exercises during Session.

For excelling in the weekly exercises in Greek Verse prescribed during Session.

1. James M'Donald, Bridge of Allan, Perthshire.
2. John M'Intosh, Glasgow.
3. Alexander Chrystal, ,,
4. Robert Massie, ,,

For Eminence in Conduct, Scholarship and Talent, throughout the Session.

Provectiores.

1. Alexander Chrystal, Glasgow.
2. David Arnot, Kilmarnock.
3. Donald Weir, Glendaruel, Argyllshire.
4. Duncan Blair, Balfron.
5. James M'Donald, Bridge of Allan.
6. James Reid, Dunblane.
7. John M'Intosh, Glasgow.
8. James Barlas, Crieff.
9. James Porter, Stranraer.

Tyrones.

1. James Brownlie, Laurieston.
2. Charles Shaw, Benbecula, Inverness-shire.
3. John Eadie, Alloa, Stirlingshire.
4. James Morrison, Auchterarder, Perthshire.
5. John Thomson, Perth.
6. William M'Call, Largs.
7. John Lang, ,,
8. James Dunlop, Beith.

Prizes in the HUMANITY CLASS.

I. For the best original Latin Verses, written during the Vacation, to

John Macfarlane, Glasgow.
John M'Kinlay, ,,

Written during the Session.

1st DIVISION—John M'Kinlay, Glasgow.
Adam Roxburgh, Kilmaurs.

2nd DIVISION—Patrick Muirhead, Glasgow.
Alexander Chrystal,   ,,

II. For the best original Essay in Latin Prose, written during the Vacation, to

John M'Kinlay, Glasgow.

Written during the Session, to

1st DIVISION—William Reid, West Kincardine.

2nd   ,,   Alexander Chrystal, Glasgow.

III. For the best Essay on the Epistolary Composition of the Romans, to

John Macfarlane, Glasgow.

IV. For the best Translation into English Verse of an Ode of Horace, to

Patrick Muirhead, Glasgow.

V. For the best Voluntary Exercises, to

Adam Roxburgh, Kilmaurs.
James Barlas, Crieff.

VI. For excelling in the Weekly Exercises, to

1st DIVISION. { John M'Kinlay, Glasgow.
Andrew Tennent,   ,,
William Reid, W. Kincardine.

2nd DIVISION. { George Paterson Frew, Perthshire.
William Macfarlane, Thornhill.

VII. For excelling in the Examination on Roman Antiquities, to

John M'Kinlay, Glasgow,
Robert Keir, Falkirk.

VIII. For excelling at the Black Stone Examination, to

COMPETITORS. { Hugh Smith, Glasgow.
Andrew Tennent,   ,,

Non-Competitors {
James Barlas, Crieff.
David Arnot, Kilmarnock.
James Douglas, Lochwinnoch.

IX. For exemplary eminence in talent, diligence and conduct, throughout the Session, to

FIRST DIVISION.

Seniores of two years' standing.

1. John M'Kinlay, Glasgow.
2. Andrew Tennent, „
. William Reid, West Kincardine.
3. Hugh Smith, Glasgow.
5. Adam Roxburgh, Kilmaurs.
6. Archibald Currie, Glasgow.

Seniores of one year's standing.

1. David Arnot, Kilmarnock.
2. John Symington, Paisley.
3. John Tannoch, Kilmarnock.
4. William Clarke, Glasgow.
5. James Halley, „
6. John Struthers, „
7. Niel MacMichael, Kilmarnock.

SECOND DIVISION.

Seniores attending the 2nd Division.

1. James Barlas, Crieff. } Equal.
   William Watt, Glasgow. }
2. George Paterson Frew, Perthshire.
3. James Macdonald, Bridge of Allan.
4. John Eadie, Alva.
5. Henry Beatson, Campbelton.

Juniores.

1. Alexander Chrystal, Glasgow.
2. Walter Ferguson, Glasgow.
3. Duncan Blair, Balfron.
4. John Paterson, Cambusnethan.
5. Laurence Craigie, Glasgow.
6. Andrew MacEwan, „
7. Alexander Murray, Stirling.
8. Patrick Muirhead, Glasgow.
9. Robert Wilson, „

GLASGOW COLLEGE, 1st MAY, 1828.

This day, the Annual Distribution of Prizes was made, in the Common Hall, by the Principal and Professors, in presence of a numerous meeting of the University, and of many Reverend and respectable Gentlemen of the City and neighbourhood, and of several distinguished strangers.

On Mr. COULTER'S DONATION.

For the best Lecture on Isaiah, ch. 53, to
James Lewis, Glasgow.

For the best Translation of Tacitus, de Moribus Germanorum, to

John Macfarlan, Glasgow.

The LORD RECTOR'S PRIZES, viz. :—

Gold Medal, for the best English Poem, to
Alex. Munro, Paisley.

Silver Medal, for the second best English Poem, to
Wm. Park, A.M., Hutchesontown.

Silver Medal, for the best English Poem by a Gowned Student, to

James MacBeth, Ayrshire.

Mr. JEFFREY'S GOLD MEDAL.

For the best Scholar in the whole Greek Class, to
John M'Kinlay, Glasgow.

DEGREES IN ARTS

Were announced to have been conferred, with first honours, or the highest Distinction in Languages, Logic, and Moral Philosophy, on

William Acworth, A.M., Kent.
Samuel Greer, A.M., Coleraine.

With second honours, or honourable Distinction in the same Department, to

John James Rankin, A.M., Glasgow.
William Baird, A.M.,   ,,

And with second honours, or honourable Distinction in Natural Philosophy and Mathematics, to

John Reid, A.M., London.
Alex. Ure, A.M., Glasgow.

———

Two Prizes given by the JURISDICTIO ORDINARIA, for the best Latin Orations in the Common Hall, were adjudged to

Robert Whyte, Kilmarnock.
John Tennent, Glasgow.

———

The Prizes of the DIVINITY CLASS were adjudged—

To Students of the 2nd Year.

For an Abridgement of the Lectures on the Evidences for Divine Revelation, to

John Thomson, Stirling.
James Law, Lanark.

For an Essay " on Miracles," to

James Lewis, Glasgow.

For an Essay " on the rapid propagation of the Gospel, and the Secondary Causes alleged by Mr. Gibbon," to

John Roxburgh, Glasgow.

For an Essay "on the Canon of the Old and New Testaments," to

Matthew Barclay, Paisley.   } equal.
William Hamilton, Kilmarnock. }

For the best Specimen of Reading, to

James Robb Grant, Glasgow.

To Students of the 1st Year.

For an Essay on the state of the Heathen World at the coming of our Saviour, to

1. John Neilson, Paisley.
2. George Craig, Glasgow.
3. Mungo Parker, Kilmarnock.

For an Essay on the Prophecies respecting the Nation of Israel, to

    1. James Bannatyne, Rothsay.
    2. John Neilson, Paisley.
    3. James M'Gown, Kincardine.

———

Prizes in the *Senior* HEBREW CLASS were adjudged—
I. For the best Philological Essay on the Hebrew word signifying "to bless," etc.,

    1. Robert Elder, A.M., Campbelton.
    2. James Law, Lanark.

II. For the best Critical Exposition of Isaiah, vii. ch., 10 v. to the end, to

    James Law, Lanark.

———

Prizes in the *Junior* HEBREW CLASS were adjudged—
I. For close attention and distinguished proficiency throughout the Session, to

    1. John Finlay Neilson, Glasgow.
    2. Thos. S. Russell, A.M., Islay, Argyllshire.

II. For the best exemplification of the Hebrew Verb, to

    1. John Finlay Neilson, Glasgow.
    2. Colin F. Campbell, Glenmore, Argyllshire.

III. For the most correct specimen of the Hebrew Noun, with the affixes, to

    James Smith, Glasgow.

———

Prizes in the CHURCH HISTORY CLASS were adjudged—
for the best Essays on the Civil and Political Institutions of the Hebrews.

    1. *To the Students of the Second Year.*

    William Hamilton, A.M., Kilmarnock.

    2. *To the Students of the First Year.*

    James Williamson, A.M., Galloway.

Prizes in the CIVIL HISTORY CLASS were adjudged—
for the best Essays on the Government of Sparta, and the Laws of Lycurgus, to

> Robert M'Corkle, A.M., Glasgow.
> James Clason, A.M., Dumblane.

LAW.

Two Prizes for excelling in the daily examinations in the SCOTTISH LAW CLASS, proposed to those Students who chose to be examined, were adjudged to

> Gabriel H. Lang, Glasgow.
> James Robertson, ,,

IN ANATOMY.

The Prize for the best Essay on the Motions of the Iris, and the power of adapting the Eye to see objects at different distances, was adjudged to

> Thomas Muir, Glasgow.

Prizes in the CHEMISTRY CLASS.

For the best appearances at the Public Examinations during the Session, to

> 1. William Nimmo, Glasgow.
> 2. William Muir, ,,
> 3. James Whitelaw, Calton.

For the two best Essays on Digestion, to

> 1. Alexander Rob, Anderston.
> 2. James Bailey, Tolderoy, Croyden.

The Prizes of the MATHEMATICAL CLASSES, for general eminence and proficiency during the Session, were adjudged to

SENIOR CLASS.

Donald Kennedy, Dornoch.
Robert Stevenson, Campsie.
Archibald Buchanan, East Kilpatrick.

Junior Class.
Senior Division.

John Pollock, Paisley.
James M'Cosh, Straiton, Ayrshire.
James Boyd, Glasgow.
John Lamont,   ,,
David M'Mutrie, Stranraer.
Archibald Bannatyne, Rothesay.

Junior Division.

James Douglas, Kilbarchan.
John Shirreff, Glasgow.
Archibald C. Tait, Edinburgh.

The Prizes of the NATURAL PHILOSOPHY CLASS, for propriety of conduct, exemplary diligence, and display of eminent ability in examinations on the subjects of the Lectures, and in Essays and Investigations connected with Physical Science, were adjudged to

Donald Kennedy, Dornoch, Sutherlandshire.
James Ewing, Concraig, Crieff.
Robert Whyte, Kilmarnock.
Archibald Galloch, Lecropt, Perthshire.
John Murdoch, Cornton, Stirlingshire.
Alexander Stevenson, Campsie.
Samuel Greer, A.M., Coleraine, Ireland.

The Prizes in the ETHIC CLASS, for the best Specimens of Composition on the subjects connected with the business of the Class, and prescribed by the Professor or chosen by the Students themselves, and for exemplary conduct and distinguished eminence, were adjudged to

Seniores.

1. John Lamont, Glasgow.
2. James Banks, Saltcoats.
3. William Graham, Tollcross.
4. Robt. Horn, Bridge of Allan, Stirlingshire

Juniores.

1. John Tait, Moffat.
2. Francis John Gardner, Edinburgh.
3. Andrew Borland Parker, Ayr.
4. { William Dunn, Down.
   { Robert Stevenson, Campsie.

For the best Poetical Compositions, to
William Henderson, Greenock.

For an Essay on the Influence of Commerce on the Knowledge and Civilization of the Ancients, a Prize given by a Gentleman who subscribes himself a well-wisher to historical research, was adjudged to
John Tennent, Glasgow.

———

The Prizes in the LOGIC CLASS, for this Session, were adjudged as follows :—

I. For general Eminence and superiority in the various Exercises and Examinations of the Class throughout the Session, to

Seniores.

1. William Hanna, Belfast.
2. Robert Cotton Mather, Birmingham.
3. William Gibb, Stirling.
4. Wm. Grierson Smith, Edinburgh.
5. John Jenkins, Swansea, Glamorganshire.
6. George Morton, Galston.
7. John Lockhart Ross, Edinburgh.
8. James Patterson, Dumbarton.

Juniores.

1. James Gardiner, Bothwell.
2. Robert Roxburgh, Kilmaurs.
3. George Gilfillan, Comrie, Perthshire.
4. William B. Galloway, Glasgow.
5. Hugh Smith,   ,,
6. John Hall Maxwell,   ,,
7. William Lumsden,
8. William Lyall, Paisley.

II.

FOR ESSAYS.

I.

(Prescribed at the end of last Session, and composed during the Vacation).

For the best Essay on the Evidence of Human Testimony; with particular reference to the question—Whether in any circumstances it can be sufficient to justify our belief in a miracle.   From the number and merit of the competing Essays on the subject, two Prizes were awarded, viz., to

John Tait, Moffat.
John MacFarlane, Glasgow.

II.

(Prescribed in the course of the present Session, and executed during the Christmas holidays).

1. For the best Poem, subject, "the Association of Ideas," to

James Fleming, Ballymoney, Antrim, Ireland.

2. For the best Essay on the question, "Is Memory to be regarded as a simple, original, and distinct Faculty of the Mind?" to

William Hanna, Belfast.

Prizes of the GREEK CLASS.

I.

Private—VACATION EXERCISES.

Essay on the true meaning of "The Sublime," as understood by Longinus ; and on the Study of Nature, both in the Physical and Moral World, as a source of this quality in Composition,

Mungo Parker, Kilmarnock.

EXERCISE DURING THE SESSION.

Translation into English Verse of Pindar's Second Olympic Ode,

Francis Garden, Glasgow.

For Eminence in the Weekly Examinations throughout the Session,

John M'Kinlay, Glasgow.

II.

Public, Senior—VACATION EXERCISES.

1. Translation into Greek Tragic Iambic Trimeters of 31 lines from Shakspeare's "Two Gentlemen of Verona," Act II., Scene 7,

John M'Kinlay, Glasgow.

2. Translation into English Verse of the "Œdipus Tyrannus" of Sophocles,

John M'Farlane, Glasgow.

3. Translation into English Prose of the Second Book of Herodotus,

Archibald Currie, Glasgow.

4. Translation into English Prose of the Fourth Book of the "Memorabilia" of Xenophon,

John M'Farlane, Glasgow.

EXERCISES DURING SESSION.

1. Translation into Homeric Hexameters of lines from Akenside's "Pleasures of Imagination,"

Alexander Chrystal, Glasgow.

2. For excelling in the Weekly Exercises in Greek Verse, prescribed throughout the Session,

1. John M'Kinlay, Glasgow.
2. James Halley,   ,,
3. Andrew Tennent,   ,,

For excelling at the Black Stone Examination,

1. Ronald Young, Kelvindock.
2. Robert Mather, Birmingham.
3. George Morton, Galston.

For eminence in talent, industry, and scholarship throughout the Session.

LOGIC SIDE.

1. Ronald Young, Kelvindock.
2. Andrew Tennent, Glasgow.
3. Neil Macmichael, Kilmarnock.
4. Robert Ranken, Paisley.
5. Alexander Patrick Stewart, Erskine.

GREEK SIDE.

1. James Halley, Glasgow.
2. David Arnott, Kilmarnock.
3. Robert Johnstone, Alva.
4. Thomas James, Croyden.
5. Alexander Crystal, Glasgow.

III.—PUBLIC—JUNIOR.

Vacation Exercises.

1. Grammatical Version of the "Introduction to the Writing of Greek,"

John Thomson, Perth.

2. Translation of Lucian's "Sale of Lives," with a Commentary,

Robert Macgowan, Greenock.

3. Translation into English Verse of Extracts from Anacreon and Tyrtæus,

John Mackintosh, Moy, Inverness-shire.

4. Translation into English Prose of Extracts from Homer, Anacreon, Tyrtæus, with a Commentary,

John Boyd, Paisley.

EXERCISES DURING THE SESSION.

For Excelling in the Weekly Exercises in Greek Verse, prescribed during Session,

1. William Tennent, Glasgow.
2. John Gardiner, Bothwell.
3. Robert Dees, Newcastle-upon-Tyne.

For Eminence in Talent, Industry, and Scholarship throughout the Session,

PROVECTIORES.

1. James Morrison, Auchterarder, Perthshire.
2. Robert Dees, Newcastle-upon-Tyne.
3. John Davie, Glasgow.
4. John Edie, Alva, Stirlingshire.
5. Patrick Muirhead, Glasgow.
6. John Gardiner, Bothwell.
7. Wm. Hislop, Wanlock-head, Dumfries-shire.
8. Wm. Bruce, Ardoch Cottage, Dumbartonshire.
9. Thomas Knox, Kilbirnie, Ayrshire.

TYRONES.

1. Robert Wilson, Glasgow.
2. James Finlay, Kirkintilloch.
3. Murdoch Ardbuckle, North Uist.
4. Andrew Reid, Rutherglen.

5. Wm. M'Kechnie, Paisley.
6. Wm. M'Gill, London.
7. Hugh M'Gowan, Cumnock.
8. Joseph Thomson, Dumfries-shire.

Prizes in the HUMANITY CLASS.

I. For the Best Original Latin Verses written during the Vacation, to

Patrick Muirhead, Glasgow.

WRITTEN DURING THE SESSION, to

1st Division—Archibald C. Tait, Edinburgh.
2nd   ,,   —Peter M'Kinlay, Glasgow.

II. For the Best Original Essay in Latin Prose, written during the Vacation, to

John M'Kinlay, Glasgow.
Alexander Chrystal, ,,

WRITTEN DURING THE SESSION, to

1st Division—{ John Hume, Hamilton. } equal.
             { Alex. Chrystal, Glasgow. }
2nd   ,,   —Peter M'Kinlay, Glasgow.

III. For the Best Essay on the Life and Writings of Livy, to

Laurence W. Craigie, Glasgow.

IV. For the Best Metrical Translation of Horace, Book 3rd, Ode 29, to

Archibald C. Tait, Edinburgh.

V. For the Best Voluntary Exercises, to

Laurence W. Craigie, Glasgow.

VI. For the Best Public Theme, to

Peter M'Kinlay, Glasgow.

VII. For Excelling in the Weekly Exercises, to

1st Division—Robert A. Johnston, Edinburgh.
             Archibald C. Tait,   ,,
             { Alexander Chrystal, Glasgow. }
             { J. Paterson, Cambusnethan. } equal.
             { James Muir, Kilmarnock. }

2nd Division—Peter M'Kinlay, Glasgow.
             John Gardiner, Bothwell.

VIII. For Excelling in the Examination on Roman Antiquities,
to

Duncan Blair, Balfron.
Josiah Bull, Newport Pagnel.

IX. For excelling at the Black Stone examination, to

COMPETITORS.
{
Archibald C. Tait, Edinburgh.
Allan M'Culloch.
Josiah Bull, Newport Pagnel.
Robert R. Dees, Newcastle.
} equal.

NON-
COMPETITORS.
{
Alexander Chrystal, Glasgow.
Robert A. Johnston, Edinburgh.
Walter Ferguson, Glasgow.

X. For Exemplary General Eminence throughout the Session,
to

FIRST DIVISION.

Seniores of two years' standing.

1. Alexander Chrystal, Glasgow.
2. Walter Ferguson,   „
3. Duncan Blair, Balfron.
4. John Paterson, Cambusnethan.
5 Alexander Murray, Stirlingshire.
6. Laurence W. Craigie, Glasgow.
7 Andrew MacEwan,   „

Seniores of one year's standing.

1. Robert Johnstone, Edinburgh.
2. Archibald C. Tait,   „
3. Robert R. Dees, Newcastle.
4. Josiah Bull, Newport Pagnel.
5. John Mackintosh, Moy, Invernesshire.
6. William Bruce, Dumbarton.

SECOND DIVISION.

Seniores attending the Second Division.

1. William Hislop, Wanlockhead.
2. Andrew Reid, Rutherglen.
3. James Finlay, Kirkintilloch.
4. John M'Neil, Lesswalt.

Juniores.

1. Peter M'Kinlay, Glasgow.
2. John Davie,   „
3. Donald Coghill,   „
4. Alexander Mein,   „
5. Alexander Taylor,   „
6. John Gardiner, Bothwell.
7. Robert Douie, Glasgow.
8. Robert Stewart,   „
9. James Chalmers,   „

Given to the Students of the 2nd Division by the Assistant.

I. For the Best appearance at the Second Reading of the Daily Sessions, to

William Turnbull, Blantyre.

II. For the best Translation of detached Chapters of Livy, connected by a Chronological Epitome, to

Seniores.

William Hislop, Wanlockhead.

Juniores.

Jas. Chalmers, Glasgow. ⎫ equal.
James Currie.   ⎭

III. For best and most numerous Voluntary Exercises, to

William Dunlop, Irvine.

GLASGOW COLLEGE, 1st MAY, 1829.

ANNUAL PRIZES.

On the 1st of May, 1829, the Annual Distribution of Prizes was made in the Common Hall, by the Lord Rector, Principal and Professors, in presence of a numerous meeting of the

University, and of many Reverend and respectable gentlemen of the City and neighbourhood.

University Prizes.

I.—In Theology.

A Silver Medal for the best Essay on the Corroborations of the Mosaic Record from the History of Language, etc., was adjudged to

Mungo Parker, A.M., Kilmarnock.

II.—In Natural Philosophy.

A Silver Medal for the best View of the Progress of the Theory of the Velocity of Sound, was adjudged to

William Park, A.M., Hutchesontown, Glasgow.

Prizes were given by the Lord Rector, Two Gold Medals.

I. For the best Essay on the Evils of Intolerance, to

William Park, A.M., Hutchesontown, Glasgow.

II. For the best Essay on the Comparative Merits of Classical Erudition and Physical Science, to

Robert M'Corkle, A.M., Glasgow.

Three Silver Medals.

I. For the best Essay on Hydrocephalus, to

Edward Dill, Ireland.

II. For the best Translation of English into Greek verse, to

James Wilson, Irvine.

III. For the best Translation from English into Latin verse, to

Archibald Campbell Tait, Edinburgh.

Mr. Ewing's Gold Medal.

For the best Account of the Causes, Completion, and Consequences of the Revolution in 1688, to

William Park, A.M , Hutchesontown, Glasgow.

On Mr. COULTER's Donation.

I. For the best Discourse on John, chap. vii. ver. 46, to
John Roxburgh, A.M., Glasgow.

II. For the best Translation from Greek into English, to
Andrew Borland Parker, Newtown, Ayr.

On Mr. WATT's Donation.

For the best Account of the Construction and Theory of the
Hydraulic Ram of Montgolfier, to
John Willison Ferguson, Glasgow.

For the best Essay on the Motion of Projectiles in a Resisting
Medium, to
William Park, A.M., Hutchesontown, Glasgow.

Mr. JEFFREY's Gold Medal,

For the best Scholar in the Humanity Class, was adjudged to
Peter Mackinlay, Laurieston, Glasgow.

Two Prizes by the JURISDICTIO ORDINARIA, for the best Latin
Orations, were adjudged to
Andrew Borland Parker, Newton, Ayr.
John M'Farlane, Glasgow.

The Prizes of the DIVINITY CLASS were adjudged as follows,
To Students of the Senior Class.

For an account of the Lectures on the Evidences for Divine
Revelation, to
James M'Gowan, A.M., Kincardine.

For an Essay during the Session "On the Nature and Proof of
the Inspiration of the Scriptures," to
William Stevenson, A.M., Lochwinnoch.
John Roxburgh, A.M., Glasgow.

For the best Specimen of Public Reading, to
Peter Millar, Stirling.

To Students of the Junior Class

For eminence in the Exercises of the Class, to
John Muir, Paisley.
Thomas Dymock, Glasgow.
John Stewart, „
Colin Young, A.M., Port-Glasgow.

For an Exercise "On the Mosaic Law," to
William Thorburn, A.M., Blantyre

For an Exercise "On the Character of Christ, as an evidence of his Divine Mission," to
James Ewing, Muthill.

———

Prizes in the HEBREW CLASS.

I. For General Eminence in the ordinary business of the Class throughout the Session, to
James Russel, Strathaven. ⎱
William Stevenson, A.M., Lochwinnoch. ⎰ Equal.

II. For the best Exemplification of the Hebrew Verb, to
1. Wm. Stevenson, A.M., Lochwinnoch.
2. Walter M'Gilvray, Islay.

III. For the best Translation into Hebrew, to
William Stevenson, A.M., Lochwinnoch.

———

Prizes in the CHURCH HISTORY CLASS were adjudged, for the best Essays on the Government, Discipline, and Worship of the Christian Church during the first two centuries.

1. *To the Students of the Third Year.*

James Clason, A.M., Dunblane.
William Hamilton, Kilmarnock.

2. *To the Students of the Second Year.*

William Williamson, Galloway.

3. *To the Students of the First Year.*

Mungo Parker, A.M , Kilmarnock.

Prizes in the CIVIL HISTORY CLASS were adjudged for the best Essay on the State of Literature at Rome during the age of Augustus, to

James M'Gowan, Kincardine.
Francis John Gardner, Edinburgh

Two Prizes for excelling in the daily examination proposed to those Students of SCOTTISH LAW who chose to be examined, were adjudged to

William Steele, Glasgow.
William Mack,   ,,

The Prizes in the ANATOMY CLASS for the best Essay on the questions " Is the blood alive? and if it be, is it the life?" were adjudged,

1. To John Taylor.
2. To William Nimmo, Glasgow.

The Essays proposed in the MEDICINE CLASS were

1. On Exanthematous Diseases.
2. The Comatose Diseases.

The Prize for the first was adjudged to

Mr. A. Ure of Glasgow.

For the second, to

Mr. Alex. Robb, Anderston.

Prizes in the CHEMISTRY CLASS.

I. For acquitting themselves best at the Regular Examinations during the Session,

1. James Toldervey, Croydon, Surrey.
2. R. R. Dees, Newcastle-on-Tyne.
3. Alexander Tod, Glasgow.

II. For the best Essay on the Theory of Vapour, to

John Taylor.

The Prizes of the MATHEMATICAL CLASSES for general eminence and proficiency during the Session were adjudged to

SENIOR CLASS.

James Boyd, A.M., Glasgow.
John Pollock, Paisley.
Archibald C. Tait, Edinburgh.
Peter Bain, Row, Dumbartonshire.

JUNIOR CLASS.

Senior Division.

Robert A. Johnstone, Alva, Stirlingshire.
James Young, Lesmahagow.
William Ritchie, Ayr.
John L. Ross, Woodburn, Edinburgh.
Duncan Blair, Balfron.

Junior Division.

Archibald Smith, Jordanhill, Renfrewshire.
William H. Edington, Glasgow.
Robert D. Mackenzie, Dumbarton.
John Barclay, Catrine, Ayrshire.
William Watson, Glasgow.

The Prizes of the NATURAL PHILOSOPHY CLASS, for propriety of conduct, exemplary diligence, and display of eminent ability in Examinations on the subjects of the Lectures, and in Essays and Investigations connected with Physical Science, were adjudged to

1. Robert Horn, Bridge of Allan, Stirlingshire.
2. John Pollock, Paisley.
3. Robert Stevenson, Campsie.
4. William Dunn, Doune, Perthshire.
5. John Lamont, Glasgow.
6. James M'Cosh, Straiton, Ayrshire.
7. Andrew Borland Parker, Newton, Ayr.

The Prizes in the ETHIC CLASS for General Eminence in the business of the Class, and for superior Excellence in Exercises written on Subjects Metaphysical and Ethical, prescribed by the Professor, or voluntarily selected by their Authors, were, by the vote of the Students themselves adjudged to

Seniores.

1. William Hanna, Belfast.
2. Robert C. Mather, Birmingham
3. William Gibb, Stirling.
4. William Harris, Glasgow.
5. John Alexander, Lochwinnoch.

Juniores.

1. William B. Galloway, Glasgow.
2. Robert D. M'Kenzie, Dumbarton.
3. William Lumsden, Glasgow.
4. James Gibson,   „

A Prize for Superior Excellence in Poetical Composition was adjudged to

George Gray, Douglas.

A Prize for the best Essay on the Origin and Nature of Ideas was adjudged to

John Tait, Moffat.

———

In the Logic Class, the Prizes for this Session were adjudged as follows :—

I.

For general eminence and superiority in the various Exercises and Examinations of the Class throughout the Session, to

Seniores.

1. Robert A. Johnstone, Alva, Stirlingshire.
2. Josiah Bull, Newport-Pagnel, Bucks.
3. James Stevenson, Kilmarnock.
4. William Rowe, Bristol.
5. Charles Wicksteed, Shrewsbury.
6. Archibald Smith, Glasgow.
7. William Connel, Lochwinnoch.
8 John Wright, Glasgow.

Juniores.

1. Laurence Williams Craigie, Glasgow
2. Walter Ferguson,   .,
3. Walter L. Colvin, Johnstone, Dumfries shire.

4. Neil Bannatyne, Glasgow.
5. Robert R. Dees, Newcastle-upon-Tyne.
6. Alexander Chrystal, Glasgow.
7. Andrew MacEwan,   ,,
8. David H. Gibb,   ,,
9. Norman MacLeod, Campsie.

II.

FOR ESSAYS.

1.

(Prescribed at the close of last Session, and composed during the Vacation.)

For the best Critical Analysis and Examination of Burke's Theory of the Sublime and Beautiful, to

William Hanna, Belfast.

For the best Essay on the nature, uses, and laws of the Dilemma as a form of argument, to

John Jenkins, Swansea, Glamorganshire.

2.

(Prescribed in the present session, and executed during the Christmas holidays.)

For the best Analysis of Perception, with especial reference to the question whether it be a simple and primary power of the understanding, to

Walter L. Colvin, Johnstone, Dumfries-shire.

For the best Poem on the progress and prospects of man as an improveable being, to

William Rowe, Bristol.

———

Prizes in the GREEK CLASS.

I.

Private — Vacation Exercises.

1. Essay on the Use and Abuse of Eloquence,
      Robert Abercrombie Johnstone, Alva.

2. Translation into English Verse of the fourth Pythian Ode of Pindar,

Andrew Borland Parker, Newtown, Ayr.

3. Translation into Greek Iambic Trimeters from Shakspeare's Merchant of Venice, Act iv. Scene 1, "The quality of mercy is not strained," etc.,

Robert Abercrombie Johnstone, Alva.

Private—Session.

1. For Excelling in the Examinations of the Class,

Andrew Borland Parker, Newton, Ayr, ⎫
Henry S. Page, Worcester. ⎭ Equal.

2. Translation into English Verse from "The Frogs" of Aristophanes,

Henry S. Page, Worcester.

II.

Public—Senior—Vacation Exercises.

1. Translation into Greek Iambic Trimeters from Shakspeare's Merchant of Venice, Act v. Scene 1, "Sweet soul, let's in, and there expect their coming," to "let no such man be trusted,—mark the musick,"

Robert Abercrombie Johnstone, Alva.

2 Translation into English Verse of "The Ajax" of Sophocles,

James Thomson, Camphill, Glasgow.

3. Translation into English Prose of the Sixth Book of Herodotus, with a complete Index of Ionicisms,

Ronald Young, Kelvindock.

4. Translation into English Prose of the Olynthiacs of Demosthenes,

Archibald Smith, *major*, Glasgow.

Public—Senior—Session.

1. For excelling at the Black-Stone Examination,

1. Robert Abercrombie Johnstone, Alva.
2. Charles Wicksteed, Shrewsbury.

2. Translation into Homeric Hexameters of lines from Cowper's Task, "Nor rural sights alone, but rural sounds," etc.,

Laurence Williams Craigie, Glasgow.

3. For eminence in talent, scholarship, and industry throughout the Session.

Logic Side.

1. Robert Abercrombie Johnstone, Alva.
2. David Arnot, Kilmarnock.
3. Robert R. Dees, Newcastle-upon-Tyne.
4. Charles Wicksteed, Shrewsbury.
5. Laurence Williams Craigie, Glasgow.

Greek Side.

1. Archibald Campbell Tait, Edinburgh.
2. Robert Wilson, *minor*, Camlachie.
3. Archibald Smith, Jordanhill.
4. David Ogilvy, Edinburgh.
5. Henry S. Page, Worcester.

4. For excelling in the Weekly Exercises in Greek Verse prescribed throughout the Session,

1. James Halley, Glasgow.
2. David Arnot, Kilmarnock.
3. Robert Abercrombie Johnstone, Alva.

III.

Public—Junior—Vacation Exercises.

1. Translation into Homeric Hexameters from Campbell's "Pleasures of Hope," "Propitious power! when rankling cares annoy," etc.,

Robert Richardson Dees, Newcastle-upon-Tyne.

2. Grammatical Version of "Exercises in Homeric and Attic Greek, Part 1st,"

James Brown, Beith.

3. Translation into English Prose of Extracts from Herodotus, with an Index of Ionicisms,

Robert Richardson Dees, Newcastle-upon-Tyne.

4. Version of the "Introduction to the writing of Greek, Parts 2nd and 4th,"

Francis Lorrain, Glasgow.

5. Translation into English Prose of Extracts from Lucian, with an index of irregular Verbs,

James Kerr, Greenhead, Glasgow.

Public—Junior—Session.

1. For eminence in talent, scholarship, and industry, throughout the Session.

Provectiores.

1. Peter M'Kinlay, Laurieston, Glasgow.
2. James Colquhoun, Falkirk.
3. John Struthers, Glasgow.
4. William Dunlop, Edinburgh.
5. Charles Puller, Paisley.
6. John Wardlaw, Glasgow.
7. Robert Dewar, Muirbank, Glasgow.
8. Clement Dukes, London.

Tyrones.

1. Alexander Ross, Glasgow.
2. James Robertson, Plean, Stirlingshire.
3. Andrew Robertson, Paisley.
4. James Barlas, Glasgow.
5. William Black, Stranraer.
6. William Murdoch, Ochiltree, Ayrshire.
7. David Gibson Fleming, Glasgow.

2. For excelling in the Exercises in Greek Verse, prescribed throughout the Session.

1. Peter M'Kinlay, Laurieston, Glasgow.
2. James Colquhoun, Falkirk.
3. William Dunlop, Edinburgh.

———

Prizes in the HUMANITY CLASS.

I. For exemplary conduct and general eminence throughout the Session.

FIRST DIVISION.

Seniores of two years' standing.

1. James Halley, Glasgow.
2. Alexander Mein,   ,,
3. Robert Patrick, Dalry, Ayrshire.
4. Wm. Bruce, Ardoch Cottage, Dumbarton.
5. Robert Stewart, Glasgow.
6. James Brown, Beith, Ayrshire.

Seniores of one year's standing.

1. David Ogilvy, Edinburgh.
2. John Blackburn, Liverpool.
3. Archibald Smith, Jordanhill, Renfrewshire.
4. John J. Campbell, Edinburgh.
5. William Dunlop,   ,,
6. James Hamilton, Strathblane.

SECOND DIVISION.

Seniores attending the Second Division.

1. Alexander Stein, Falkirk.
2. James Robertson, Plean, Stirlingshire.
3. Archibald Denniston, Greenock.
4. Thomas Mathew, Edinburgh.

Juniores.

1. James Colquhoun, Falkirk.
2. John Wardlaw, Glasgow.
3. James Barlas,   ,,
4. Thomas Watson,   ,,
5. James Small, Stirling.
6. John Muir, Glasgow.
7. Alexander Ross, Glasgow.
8. Andrew Melville, Dumfries.
9. James G. Morrison, Glasgow.

II. For excelling at the Blackstone Examination.

COMPETITORS.
{ Archibald Smith, Jordanhill.
  Peter M'Kinlay, Laurieston, Glasgow.
  David Ogilvy, Edinburgh.

NON-COMPETITORS.
{ Alexander Mein, Glasgow.
  John J. Campbell, Edinburgh.
  Dugald F. Campbell, Newton Lodge, Glasgow.

III. For Excelling in the Weekly Exercises.

1st DIVISION.
{ Peter M'Kinlay, Laurieston, Glasgow
  James Halley,   ,,
  David Ogilvy, Edinburgh.

2nd DIVISION.
{ James Colquhoun, Falkirk.
  John Wardlaw, Glasgow.

IV. For the best Original Latin Verses, written during the Session,

   1st DIVISION.—James Halley, Glasgow.
           William Dunlop, Edinburgh.

   2nd DIVISION.—James Colquhoun, Falkirk.

V. For the best Essay in Latin Prose, written during the Vacation,

        Peter M'Kinlay, Laurieston, Glasgow.

Written during the Session.

   1st DIVISION—Francis Lorrain, Glasgow.

   2nd   ,,   James Colquhoun, Falkirk.
           John Wardlaw, Glasgow.

VI. For the best Essays on the defects of the Republican Constitution of Rome, to

        Andrew Ross, Glasgow.

VII. For the best Translation of the 2nd Epode of Horace,

        James Colquhoun, Falkirk.
        Andrew Robertson, Paisley.

VIII. For the best Voluntary Exercises,

        James Halley, Glasgow.

IX. For excelling in the Examination on Roman Antiquities,

        Clement Dukes, London.

GLASGOW COLLEGE, 1st MAY, 1830.

This day, the Annual Distribution of Prizes was made in the Common Hall, by the Principal and Professors, in presence of a numerous meeting of the University, and of many Reverend and respectable Gentlemen of the City and Neighbourhood, and of several distinguished strangers.

UNIVERSITY PRIZES.

I.—IN THEOLOGY.

A Silver Medal for the best Essay on the Character and Peculiarities of Hebrew Poetry, was adjudged to

        Robert M'Corkle, A.M., Glasgow.

The Gart٦ore Gold Medal.

For the best Essay on the Expediency of throwing open the Trade to the East Indies, was adjudged to

Mungo Parker, A.M., Kilmarnock.

On Mr. Coulter's Donation.

I. For the best Lecture on Luke, chap. 13, v. 1-9, to

John Roxburgh, A.M., Glasgow.

II. For the best Essay on the Nature and Classification of the Passions, to

Thomas Stark, Chryston.

III. For the best Translation into English of the Third Book of Cicero's Tusculan Questions, to

Adam Roxburgh, Kilmaurs.

Mr. Jeffrey's Gold Medal.

For the best Scholar in the Greek Class, to

James Halley, Glasgow.

Two Prizes by the Jurisdictio Ordinaria, for the best Latin Orations, were adjudged, to

William Reid, West Kincardine.

Walter L. Colvin, A.M., Johnston, Dumfries-shire.

The Prizes of the Divinity Classes were adjudged,

To Students of the Senior Class.

For an Account of the Lectures on the Evidences for Divine Revelation, to

Colin Young, A.M., Port-Glasgow.

For an Essay on " Faith in Christ," to

Robert Stevenson, Stirling.

For an Essay "On the Duration of Future Punishments," to

John Roxburgh, A.M., Glasgow.⎫
Robert M'Corkle, A.M.,   „   ⎬ Equal.

For the best specimen of Public Reading, to

Francis Porter, A.M., Ireland.

To Students of the Junior Class.

For Eminence in the general Exercises of the Class, to

Jonathan Ranken Anderson, Paisley.
David Thomas, Glasgow.
John Tait, Moffat.
John Macfarlane, Glasgow.
John Campbell, Balquhidder.
John Pollock, Paisley.
Andrew Borland Parker, Ayr.
Robert Stevenson, Campsie.

For an Essay " On the Character and Conduct of Christ, as an evidence of his Divine Mission," to

Jonathan R. Anderson, Paisley.
John Macfarlane, Glasgow.

For an Essay on the " Genuineness of the Pentateuch," to   .

John Pollock, Paisley.

———

Prizes in the CHURCH HISTORY CLASS were adjudged, for the best Essays on the state of the Romish Church since the Reformation to the present times,

1. *To the Students of the Third Year.*

Wm. Nisbet, Glasgow.

2. *To the Students of the Second Year.*

Thomas Dymock, Glasgow.

3. *To the Students of the First Year.*

Archibald Kirkland, Cambusnethan.

———

Prizes in the CIVIL HISTORY CLASS were adjudged,

For the best Essays on the Causes which retarded the progress of Literature and Science among the ancient Eastern Nations.

Robert Hill White, Inch, }
James Law, Lanark,   } Equal.

———

Prizes in the HEBREW CLASS.

I. For exemplary conduct and eminent proficiency, to

1. James Boyd, A.M., Glasgow.
2. Duncan M'Intosh, Renton, Dumbartonshire.
3. Thomas Dymock, Glasgow.

II. For the best written specimen of the Hebrew Verb, to

    1. William Norval, A.M., Glasgow.

    2. Andrew Borland Parker, Ayr.

III. For the best Critical Analysis of the 16th Psalm, to

    1. George Stein, Londonderry, Ireland.

    2. Andrew Borland Parker, Ayr.

IV. For the best Hebrew Translation of 24 Verses selected from the Apocryphal Greek Book of The Wisdom of Solomon and Baruch, to

    1. Duncan M'Intosh, Renton, Dumbartonshire.

    2. James Boyd, A.M., Glasgow.

V. For excelling in an Examination on the Masoretic Hebrew, of certain passages in the Book of Genesis and Psalms, to

    Duncan M'Intosh, Renton, Dumbartonshire.

Two Prizes for excelling in the daily examination, proposed to those Students of SCOTTISH LAW who chose to be examined, were adjudged to

    John Tennant, Glasgow.

    Alexander Fleck, ,,

The Prizes in the MEDICINE CLASS were adjudged,

I. For the best Essay on Fever, to

    William Brown, A.M., Kilmacolm.

II. For the best Account of the Stethoscope, to

    William Travers Cox, Dublin.

The Subjects announced for the Prize Essays in the ANATOMY CLASS for next year were, 1st, The Anatomy and Physiology of the Liver, and the 2nd On Secretion.

Prizes in the CHEMISTRY CLASS.

For the best Essay on Galvanism, to

    Robert Dundas Thomson, Berwickshire.

For the best appearance at the Examinations throughout the Session, to

    1. William Baird, A.M., Fintry.

    2. Charles Freebairn Sloan, Ayr.

    3. David Bell, Carlisle.

The Prizes of the MATHEMATICAL CLASSES for General Eminence and Proficiency during the Session, were adjudged to

SENIOR CLASS.

1 Neil M'Michael, Kilmarnock.
2. William Brown Galloway, Glasgow.
3. Archibald Smith, Jordanhill.
4. Robert Neilson, Edinburgh.
5. William Kell, Kelso.

JUNIOR CLASS.

Senior Division.

1. James Fleming, Ballimoney.
2. Andrew Donald, Lesmahagow.
3. William Beckett, Paisley.
4. James Steven, Eaglesham.
5. Angus M'Master, Shiskan, Arran.

Junior Division

1. Alexander Chrystal, Glasgow. } Equal.
   William M'Goun, Greenock. }
2. John Kinross, Dumblane.
3. David H. Gibb, Glasgow.
4 Robert Sturrock, Dundee.
5 William Dunlop, Edinburgh.

———

The Prizes of the NATURAL PHILOSOPHY CLASS, for propriety of conduct, exemplary diligence, and display of eminent abilities in examinations on the subjects of the Lectures ; and in Essays, and Investigations connected with Physical Science, were adjudged to

1. William Hanna, A.M., Belfast.
2. Neil M'Michael, Kilmarnock.
3. James Young, Lesmahagow.
4. John Alexander, Lochwinnoch.
5. Robert J. Neilson, A.M., Edinburgh
6. John M'Cosh, Maybole.
7. William Lumsden, Glasgow.

The Prizes of the ETHIC CLASS, given for general eminence in the Composition of Exercises, and in the other duties and business of the Class, were adjudged

1st, In the *Senior Division* of the Class, to

1. James Stevenson, Kilmarnock.
2. James Barclay, Glasgow.
3. William Rowe, Bristol.
4. John Davidson, Lanark.
5. Charles Wickstead, A.B., Shrewsbury.

2nd, In the *Junior Division*, to

1. David Hutchison Gibb, Glasgow.
2. Robert Frew, Perth.
3. William Wardrop, Beith.
4. Laurence Craigie, Glasgow.
5. Cunningham Smith,   ,,
6. Robert Stevenson, Campsie.

A Prize for Poetical Exercises was adjudged to

James Fleming, Ballimoney, Antrim.

A Prize for an Essay on Habit, proposed to the Students of last year, at the close of the Session 1828-29, was adjudged to

Thomas Stark, Chryston.

In the LOGIC CLASS the Prizes for this Session were adjudged as follows :—

I.

For general Eminence and Superiority in the various Exercises and Examinations of the Class throughout the Session, to

Seniores.

1. John M. Mackenzie, St. Neots, Huntingdonshire.
2. Archibald Swinton, Edinburgh.
3. Arch. C. Tait,   ,,
4. John Leechman, Glasgow.
5. James Douglas, Kilbarchan.
6. Geo. H. Wells, Warrington.
7. David Lloyd, Cardiganshire.
8. J. R. Howison Craufurd, Craufurdland, Ayrshire.
9. John Paterson, Cambusnethan.

Juniores.

1. James Halley, Glasgow.
2. John Blackburn, Liverpool.
3. John James Campbell, Edinburgh.
4. James Robertson, Plean, Stirlingshire.
5. Archibald Smith, Jordanhill.
6. James Patrick Muirhead, Glasgow.
7. Robert Stewart,   ,,
8. John Campbell, Newton-lodge, Glasgow.
9. William W. Watson,   ,,

II.
For Essays.

1.

(Prescribed at the close of last Session, and composed during the Vacation.)

For the best "Essay on Experience as a source of moral evidence," to

William Rowe, Bristol.

For the best "Account historical and critical of the Pastoral Drama," to

Laurence W. Craigie, Glasgow.

2.

(Prescribed in the present Session, and executed during the Christmas holidays.)

For the best Essay on the question "Are all the Secondary Laws of Association reducible to these two :— (1) The frequency of the association between the suggesting and the suggested thought or feeling—and (2) the vividness of the associated feelings or ideas themselves," to

Senior Division.

James Douglas, Kilbarchan.

Junior Division.

James Halley, Glasgow.

3.

(Competed for by the Students of the Private Class).

For the best "Analytic Sketch of the Intellectual Powers," to

Ebenezer Wallace, Glasgow.

Prizes in the GREEK CLASS.

I.

Private—Vacation Exercises.

1. Essay on the critical character of Aristotle,

Andrew Borland Parker, Ayr.

2. Translation into English verse of the ninth Pythian Ode of Pindar,

Andrew Borland Parker, Ayr.

3. Translation into Greek Iambic Trimeters, from Shakspeare's Twelfth Night, Act I. Scene 2, " What's she ? " etc.,

James Halley, Glasgow.

Private—Session.

4. Essay on the discussion by Longinus, of Passion, as a source of the sublime,

Robert Cotton Mather, England.

II.

Public—Senior—Vacation Exercises.

1. Translation into Greek Tragic Iambic Trimeters, from Shakspeare's Measure for Measure, Act I. Scene 1, " Always obedient to your Grace's will," to " of your Commissions,"

James Halley, Glasgow.

2. Translation into English verse of the " Trachiniæ " of Sophocles,

John Blackburn, Liverpool.

3. Translation into English Prose of the ninth book of Herodotus, with an index of Ionicisms,

Laurence Williams Craigie, Glasgow.

4. Translation into English Prose of the Corinthian and Corcyræan Speeches at Athens, Thucy. B. I., c. 32-43,

Archibald Campbell Tait, Edinburgh.

Public—Senior—Session.

1. For excelling at the Black-Stone Examination, to

1. James Halley, Glasgow.
2. Archibald Campbell Tait, Edinburgh.
3. Archibald Smith, Jordanhill.

2. Translation into Greek Elegiac Verse, from Qvid's Heroides, "Briseis Achilli," v. 57-80,

James Halley, Glasgow.

3. For eminence in talent, scholarship, and industry throughout the Session,

Logic Side.

1. Archibald Campbell Tait, Edinburgh.
2. Archibald Smith, Jordanhill.
3. John M. Mackenzie, St. Neots, Huntingdonshire.
4. James Morrison, Auchterarder.
5. John Paterson, Cambusnethan.

Greek Side.

1. James Colquhoun, Glasgow.
2. Robert Dewar, Muirbank, Glasgow.
3. Charles Pullar, Paisley.
4. William Dunlop, Edinburgh.

4. For excelling in the Weekly Exercises in Greek Verse prescribed throughout the Session,

1. Peter M'Kinlay, Laurieston, Glasgow.
2. James Colquhoun,   „
3. Archibald C. Tait, Edinburgh ; and
   Robert Dewar, Muirbank.

III.—*Public—Junior.*

Vacation Exercises.

1. Translation into Homeric Hexameters, from Goldsmith's Traveller, "Yet still, even here, content can spread a charm," etc.,

Peter M'Kinlay, Laurieston, Glasgow.

2. Grammatical version of "Exercises in Homeric and Attic Greek, Part 1st,"

Peter M'Kinlay, Laurieston, Glasgow.

3. Translation into English Prose of Lucian's "Sale of Lives," with Historical notes,

James Colquhoun, Glasgow.

4. Version of the "Introduction to the Writing of Greek, Parts I. and II.,"

Samuel Davidson, Paisley.

5. Translation into English Prose of the Extracts from Anacreon and Tyrtæus, with a list of the irregular Verbs, and Ionic forms,
James Robertson, Plean, Stirlingshire.

Public—Junior—Session.

1. For eminence in talent, scholarship, and industry, throughout the Session.

Provectiores.

1. James Robertson, Plean, Stirlingshire.
2. George Forsyth, Glasgow.
3. John Johnstone, Greenock.
4. Alexander Ross, Glasgow.
5. John Turner,   ,,
6. Andrew Robertson, Paisley.
7. William Black, Stranraer.
8. James Murdoch, Ayr.

Tyrones.

1. John M. Symington, Paisley.
2. Robert Frame, Glasgow.
3. William Arnott, Perth.
4. James Clarke, Kilmun, Cowal.
5. William Fulton, Stewarton.
6. John M'Kinlay, Renton.

2. For Excelling in the Exercises in Greek Verse, prescribed throughout the Session,

1. George Lyon, Glasgow.
2. Alex. Campbell, Newton Lodge, Glasgow.
3. Alexander Ross,   ,,

Prizes in the HUMANITY CLASS.

I. For exemplary conduct and general eminence throughout the Session.

FIRST DIVISION.

Seniores of two years' standing

James Colquhoun, Glasgow.
John Wardlaw,   ,,
James Barlas,   ..
John Muir,   ,,
Alexander Ross,   ,,
Thomas Mathew, Kincardine.

Seniores of one year's standing.

George Robinson, Edinburgh.
John M. Symington, Paisley.
George Gordon, Edinburgh.
Mungo Muir, Kilmarnock.
Walter M'Hutchison, Glasgow.
James Bruce, Kilmarnock.

SECOND DIVISION.

Seniores attending the Second Division.

Robert Frame, Glasgow.
William Fulton, Stewarton.
William Arnot, Perth.
John M'Kinlay, Renton, Dumbartonshire.

Juniores.

George Forsyth, Glasgow.
John Johnston, Greenock.
John Turner, Glasgow.
John Neilson,   ,,
John Cochran,   ,,
Adam Walker, New Kilpatrick.
Morton Shand, Glasgow.
Robert Chrystal,   ,,
James Gourlay,   ,,

II. For excelling at the Blackstone Examination.

COMPETITORS. { James Colquhoun, Glasgow.
{ G. Robinson, Edinburgh. } Equal.
{ James Barlas, Glasgow.   }

NON-
COMPETITORS. { John Wardlaw, Glasgow.
{ Andrew Melville, Dumfries.
{ James Bruce, Kilmarnock.

III. For excelling in the Weekly Exercises.

1st DIVISION. { James Currie, Dumfries.
{ James Colquhoun, Glasgow.
{ Hugh Jaffrey, Irvine.

2nd DIVISION. { John Johnston, Greenock.
{ George Forsyth, Glasgow.

IV. For the best Original Latin Verses, written during the Vacation, to

James Colquhoun, Glasgow.

Written during the Session.

1st DIVISION—James Colquhoun, Glasgow.
John Struthers, Waterbeck, Dumfries-shire.

2nd DIVISION—George Forsyth, Glasgow.

V. For the best Essay in Latin Prose, written during the Vacation, to

James Colquhoun, Glasgow.

Written during the Session.

1st DIVISION—William Burnie, Moffat.

2nd   ,,   —John D. Muter, Glasgow.

VI. For the best English Poem founded on Tacitus' Annals, I. 61.

James Colquhoun, Glasgow.

VII. For the best Translation into English Verse of Hor. Epist. I. 10.

James Colquhoun, Glasgow.

VIII. Best biographical and critical account of the poet Claudian,

James Colquhoun, Glasgow.
John Wardlaw,   ,,

IX. For the best notes of the Lectures on Roman Antiquities,

James Colquhoun, Glasgow.
Colin Mitchell,   ,,

————

GLASGOW COLLEGE, 30th APRIL, 1831.

This day, the Annual Distribution of Prizes was made in the Common Hall, by the Principal and Professors, in presence of a numerous meeting of the University, and of many Reverend and respectable Gentlemen of the City and neighbourhood, and of several distinguished strangers.

UNIVERSITY PRIZES.

I. In THEOLOGY.

A Silver Medal, for the best Essay on the Religion of the ancient Persians,

John MacFarlan, Glasgow.

Mr. EWING'S GOLD MEDAL.

For the best Account of the Competition between Bruce and Baliol for the Crown of Scotland,

Robert M'Corkle, A.M., Glasgow.

On Mr. COULTER'S Donation.

I. For the best Discourse on 1st Thess. v. 22,

Mungo Parker, Kilmarnock.

II. For the best Translation from Greek into English,

Alexander Davidson, Cadder.

Mr. JEFFREY'S GOLD MEDAL.

For the best Scholar in the Humanity Class, to

Andrew Ramsay Campbell, Garscube.

On Mr. WATT's Donation.

I. For the best Account of the Chemical Theory of Malting Grain,

Andrew B. Parker, Ayr.

II. For the best Essay on the theory and uses of the Pendulum,

John Pollock, A.M., Paisley.

The MARQUIS of LANSDOWNE'S Prizes.

For excelling in the Examination for a Degree in Arts, in Physical Science, to

Neil M'Michael, A.M., Kilmarnock.

And in General Literature, to

James Halley, A.B., Glasgow.

The Degree of A.M., was taken, with highest honours in Literature, by

David Arnot, Riccarton.

With second honours in Literature, by

John Jenkins, Wales.
Robt. Cotton Mather, England.

And in Physical Science, by -

Neil M'Michael, Kilmarnock.

The degree of A.B. was taken, with highest honours, by

James Halley, Glasgow.

Two Prizes by the JURISDICTIO ORDINARIA, for the best Latin Orations, were adjudged to

David Arnot, A.M., Riccarton.
Alexander Davidson, Cadder.

The Prizes of the DIVINITY CLASSES were adjudged—

To Students of the Senior Class.

For an Account of the Lectures on the Evidences for Divine Revelation, to

1. John Pollock, A.M., Paisley.
2. John Campbell, Balquhidder.

For an Essay on the Miracles of our Lord and his Apostles, to

Robert Stevenson, A.M., Campsie.

For an Essay on the Divine Authority of the Old Testament Scriptures, to

John Pollock, A.M., Paisley.

For an Essay on the Proof arising from the rapid and extensive Propagation of the Gospel, to

John Macfarlane, Glasgow.

(The above Exercises were executed during the Summer Vacation).

For an Essay on the Goodness of God, to
>> Peter M'Moreland, Greenock.

For an Essay on the Justice of God, to
>> John Pollock, A.M., Paisley.

For an Essay on Divine Providence, to
>> Andrew Borland Parker, Ayr.

For the best Specimen of Public Reading, to
>> William Norval, A.M.,   ⟩ Glasgow.
>> William Chalmers, A.M., ⟩ Aberdeen.

To Students of the Junior Class.

For Eminence in the general Exercises of the Class, to
>> Mathew Graham, Glasgow.
>> Daniel Cameron,   ,,
>> George R. Kennedy, Dornoch.

For an Essay on the Internal Evidence of Christianity, to
>> Mathew Graham, Glasgow.

Prizes in the CHURCH HISTORY CLASS were adjudged—
for the best Essays on the Jewish Sects.

1. *To the Students of the Third Year.*

>> Thomas Dymock, Glasgow.

2. *To the Students of the Second Year.*

Andrew Borland Parker, Ayr.
Archibald Kirkland, Cambusnethan.

3. *To the Students of the First Year.*

>> John Pollock, A.M., Paisley.

A Prize in the CIVIL HISTORY CLASS was adjudged—
for the best Essay on the History of Rome during the Regal Government,
>> John Blackburn, Liverpool.

Prizes of the HEBREW CLASSES.
Senior Class.

I. For the best Original Composition in Biblical Hebrew, to
>> William Boyd, Largs.

II. For the best comparative view of the Hebrew and Arabic Accidence, to

1. William Boyd, Largs.
2. Andrew Borland Parker, Ayr.

Junior Class.

I. For eminent proficiency in the business of the class, to

1. James Ewing, Muthill.
2. Mathew Graham, Glasgow.
3. Robert Blair,   ,,

II. For the best Essay on the New Testament Greek, to

Alexander Davidson, **Cadder.**

III. For excelling in the performance of the Weekly Exercises, to

Matthew Graham, Glasgow.

LAW.

Two Prizes for excelling in the daily examinations, proposed to those Students of SCOTTISH LAW who chose to be examined, were adjudged to

John Shirreff, Glasgow.
James Scott Richardson, Glasgow.

Two Prizes were given in the ANATOMY CLASS.
One for the best Essay on Secretion, was given to

Robert Dundas Thomson.

Another for the best Essay on the question, " Is Organization the cause of Vitality, or Vitality the cause of Organization ? " was given to

Alex. Anderson.

Prizes in the CHEMISTRY CLASS.
For the best Essay on Respiration,

John Borland, Kilmarnock.

For the best appearance at the public Examinations of the Class, during the Session.

Second Year's Students.

William Frazer Tolmie, Glasgow.
William Birkmyre, Paisley.

First Year's Students.

John Mackinlay, Renton.
William Dering Walker, New Rumney, Kent.
James Macnair, Glasgow.

NATURAL HISTORY.

For General Eminence, to

Mr. Andrew Borland Parker, Ayr.
Mr. James Young, Lesmahagow.
Mr. Thomas Easton M'Fadyen, Glasgow.

For the best Essay on the Geology of the Deluge, to
Mr. Andrew Borland Parker, Ayr.

Prizes of the MATHEMATICAL CLASSES.

Senior Class.

Prizes for general Eminence throughout the Session,

1. Thomas Morton, Kilmarnock.
2. Archibald Smith, Jordanhill.
3. Robert M'Goun, Greenock.
4. Alexander Chrystal, Glasgow.
5. Robert Kay, Kilmarnock.

JUNIOR CLASS.

Senior Division.

Prizes for general Eminence.

1. John M'Cubbin, Glasgow.
2. Daniel Gunn, Christ Church, Hampshire.
3. John Paterson, Ochiltree, Ayrshire.
4. John Currie, Newfield, Dumfries-shire.
5. Alexander Stewart, Doune, Perthshire.

Junior Division.

1. James Halley, Glasgow.
2. John Cross, Paisley.
3. James Colquhoun, Glasgow.
4. John Blyth, Nunwood, Dumfries-shire.
5. Andrew C. Brisbane Neil, Largs, Ayrshire.

Prizes for ALGEBRAIC EXERCISES.

1. John M'Cubbin, Glasgow.
2. George Morton, Galston, Ayrshire.
3. { George Wells, Warrington, Lancashire.
     James Colquhoun, Glasgow.   } Equal.
     John Cross, Paisley.

The Prizes of the NATURAL PHILOSOPHY CLASS, for propriety of conduct, exemplary diligence, and display of eminent abilities in examinations on the subjects of the Lectures ; and in Essays and Investigations connected with Physical Science, were adjudged to

1. Andrew Donald, Lesmahagow.
2. William Beckett, Paisley.
3. James Steven, Eaglesham.
4. George D. Thomson, Kilmarnock.
5. John Kinross, Dunblane.
6 and 7. { James Stevenson, Kilmarnock.
equal.   { John Davidson, Lanark.
8. Alexander Davidson, Cadder.

A Prize was given for eminent talent and exemplary diligence in performing voluntarily the various Exercises, to a Student of the Private Class,

Thomas Morton, Kilmarnock.

The Prizes of the ETHIC CLASS, given for general eminence in the Composition of Exercises, and in the other duties and business of the Class, were adjudged—

1st, In the Senior Division.

1. John Morell M'Kenzie, St. Neot's, Huntingdonshire.
2. John Paterson, Cambusnethan.
3. Robert Walter Stewart, Erskine.
4. Jn. Morrison Whitelaw, Berwick-on-Tweed.
5. Daniel Penman, Muirkirk.

In the Junior Division.

1. Jas. Halley, B.A., Glasgow.
2. John Blackburn, Liverpool.
3. James Patk. Muirhead, Glasgow.
4. Andrew Thomson, Sanquhar.
5. William M'Kechnie, Paisley.

For excelling in Poetical Composition,
John Morrison Whitelaw, Berwick.
James P. Muirhead, Glasgow.

For the best Essay on Instinct,
James J. Beck, Capetown, South Africa.

———

In the LOGIC CLASS the Prizes for this Session were adjudged as follows :—

I.

For general eminence and superiority in the various Exercises and Examinations of the Class throughout the Session, to

Seniores.

1. Christopher Dunkin, Huntingdonshire.
2. Henry Wilkes, Birmingham.
3. James C. Gallaway, London.
4. William Arnot, Perthshire.
5. Andrew Robertson, Paisley.
6. Edward Napier, Montrose.
7. Matthew Lindsay, Lauriston.

Juniores.

1. James Forrest, Greenock.
2. James Colquhoun, Glasgow.
3. Colin G. Mitchell, Newton-hill.
4. Andrew Melville, Dumfries.
5. Robert Douie, Glasgow.
6. Mungo F. Muir, Kilmarnock.
7. { George A. Eccles, Glasgow. } equal.
   { John W. Thomson, Kilmarnock. }

II.

For Essays.

1.

(Prescribed at the close of last Session, and composed during the Vacation).

For the best Essay on Analogy as a Species of Moral Evidence, to

John M. Mackenzie, St. Neot's, Huntingdonshire.

2.

(Prescribed in the present Session, and executed during the Christmas holidays).

For the best Specimen of the Socratic Dialogue—Subject—Temperance Societies, to

Matthew Lindsay, Lauriston.

3.

(Competed for by Students of the Private Class).

For the best Critical examination of Sir Walter Scott's History of Scotland, with reference to the chief requisites of Historical Composition, to

James R. Campbell, Glasgow.

Prizes in the Greek Class.

I.

Private—Vacation Exercises.

1. Essay on the origin, use, and proper limits of Metaphysical Language in Composition,

Adam Roxburgh, Kilmaurs.

2. Translation into Greek Comic Iambic Trimeters, from Shakspeare's Tempest, Act I. Sc. ii., "As wicked dew as e'er my mother brush'd," to "the honour of my child,"

Alexander Chrystal, Glasgow.

Private—Session.

1. Essay on Aristotle's rhetorical tests of absolute and comparative good, and of the honourable and the base, considered with reference to Morality,

Charles **Wicksteed**, A.B., Shrewsbury.

2. Translation into English Verse of the 1st Choral Interlude of the Ædipus Tyrannus of Sophocles,

Adam Roxburgh, Kilmaurs.

II.

Public—Senior—Vacation Exercises.

1. Translation into Greek Tragic Iambic Trimeters of Cowper's Verses, supposed to be written by Alexander Selkirk,

James Colquhoun, Glasgow.

2. Translation into Greek Attic Prose from Goldsmith's History of Greece,

James Colquhoun, Glasgow.

3. Translation into English Verse of the Choral Interludes of the Hippolytus of Euripides,

Archibald Smith, Jordanhill.

4. Translation of the Panegyric Oration of Isocrates,

John Wardlaw, Glasgow.

Public—Senior—Session.

1. For excelling at the Black-stone examination,
    1. James Colquhoun, Glasgow.
    2. George Robinson, Ruchill.

2. For the best Poem in Greek Elegiac Verse,
    James Currie, Newfield, Dumfries-shire.

3. For eminence in Talent, Scholarship, and Industry throughout the Session,

Logic Side.

1. James Colquhoun, Glasgow.
2. George Robinson, Ruchill.
3. William Arnot, Perth.
4. Alexander Ross, Glasgow.

Greek Side.

1. Archibald Smith, Jordanhill.
2. David Ogilvy, Edinburgh.
3. Alexander Stewart, Erskine.
4. James Currie, Newfield, Dumfries-shire.
5. John Wardlaw, Glasgow.
6. Andrew Ramsay Campbell, Garscube.

4. For excelling in the weekly Exercises in Greek Verse and Prose prescribed throughout the Session,

1. Archibald Smith, Jordanhill.
2. David Ogilvy, Edinburgh.
3. John Wardlaw, Glasgow.

III. Public Junior.

Vacation Exercises.

1. Translation of the first Idyl of Theocritus, with an Index of the Doric forms,

James Robertson, Plean, Stirling.

2. Translation of Extracts from Herodotus, with an Index of Ionicisms and of the irregular Verbs,

John W. Thomson, Kilmarnock.

3. Translation of Extracts from Homer and Tyrtæus, with an Index of Epic and Ionic forms,

William Fulton, Stewarton.

4. Translation of Extracts from Lucian's Dialogues, with an Index of the irregular Verbs,

Henry Bryce, Helensburgh.

Public—Junior—Session.

1. For eminence in talent, scholarship, and industry, throughout the Session.

Provectiores.

1. William Fulton, Stewarton.
2. Anthony Gowan, Whitehaven.
3. Andrew Johnston, Calton, Glasgow.
4. John Frame, Bothwell.
5. John Thomson, Kilmarnock.

6. Robert Hervey, Glasgow.
7. Thomas D. D. Graham, Glasgow.
8. David Wharton, Greenock.

Tyrones.

1. Thomas Stirratt, Glasgow.
2. Duncan Clark, Dunoon, Argyllshire.
3. Moncrieff Mitchell, Glasgow.
4. James Cameron, Gourock.
5. Archibald Roy, Dunblane, Perthshire.
6. John Millar, East Kilbride.

2. For excelling in Exercises in Greek Verse and Prose.
   1. David Gray, Kincardine, Blairdrummond. ⎫ equal
      William Urquhart, Fairhill, Hamilton.   ⎬
   2. William Fulton, Stewarton.

Prizes in the HUMANITY CLASS.

I. For Exemplary Conduct and General Eminence throughout the Session,

FIRST DIVISION.

Seniores of two years' standing.

1. John Johnston, Greenock.
2. George Forsyth, Glasgow.
3. John Gardiner, Bothwell.
4. John Turner, Glasgow.
5. William Fulton, Stewarton.
6. James Hamilton, Strathblane.

Seniores of one year's standing.

1. Alexander Dorsey, Glasgow.
2. David Wharton, Greenock.
3. John Thomson, Kilmarnock.
4. John Frame, Bothwell.
5. Alexander Rowand, Glasgow.
6. Anthony T. Gowan, Whitehaven.

SECOND or JUNIOR DIVISION.

1. George Stevenson, Campsie.
2. Duncan Clark, Dunoon.

      3. William Thomson, Stirling.
      4. William Urquhart, Fairhill, Hamilton.
      5. John Morier, Glasgow.
      6. David Stewart, Erskine.
      7. William Stirling, Craigie, Ayrshire.
      8. David Gray, Kincardine, Perthshire.
      9. William Taylor, Liston.

II. For excelling at the Black Stone Examination,
      1. John Gardiner, Bothwell.
      2. Andrew R. Campbell, Garscube.
      3. George Forsyth, Glasgow.

III. For excelling in the Weekly Exercises,

1st DIVISION. { 1. John Johnston, Greenock.
2. John Gardiner, Bothwell.
3. James Hamilton, Strathblane.

2nd DIVISION. { 1. Wm. Urquhart, Fairhill, Hamilton.
2. David Gray, Kincardine, Perthshire.

IV. For Single Exercises.

1. For the best Verse Exercise written during the vacation,
      William Fulton, Stewarton.

For the best written during the session,
    1st DIVISION—Andrew R. Campbell, Garscube.
    2nd   ,,   —David Stewart, Erskine.

2. For the best Essay in Latin Prose, written during the vacation,
      William Fulton, Stewarton.

For the best written during the Session,
    1st DIVISION—Andrew R. Campbell, Garscube.
    2nd   ,,   —David Stewart, Erskine.

3. For the best Translation into English Verse of the Elegy of Ovid on the death of Tibullus, Amorum 3, 9.
      Andrew R. Campbell, Garscube.

4. For ne oest Biographical and Critical Account of the poet Silius Italicus,
      John Turner, Glasgow.

GLASGOW COLLEGE, 27th APRIL, 1832.

This day, the Annual Distribution of Prizes was made in the Common Hall, by the Principal and Professors, in presence of a numerous meeting of the University, and of many Reverend and respectable Gentlemen of the City and neighbourhood.

UNIVERSITY PRIZES.

I. IN THEOLOGY.

A Silver Medal for the best Account of the Manuscripts of the Old Testament,
John Pollock, A.M., Paisley.

GARTMORE GOLD MEDAL,

For the best Historical Account of the Scottish Parliament previous to the Union,
Andrew Borland Parker, A.M., Ayr.

On Mr. COULTER'S DONATION.

I. For the best Lecture on the 84th Psalm,

II. For the best Essay on Intuitive Evidence,

John Campbell, Port-Glasgow.
Thomas Stark, Cadder.

III. For the best Translation from Latin into English,
James Colquhoun, Glasgow.

Mr. JEFFREY'S GOLD MEDAL.

For the best Scholar in the Greek Class, to
James Currie, Dumfries-shire.

On Mr. WATT'S DONATION.

For the best Essay on the connection between the rate at which Sound passes through the Gases and their specific gravities,
Andrew B. Parker, A.M., Ayr.

The Degree of A.M., was taken, with the highest honours in Literature, by
Andrew B. Parker, Ayr.

Two Prizes by the JURISDICTIO ORDINARIA for the best Latin
Orations, were adjudged to

      Robert Walter Stewart, A.M., Erskine.
Archibald Currie, Glasgow.

The Prizes of the DIVINITY CLASSES were adjudged to

Students of the Senior Class.

For an Abridgement of the Lectures on the Evidences for
Divine Revelation, to
      Robert Dalglish, Kilbride.

For an Essay on the Character of Christ, as a proof of his
Divine Commission, to
      Matthew Graham, Glasgow.

(The above Exercises were executed during the Summer
Vacation).

For the best Specimen of Public Reading among Students of
the second year, was adjudged to
      Andrew Sutherland, Glasgow.

For Exercises during the Session, in the Senior Class, by
Students of the second and third years.

A Prize for an Essay " On the Subjects and Manner of Christ's
Teaching," was adjudged to
      John Pollock, A.M., Paisley, of the 3rd year.
Wm. Braid, Kirkintilloch, of the 2nd year.

For an Essay " On Views Preliminary to the consideration of
the Death of Christ," to
      James Reid, Dunblane, of the 3rd year.
Matthew Graham, Glasgow, of the 2nd year.
Thomas Stark, Chryston, of the 2nd year.

To Students of the Junior Class.

For Eminence in the General Exercises of the Class, to
      James Stevenson, A.M., Kilmarnock.
John Davidson, A.M., Lanark.
William Lyall, Paisley.
Archibald Duncan Bute

For the best Essay on Testimony in its connexion with the Evidence for Christianity, to

James Stevenson, A.M., Kilmarnock.

To Students of the Class for Sacred Criticism.

For an Essay on Figurative Language, applied to the illustration of the Language of Scripture, particularly of the origin and nature of Parables, to

Andrew Borland Parker, A.M., Ayr.

For an Essay on the Influence of Moral qualities upon Style, applied to the illustration of the Style of the Writings of the New Testament, to

John Pollock, A.M., Paisley.

———

Prizes in the CHURCH HISTORY CLASS were adjudged for the best Essays on the Apostolic Fathers, with an Analysis of their Writings.

1. *To Students of the Third Year.*

Archibald Kirkland, Cambusnethan.
William Douglas, Inch.

To the Students of the Second Year.

John Pollock, A.M., Paisley.

3. *To the Students of the First Year.*

Robert Stevenson, A.M., Campsie.

———

A Prize in the CIVIL HISTORY CLASS was adjudged for the best Essay on the Government of Athens contrasted with that of Sparta, to

Duncan Blair, Balfron.

———

Prizes in the HEBREW CLASS.

For general eminence in the business of the Class.

First or Senior Division:

1. John Pollock, A.M., Paisley.
2. Mr. Duncan Blair, Balfron.
   Mr. John Haddin, Glasgow. } Equal.

Second or Junior Division.

1. Mr. John Paterson, Cambusnethan.
2. Mr. James Young, Lesmahagow.
3. Mr. Robert Stevenson, Campsie.

For excelling in the Writing of the Essays prescribed during the Session.

First Division.

John Pollock, A.M., Paisley.

Second Division.   } Equal.

Mr. Will. Brown Galloway, Glasgow.

LAW.

Two Prizes for Excelling in the Daily Examinations proposed to those Students of SCOTTISH LAW who chose to be examined, were adjudged to

John Walker. Glasgow.
Peter Finlayson, „

ANATOMY.

For the best Essay on the influence of the Brain and Nerves on the several functions of the Animal Economy, to

John Balbirnie, A.M., Glasgow.

MEDICINE.

For general Eminence.

Price Carfrae Brown, M.D., Jamaica.

Prizes in the CHEMISTRY CLASS.

For the best Essay on the Chemical Constitution of Urine and Calculi.

Mr. James Bruce, Kilmarnock.

For the best appearance during the regular Examinations of the Class during the Session.

Price Carfrae Brown, M.D., Jamaica.
Henry Marshall Hughes, London.
Francis Bossey,   „

NATURAL HISTORY.

Prizes for General Eminence,

Mr. Wm. Brown Galloway, A.M., Glasgow.
,, John Pollock, A.M., Paisley.
,, James Steven, Eaglesham.

SENIOR MATHEMATICAL CLASS.

Prizes for proficiency in the Class,

1. John M'Cubbin, Glasgow.
2. Wm. Ferrie, Kilconquhar, Fife.
3. Andrew Robertson, Girvan, Ayrshire.

Prizes for superior merit in performing the Exercises,

1. John M'Cubbin, Glasgow.
2. Wm. Ferrie, Kilconquhar, Fife.

JUNIOR MATHEMATICS.

Prizes for proficiency in the Class,

1st Division.

1. Thomas A. Bryce, Belfast.
2. William Arnot, Perth.
3. John M'Kail, Coylton, Ayrshire.
4. James Galloway, London.

2nd Division.

1. John M'Carter, Ireland.
2. Nathan Rogers,   ,,
3. George Robinson, Ruchill, Glasgow.

3rd Division.

1. Colin G. Mitchell, Glasgow.
2. David Playfair, Dalmarnock, Glasgow.
3. Thomas Thomson,   ,,
4. Isaac Cust, Durham.

Prizes for superior merit in performing the Exercises.

1st Division.

1. James Cook Neil, Eldon Place, Tradeston, Glasgow.
2. Thomas A. Bryce, Belfast.

2nd Division.

1. John M'Carter, Ireland.

Equal 2. {Nathan Rogers,   ,,
           {George Robinson, Ruchill, Glasgow.

3rd Division.

1. David Playfair, Dalmarnock, Glasgow.

Equal. 2. {Colin Mitchell,   ,,
          {Thomas Thomson,
          {Isaac Cust, Durham.

Superior merit in Trigonometry.

John M'Kail, Coylton, Ayrshire.

The Prizes of the NATURAL PHILOSOPHY CLASS, for propriety of conduct, exemplary diligence, and display of eminent abilities in Examinations on the Subjects of the Lectures ; and in Essays and Investigations connected with Physical Science, were adjudged to

1. Archibald Smith, Jordanhill.
2. James Halley, A.B., Glasgow.
3. George Morton, Galston.
4. Andrew C. B. Neill, Largs,
5. William Ferrie, Kilconquhar.
6. Daniel Penman, Muirkirk.
7. Archibald Currie, Glasgow.

The Prizes in the ETHIC CLASS, given for general eminence, and more particularly for the industry, ability, and acquirements exhibited in the weekly and in the voluntary Exercises on Ethical Subjects, which were read in the Class, were adjudged

In the Senior Division, to

1. Henry Wilks, Canada.
2. {James Galloway, London.
   {Matthew Lindsay, Glasgow.
3. Andrew Robertson, Paisley.
4. John Sheriff, Glasgow.

And in the Junior Division, to

1. James Forrest, Greenock.
2. James Robertson, Plean, Stirlingshire.
3. James Colquhoun, Glasgow.
4. Mungo Muir, Kilmarnock.

A Prize for Essays in Verse, was adjudged to
Andrew Ross, Glasgow.

In the LOGIC CLASS, the Prizes for this Session were adjudged as follows :—

I.

For general eminence and superiority in the various Exercises and Examinations of the Class throughout the Session, to

Senior Division.

1. Robert M'Dowell, County Antrim, Ireland.
2. John Robertson, Aberdeen.
3. James R. Campbell, Glasgow.
4. Anthony Gowan, Whitehaven, Cumberland.
5. James Connell, Edinburgh.

Middle Division.

1. James Hamilton, Strathblane.
2. And. Ramsay Campbell, Garscube.
3. John Wardlaw, Glasgow.
4. John Cochrane,   „
5. James Currie, Dumfries-shire.

Junior Division.

1. Robert Hadfield, Manchester.
2. James Dennistoun, *minor*, Dumfries.
3. John Crawford, Greenhaugh, Govan.
4. Thomas Watson, Glasgow.
5. Frederick Wilkes, Upper Canada.

II.

FOR ESSAYS.

1.

(Prescribed at the close of last Session, and composed during the Vacation).

For the best Critical Analysis and Examination of Sir Joshua Reynolds's Theory of Beauty, to

Andrew Robertson, Paisley.

2.

(Prescribed in the present Session, and executed during the Christmas holidays).

PROSE.—For the best Essay on Judgment or the Judging Faculty, to
James R. Campbell, Glasgow.

VERSE.—For the Best Poem on Creative Imagination, to
George Duncan, Govanhaugh, Hutchesontown.

3.

(Competed for by the Students of the *Private Class*).

For the best Essay explaining and exemplifying Lord Bacon's fourfold division of the Idols of the human understanding, to
James Mason, Kilmarnock.

Prizes in the GREEK CLASS.

I.

Private—Vacation Exercises.

1. Analytical Abridgement of Aristotle's Rhetoric, as prelected on in the Class,
James Patrick Muirhead, Glasgow.

2. Translation into English Verse of the 2nd Olympic Ode of Pindar,
James Patrick Muirhead, Glasgow.

3. Translation into Homeric Hexameters of Psalm 139,
James Colquhoun, Glasgow.

Private—Session.

For Excelling in the Voluntary Examinations on the business of the Class,
1. James Colquhoun, Glasgow.
2. George Robinson, Ruchill.
3. Alexander Patrick Stewart, Erskine.

II.

Public—Senior — Vacation Exercises.

1. Translation into Greek Iambic Trimeters, from Shakspeare's Taming of the Shrew, Act V., Scene II., " Fy, fy, unknit that

threat'ning unkind brow," to "Should well agree with our external parts,

Ramsay Campbell, Garscube.

2. Translation into Attic Prose of Hume's Character of Charles I., from "Some historians have rashly questioned," to "which form an accomplished Prince,"

William Dunlop, Edinburgh.

3. Translation into English Prose of Herodotus, B. II., from C. 99 to end, with an Index of Ionic forms,

John Cochran, Glasgow.

Public—Senior—Session.

1. For excelling at the Blackstone Examination,

1. James Hamilton, Strathblane.
2. Ramsay Campbell, Garscube.
3. John Wardlaw, Glasgow.

2. For the best poem in Greek Verse on the Cyreian Greeks in sight of the sea,

James Connell, Edinburgh.

3. For excelling in ability, scholarship, and assiduity throughout the Session,

Logic Side.

1. Ramsay Campbell, Garscube.
2. James Connell, Edinburgh.
3. George Forsyth, Glasgow.
4. Antony Gowan, Whitehaven.
5. James Hamilton, Strathblane.

Greek Side.

1. John Gardiner, Bothwell.
2. William Fulton, Stewarton.
3. Alexander Ogilvy, Forfarshire.
4. Peter Waddell, Finnieston, Glasgow.
5. George Stevenson, Campsie.

4. For excelling in the Weekly Exercises in Greek Verse and Prose, throughout the Session,

1. Henry Cadogan Hastings, Glasgow.
2. John Wardlaw,   ,,
3. Ramsay Campbell, Garscube.

III.

Public—Junior—Vacation Exercises.

1. Abridgement of first three books of Xenophon's Anabasis, with Historical and Geographical Notes,

William Fulton, Stewarton.

2. Version of "Exercises in Homeric and Attic Greek, Part I.," with exemplifying Words and Phrases underlined,

William Fulton, Stewarton.

3. Translation of Lucian's "Sale of Lives," with an index of irregular verbs,

James Gray, Kincardine, Blairdrummond.

4. Version of "Introduction, etc.," Parts I. and IL, with exemplifying words and phrases underlined,

Frederick Thomas Wilkes, Upper Canada.

5. Translation of Extracts from Homer and Anacreon, with an Index of Epic and Ionic forms,

Robert Kingan, Glasgow.

Public—Junior—Session.

1 For excelling in Ability, Scholarship, and Assiduity throughout the Session.

Provectiores.

1. Thomas Stirrat, Glasgow.
2. Robert Kingan,   ,,
3. William Young, Kilsyth.
4. Duncan Clark, Dunoon.
5. Charles Young, Batavia.
6. John Miller, East Kilbride.
7. James Newman, Glasgow.
8. James Reid, Coilton, Ayrshire.

Tyrones.

1. David Patrick, Dalry, Ayrshire.
2. Charles M'Rae, Barvas, Ross-shire.
3. John Fraser, Glasgow.
4. Henry Cleland,   ,,
5. Peter Bannatyne, ,,
6. Alexander Campbell, Oban.

2. For excelling in Greek Versification.
   1. Robert Reddie, Glasgow.
   2. Thomas Stirratt,   ,,

Prizes in the HUMANITY CLASS.

I.

Private—Session.

1. Essay on writings of Horace, embracing an account of the rise and progress of Lyric and Satiric Poetry among the Romans,
Michael Connal, Glasgow.

2. Imitation in English verse of Horace, Sat. IX., Bk. I.
William Urquhart, Fairhill, Lanarkshire.

II.

Public—Senior—Vacation Exercises.

1. Latin Ode on the subject, " Nihil est ab omni parte beatum,"
William Fulton, Stewarton.

2. English verses on the Story of Sophonisba and Massinissa, as related by Livy, Bk. XXX.
Alexander Dorsey, Glasgow.

Public—Senior—Session.

1. For excelling at the Black Stone Examination,
      1. Thomas Thomson, Glasgow.
      2. Alexander Ogilvy, Forfarshire.
      3. James Nixon Porter.

2. Latin Verses on the subject " Pestis,"
David Stewart, Erskine.

3. Latin Essay on the History of the first Punic war,
William Little, Glasgow.

4. For Eminence in Talent, Scholarship, and Industry throughout the Session.

Students of the Second Year.

1. Thomas Stirrat, Glasgow.
2. Alexander Dorsey,   ,,
3. John Blythe, Savanna-la-Mar, Jamaica.

4. George Stevenson, Campsie, Stirlingshire.
5. Peter Waddell, Finnieston House, Glasgow.
6. William Thomson, Stirling.

Students of the First Year.

1. John M'Murrich, Arrochar.
2. Alexander Ogilvy, Forfarshire.
3. John Lightbody, Walmer, Kent.
4. John Storrie, Paisley.
5. Robert Newlands, Lesmahago.
6. William Little, Glasgow.

5. For excelling in the Weekly Exercises in Latin Prose, prescribed throughout the Session,

1. Thomas Stirrat, Glasgow.
2. William Urquhart, Fairhill, Lanarkshire.
3. David Gray, Kincardine, by Blair-Drummond.

6. For excelling in the Exercises in Latin Verse, prescribed during the Session,

William Urquhart, Fairhill, Lanarkshire.

III.

Public—Junior—Vacation Exercises.

Essay on the Life and Writings of Lucan,
James Thomson, Edinburgh.

Public—Junior—Session.

1. Latin Verses on the subject " In Novum Annum,"
John Walker, New Kilpatrick.

2. An Abridgement in Latin Prose of the Jugurthine War,
Joseph Edward Heap, Berwick-upon-Tweed.

3. An Essay on the changes which took place in the Roman Constitution from the expulsion of the Kings to the death of Augustus,
John Fraser, Glasgow.

4. For eminence in Talent, Scholarship, and Industry throughout the Session,

1. John Fraser, Glasgow.
2. Charles William Young, Batavia, Java.
3. John Walker, New Kilpatrick. .

4. Joseph Edward Heap, Berwick-upon-Tweed.
5. John Sharp, Richmond St., Glasgow.
6. James Kirk, Glasgow.
7. Daniel M'Kenzie, Craig-Park.

5. For excelling in the Exercises in Latin Prose prescribed weekly during the Session,

    1. Daniel M'Kenzie, Craig-Park.
    2. Charles William Young, Batavia, Java.
    3. John Walker, New Kilpatrick.

6. For excelling in the Exercises in Latin Verse prescribed during the Session,
    Charles William Young, Batavia, Java.

GLASGOW COLLEGE, 1st May, 1833.

Annual Prizes.

On the 1st of May, 1833, the Annual Distribution of Prizes was made in the Common Hall, by the Lord Rector, Principal, and Professors, in presence of a numerous meeting of the University, and of many Reverend and respectable Gentlemen of the City and neighbourhood.

University Prizes.

In Theology.

A Silver Medal for the best Account of the Manuscripts of the New Testament, to
    Andrew Borland Parker, A.M., Ayr.

Mr. Ewing's Gold Medal.

For the best Historical Account of the Wars of the Two Roses, to
    Andrew Borland Parker, A.M., Ayr.

On Mr. Coulter's Donation.

I. For the best Discourse on 1st Peter iii. 15, to
    John Campbell, Port-Glasgow.

II. For the best Translation of the Ethical Characters of Theophrastus, to
James Currie, Dumfries-shire.

———

On the Donation of Mr. Watt.

For the best Essay on the Conditions of Stability in Floating Bodies, to
A. C. Brisbane Neil, Ayrshire.

———

The Lord Advocate's Gold Medal.

To the best Student in the Humanity Class,
Thomas Taylor, Sunderland.

———

A Prize by the Jurisdictio Ordinaria, for a Latin Oration prepared for the Common Hall, was adjudged to
William Arnot, Perth.

———

On a Special Donation.

For the best Essay on Employing a Redundant Population, to
James Thomson, Forfarshire.

———

The Prizes of the Divinity Class were adjudged as follows:—

To Students of the Senior Class.

For an Essay on the Nature of Internal Evidence, to
James Stevenson, A.M., Kilmarnock.

For an Essay on the Internal Evidence of Christianity, to
James Stevenson, A.M., Kilmarnock.

(The above Exercises were executed during the Vacation.)

For an Essay on Prayer, to
Matthew Graham, Glasgow, of the 3rd year.
James Stevenson, A.M., of the 2nd year.

For an Essay on Future Punishment, to
Matthew Graham, Glasgow, of the 3rd year.
John Campbell, Port-Glasgow, of the 3rd year.
John Kinross, A.M., Dumblane, of the 2nd year.

For the best Specimen of Public Reading, to
    William Shand, A.M., Wishawtown.
        To Students of the Junior Class.
For excelling in the Class Exercises, to
        James Halley, A.B., Glasgow.
        William Graham, Glasgow.
        Alexander Stewart, A.M., Doune.
For the best Essays on the Corroborations to the Mosaic
History, arising from Heathen Writers and the Traditions of
Nations, to
        James Halley, A.B., Glasgow.
        William Graham,   ,,
        John Wright, Barony, Glasgow.
        ————
        Prizes in the HEBREW CLASSES.
            JUNIOR CLASS.
For General Eminence in the Business of the Class,
        James Halley, A.B., Glasgow.
        James Landels Rose,   ,,
        John Murray Auld, Stevenson.
For excelling in the writing of the Essays prescribed during the
Session, to
        James Stevenson, A.M., Kilmarnock.
            SENIOR CLASS.
For General Eminence in the Business of the Class, to
        Robert Paisley, Glasgow.
For excelling in the writing of the Essay, prescribed during the
Session, to
        John Pollock, A.M., Paisley.
        ————

Prizes in the CHURCH HISTORY CLASS were adjudged for the
best Essays on the History of the Lutheran Church, from the
Reformation till the present times.
        1. *To the Students of the Third year.*
        John Pollock, A.M., Paisley.
        William Dunn, Kilmadock.
        2. *To the Students of the Second year.*
        James Stevenson, A.M., Kilmarnock.

3. *To the Students of the First year.*
Robert Patrick, Dalry, Ayrshire.

A Prize in the CIVIL HISTORY CLASS was adjudged for the best Essay on the Causes which retarded the Progress of the Arts and Sciences among the Egyptians, to
James Young, Lesmahagow.

LAW.

Two Prizes for excelling in the Daily Examinations, proposed to those Students of SCOTTISH LAW who chose to be examined, were adjudged to
Robert D. Mackenzie, A.M., Dumbarton
John Wilson, Glasgow.

ANATOMY.

The Prize for the best Essay on the Structure and Functions of the Brain, with a Review of the Doctrines of Gall and Spurzheim, was adjudged to
John Balbirnie, A.M.

Prizes in the CHEMISTRY CLASS.
For the best Essays on the Blood, to
John Henry Frame, Bothwell.
Alexander Riddel, Blantyre.

For the best appearances at the regular Examinations of the Class,
Second Year's Students.

Le Baron Botsford, New Brunswick.

First Year's Students.

John Henry Frame, Bothwell.
James Maclune, Kirkcudbright.

Prizes in the MATHEMATICAL CLASSES.

For Ability, Diligence, and Proficiency, during the Session, in the Daily Examinations, and in the Performance of Exercises,

SENIOR CLASS.

1. Thomas A. Bryce, Belfast.
2. Daniel Penman, Muirkirk.
3. Andrew Anderson, Glasgow.
4. David Playfair, Dalmarnock.

JUNIOR CLASS.

Senior Division.

1. Robert C. Brown, Belfast.
2. John Millar, East Kilbride.
3. John Lyon, Rothsay.
4. John Johnston, Greenock.
5. William Young, Kilsyth.
6. Robert M'Dowell, County Antrim.

Junior Division.

1. John Shearer, Campsie.
2. James Dennistoun, Dumfries.
3. David Baird, Greenock.

EXAMINATIONS.

I. On the Senior Mathematical Course,

Thomas A. Bryce, Belfast.} Equal.
Daniel Penman, Muirkirk.}

II. On the Junior Mathematical Course,

1. John Shearer, Campsie.
2. William Turner, Shotts.

III. On the application of the Senior Course, in the Solution of Problems not previously known to the Students,

John Cunningham, Glasgow.

IV. On a similar application of the Junior Course, and on Voluntary Reading, in addition to the Course,

William Young, Kilsyth.

———

The Prizes of the NATURAL PHILOSOPHY CLASS, for propriety of Conduct, Exemplary Diligence, and display of Eminent Abilities in Examinations on the subjects of the Lectures, and in Essays and Investigations connected with Physical Science, were adjudged to

1. John M'Cubbin, Glasgow.
2. John M'Carter, A.M., Londonderry, Ireland.
3. John M'Kail, Coylton, Ayrshire.
4. David Playfair, Dalmarnock, Glasgow.
5. James Pearson, Tolcross,   ,,

The Prizes in the ETHIC CLASS, given for General Eminence, and more particularly for the Industry, Ability, and Acquirements exhibited in the Weekly and in the Voluntary Exercises on Ethical Subjects, which were read in the Class, were adjudged to

Seniores.

1. Robert M'Dowell, County of Antrim.
2. Edmund Hartnell, Warwickshire.
3. James Robertson Campbell, Glasgow.
4. James Hamilton, Strathblane.
5. John Cunningham, Glasgow.

Juniores.

1. James Dennistoun, Dumfries-shire.
2. James Thomson, Forfarshire.

A Prize, given for the best Essay on the Origin and Progress of Civil Society, written during the Summer vacation, was adjudged to

Alexander Patrick Stewart, Erskine.

And a Prize for Poetical Essays written during the Session, was adjudged to

Archibald Kirkland, Strathaven.

NATURAL HISTORY.

For the best Essay upon the Geology of the Deluge, to
Alex. Stewart, A.M., Doune, Perthshire.

For General Eminence, to
James H. Bruce, Kilmarnock.
Duncan Blair, Balfron, Stirlingshire. ⎫
Dr. Price Brown, Jamaica.   ⎬ Equal.
Daniel Curdie, A.M., Arran.   ⎭

Geography and Popular Astronomy.

1. Moses Hueston, Londonderry.
2. Alexander P. Stewart, Erskine.
3. James Hamilton, Strathblane.

In the Logic Class the Prizes for this Session were adjudged as follows :—

I.

For General Eminence and Superiority in the various Exercises and Examinations of the Class, throughout the Session, to

First Division.

1. Abraham Hume, County Down, Ireland.
2. Alexander Campbell, Oban, Argyllshire.
3. Charles Rattray, Aberdeen.
4. John Moir, Perth.

Second Division.

1. John Campbell, Possil.
2. John Gardiner, Bothwell.
3. Samuel S. Allison, County Derry, Ireland.
4. Henry C. Hastings, Glasgow.
5. Henry C. Grey, Edinburgh.

Third Division.

1. William Urquhart, Fairhill, Hamilton.
2. Robert C. Campbell, Glasgow.
3. Francis Maxwell, Dargavel.
4. Thomas Thomson, Glasgow.
5. Colin Campbell,   ,,
6. William Graham, Meadowside, Glasgow.

II.

For Essays.

I.

(Prescribed at the close of last Session, and composed during the Vacation).

For the best Essay on the Philosophy of Des Cartes, as compared with that of his cotemporary, Lord Bacon, to

James Dennistoun, Dumfries.

2.

(Prescribed in the present Session, and executed during the Christmas holidays).

PROSE—For the best Essay on Creative Imagination, illustrated by Milton's description of Chaos, and Satan's journey through it, to

Henry C. Grey, Edinburgh.

VERSE—For the best copy of Verses—subject, Day-dreams, or the Dangers of the Imagination, to

William Urquhart, Fairhill, Hamilton.

Prizes in the GREEK CLASS.

I.

Private—Vacation Exercises.

1. Essay on the Applicability of Aristotle's Rhetorical doctrines to the different kinds of Public Speaking at the present day, to

James Hamilton, Strathblane.

2. Translation into English Verse of Æschylus' Supplices, v 620-690, to

Alexander P. Stewart, Erskine.

3. Translation into Greek Iambic Trimeters of Job, cap. iv. v. 12-21, to

William Fulton, Stewarton.

Private—Session.

Criticism on Pope's Translation of the Iliad, Book III., to

Thomas D. D. Graham, Gartmore.

II.

Public—Senior—Vacation Exercises.

1. Translation into Greek Iambic Trimeters of Shakespeare's Measure for Measure, Act II., Sc. 2, from "The law hath not been dead, though it hath slept," to "As make the Angels weep," to

James Davidson, Glasgow.

2. Translation into Attic Greek Prose of the Character of Hannibal, Livy, Book xxi. cap. 4, to

William Fulton, Stewarton.

3. Free Translation into English Verse of Aristophanes' Plutus,
v. 507-561, to

William Stirling, Craigie.

4. Abridgement of the last four books of Xenophon's Anabasis,
with notes, to

William Urquhart, Fairhill, Hamilton.

Public—Senior—Session.

1. For excelling at the Black-stone Examination,

    1. John Turner, Glasgow.
    2. John Gardiner, Bothwell.
    3. Thomas D. D. Graham, Gartmore.

2. Translation into Homeric Hexameters of Lord Byron's Lara,
Canto I., v. 628-645, to

John Johnstone, Greenock.

3. For excelling in ability, scholarship, and assiduity, throughout
the Session,

LOGIC SIDE.

    1. John Turner, Glasgow.
    2. William Arnott, Perth.
    3. Peter H. Waddell, Garnethill, Glasgow.
    4. Thomas Stirrat, Glasgow.
    5. { George Stevenson, Campsie. } Equal.
       { James Davidson, Glasgow. }

GREEK SIDE.

    1. William Fulton, Stewarton.
    2. John Johnstone, Greenock.
    3. Thomas Taylor, Sunderland.
    4. James Cameron, *minor*, Glasgow.
    5. Charles Young, Batavia.

4. For excelling in the Weekly Exercises, in Greek Verse and
Prose, throughout the Session, to

    1. William Fulton, Stewarton.
    2. { John Johnstone, Greenock. } Equal.
       { Thomas Taylor, Sunderland. }
    3. { James Montgomerie, Glasgow. } Equal.
       { John Turner, Glasgow. }

III.

Public—Junior—Vacation Exercises.

1. Life of Xenophon, with Illustrations of his character and style, from the Anabasis, to

Daniel Mackenzie, Craigpark, Glasgow.

2. Translation into Attic Greek Prose of Cæsar de Bello Gallico, L. I., cap. 17, to

John Macindoe, Glasgow.

3. Reduction into Attic Greek of the last three Extracts from Herodotus, with a translation into English, and an index of Ionic forms, to

Clermont Marucheau, St. Lucia.

4. Life of Lucian, with Illustrations of his style and character, from the Dialogues read in the Class, to

John Fraser, Glasgow.

5. Free translation of Lucian's Dialogues contained in the Extracts, with a list of anomalous verbs, to

David Stewart, Erskine.

Public—Junior—Session.

For excelling in Ability, Scholarship, and Assiduity throughout the Session.

Provectiores.

1. Henry William Beckwith, Stockton.
2. James Patrick, Dalry, Ayrshire.
3. Robert Little, Glasgow.
4. John Miller,   ,,
5. David Stewart, Erskine.
6. Alexander Oswald Mitchell, Glasgow.

Tyrones.

1. John Edmond, Balfron.
2. Archibald Arnott, Annandale.

3. Niel Taylor, Dunoon.
4. William Robertson, Plean, Stirlingshire.
5. John Sharpe, Glasgow.
6. William Barlas, ,,

Prizes of the HUMANITY CLASS.

Vacation Exercises—Private.

1. For an Essay in English Prose, on the Silver Age of Latin Poetry, to

William Little, Glasgow.

2. For an imitation in English Verse of the III. Satire of Persius, to

Michael Connal, Glasgow.

Public—Senior.

1. For an Essay in English Prose on the Subject, "Rome in the age of Augustus," to

Alexander Dorsey, Glasgow.

2. For a copy of Latin Verse, on the subject "Naves vi vaporis impulsæ," to

David Stewart, Erskine.

Public—Junior.

1. For an Essay in English Prose, on the Life and Writings of Virgil, to

John Walker, New Kilpatrick.

2. For a translation into English Prose of the fifth book of Livy, to

John Walker, New Kilpatrick.

3. For a copy of Latin Verses, on the subject "Autumnus," to
   John Walker, New Kilpatrick.

Session—Public—Senior.

Prizes for General Eminence throughout the Session.

Students of the Second Year.

1. John Storie, Paisley.
2. Charles William Young, Batavia, Java.
3. James Kirk, Glasgow.
4. John Walker, New Kilpatrick.
5. John Sharpe, Richmond Street, Glasgow.
6. Joseph Heap, Berwick-upon-Tweed.

Students of the First Year.

1. John Edmond, Balfron, Stirlingshire.
2. Henry Bell, Paisley.
3. Robert Little, Glasgow.
4. James Montgomery, Glasgow.
5. John Morgan, Tully-Allan, Perthshire.
6. James M'Cune Smith, New-York.
7. James Knox, Port-Glasgow.

Prizes for excelling at the Black-stone Examination.

1. Thomas Taylor, Union Street, Sunderland.
2. James Montgomery, Glasgow.
3. { Henry Bell, Paisley.
     { John Sharpe, Richmond Street, Glasgow. } Equal.

Prizes for excelling in the Weekly Exercises.

1. Charles William Young, Batavia, Java.
2. Thomas Taylor, Union Street, Sunderland.
3. { John Walker, New Kilpatrick. } Equal.
     { Robert Reddie, Glasgow. }

Prizes for Exercises prescribed during the Session.

1. For an Essay in English Prose, on the Life and Political. Character of Cicero,

Antony Marucheau, St. Lucia.
Charles William Young, Batavia, Java. }Equal.
William Daniel, Edinburgh.

2. For an Abridged Account in Latin Prose, of the Second Punic War, to

James Montgomery, Glasgow.

3. For a copy of Latin Verses on the subject, "Sirenum Voces," to

John Walker, New Kilpatrick.

4. For a copy of Latin Verses on the subject, "Horti Hesperidum," to

John Walker, New Kilpatrick.

Public—Junior.

Prizes for General Eminence throughout the Session,

1. Henry William Beckwith, Stockton-upon-Tees.
2. Charles Griffin, Glasgow.
3. Robert Auld,   ,,
4. Alexander Oswald Mitchell, Glasgow.
5. Hugh Murckland, Stewarton, Ayrshire.
6. Robert Forrester Proudfoot, Strathaven.
7. Andrew Mitchell, Glasgow.

Prizes for excelling in the Weekly Exercises.

1. Henry William Beckwith, Stockton-upon-Tees.
2. Charles Griffin, Glasgow.
3. Alexander Oswald Mitchell, Glasgow.

Prizes for Exercises prescribed during the Session.

1. For a translation into English Prose of the Eclogues and first Georgic of Virgil, to

William Finlay, Moss, Stirlingshire.

2. For an abridged Account in Latin Prose of the Wars of the Romans with Pyrrhus, to

Henry William Beckwith, Stockton-upon-Tees.

3. For a copy of Latin Verses on the subject " Intractabilis Bruma," to

John Stirling, Glasgow.

INDEX.

Lightning Source UK Ltd.
Milton Keynes UK
UKHW012340281118
333023UK00012B/1225/P